THE PROTESTERS

THE PROTESTERS

Alan Eyre

THE CHRISTADELPHIAN
404 SHAFTMOOR LANE
BIRMINGHAM B28 8SZ
1985

First published 1975

Second edition 1985

Copyright © by the Christadelphian Magazine and Publishing Association Ltd.

ISBN 0 85189 087 3

Printed in Great Britain by Billing & Sons Limited, Worcester

PREFACE

THE members of a comparatively small community, who have sought from its foundation to base their beliefs and their life upon what is revealed in the Scriptures, the Word of God, have inevitably a keen interest in the career and fate of those devout believers in God of former centuries, whose aim and attitude were the same. Unfortunately the historical details and evidence were not easy to come by, scattered as they are among various writings in different languages and spread over a period of many centuries.

Alan Eyre has put us all in his debt by the massive research he has done into the religious opinions and political fortunes of those early students of Scripture. The breadth of his investigations is revealed by the impressive Bibliography at the end of this volume, and by the evidence in the text itself of the use he has made of his sources.

One or two impressions inevitably emerge from a reading of this book. Whatever may be the ultimate verdict of God upon them individually, there is no doubting the tremendous zeal and earnestness with which some of these early believers applied themselves to the study of Scripture. It is a matter of great encouragement to us, whose religious views are regarded as unorthodox by our contemporaries, to find that in a number of cases where major doctrines are concerned, these early believers had come to the same conclusions as ourselves. And how should it be otherwise, for we have sought to do what they did—go back to the Scriptures alone in our search for truth.

Another, genuinely shocking, discovery is to realise how swiftly the leaders of the "official" Protestant reformation in the 16th and 17th centuries reverted to ideas which they had originally condemned in Catholicism, and with what ruthlessness they treated the "protesters" who insisted on relying only upon the Word of God.

Not the least striking feature of the narrative of this book is the revelation of the tremendous spirit of faith, love and devotion to God shown by some of these believers of former times who suffered almost indescribable tortures for the sake of their convictions. Would we today, who profess the same faith in God and in His Word, show the same firm courage if persecution became our lot? May the reflection send us all back to the Scriptures themselves as the source of all truth and inspiration.

November 1975   F.T.P.

NOTE TO THE 1985 EDITION

THIS new edition has given the author the opportunity to take account of helpful correspondence received on a number of matters, as well as important information gleaned from his further researches since 1970, when the material which in due course became the First Edition was essentially complete. The greater part of *The Protesters* remains unchanged, but corrections and emendations have been incorporated, an index has been compiled, and new sections have been added particularly to extend the history of the movements of the brethren who took the Gospel to Romania and Russia, and to expand the period between the 1660 European expulsions and the 19th century.

Since the appearance of this material in book form in 1975, a companion volume, *Brethren in Christ*, has been published by the Australian Christadelphian Scripture Study Service, 1983. The author has also contributed further articles to the pages of *The Christadelphian*. *The Protesters* continues, however, to offer a self-contained narrative and the new edition will be welcomed by those who already have the earlier edition as well as others who may not yet have entered the fascinating world of the disciples of centuries past.

J.H.M.

CONTENTS

Preface v
Note to the 1985 Edition vi
Illustrations in Text, Plates and Maps ix
Illustration Credits x
Introduction 1
1 The Source of the Ideal 5
2 The Vaudois of the Alps 12
3 Stirrings in Switzerland 18
4 Year of Decision—1525 27
5 Debates and Dungeons 41
6 Balthasar Hübmaier in Moravia 50
7 The Fiery Trial 57
8 Scattered Abroad 67
9 Troubled Times in Lutheran Lands 75
10 Strangers and Pilgrims 89
11 Principles and Practice 99
12 Lightstand in Poland 111
13 The Irrepressible Headmaster 131
14 Struggles in the Seventeenth Century 142
15 "Until the Day Dawn"—Lone Lights of the
   Eighteenth Century 156
16 Witness to Truth in 1807 168
17 Old Wine in New Bottles 176
18 John Thomas 185
19 The Faith at the End of the Age 196
20 Epilogue 212
Selected Bibliography of Sources 215
Index 221

ILLUSTRATIONS IN TEXT

"Peter" Waldo	17
Record of Imprisonment in the New Tower, Zürich	40
Hübmaier, from an old Woodcut	43
Edict of Ferdinand, 1528	68
Title-page of the *Brüderliche Vereynigung*, 1527	71
Ferdinand I	74
Title-page of Hymn Book of the Brethren of Christ, 1564	101
Title-page of the Raków Catechism, 1605	119
The Crypt School, Gloucester, where John Biddle lived and wrote	132
John Locke's Notes on Volkel's *De Vera Religione*	143
A Print-shop of the Brethren in Christ	155
A Page from "A Brief Discourse ...", 1757	158
Title-page of John Begg's *A Connected View*	178
John Thomas and Robert Roberts	192
A Ticket for the Birmingham Town Hall Lectures	199
Vladimir Doubrovsky	209

LIST OF PLATES (*Centre pages*)

Council House in Zürich, 1525	I
Statute of Zwingli	I
The Fraumünster in Zürich	II
One of the Brethren being burned at the Stake	III
A Bible Class held for safety in mid-river	IV
Typical Pages of John Biddle's *Twofold Catechism*	V
Title-page of Calvin's *Brieue Instruction*	VI
Cages for imprisoning the Brethren, Nürnberg	VI
Seventeenth Century Meeting Hall of the Brethren in Hessen	VII
An early Nineteenth Century Meeting House in Illinois	VII
Taking Communion Wine, 18th Century	VIII

MAPS

N.E. Switzerland, 1525	29
Travels of Michael Sattler	58
Central Europe, 1536	76
Poland, 1600	113

ILLUSTRATION CREDITS

Austrian National Library 68, 71, 74
Bodleian Library, Oxford V, 143
British Library VI (lower), 119
Christadelphian Office, Birmingham 192, 199
Furter Verlag I (upper)
Guildhall Library, London VIII
Paul Hatch VII (lower)
Library of Congress, Washington VII (upper), 43, 158
M. Martini, Geneva 17
National Library of Scotland 178
Stadtsbibliothek Zürich I (lower), III, IV, 101
S.B.J. Zilverberg, Bussum 155

The remainder are by the author

INTRODUCTION

As a Christadelphian, the author has witnessed a tremendous change during the past few years in the community of which he is a member. When, thirty years ago, he began the research on which this book is based, most new members were connected with existing Christadelphian families in Britain, the "old" Commonwealth and the United States. They were generally aware, at least to a degree, of the "traditions" of the body. Today, in the mid-1980s, half of those obeying the Gospel call are non-European, and there are Christadelphian lightstands upholding Bible truth in forty-five countries across the globe. Even in such English-speaking areas as south-eastern Australia and the eastern seaboard of the United States, where ecclesias more than a century old exist, a considerable proportion of the present membership has become such only within the past decade. This is, of course, most gratifying, and a healthy indication that Christadelphians are not, as one famous encyclopaedia has it, followers of one John Thomas, but followers of Christ, even as he and others were. But as a widening distance of time separates this new generation from Christadelphian "pioneers", so appreciation of the furnace through which this faith was refined grows less. There are many, who, while knowing and loving Bible truth, would like to know more of those who struggled to preserve it for us.

There are, however, other reasons which have prompted this study. The writer, once naively and unquestioningly accepting the view that Dr. John Thomas "discovered", as if from a void, the totality of Bible truth as believed by Christadelphians, was amazed to discover source after source which showed that this was at least a serious misrepresentation. It is indeed one which he believes John Thomas himself, were he alive, would be the first to repudiate, as the abundant quotations from earlier sources in his journals indicate. The nineteenth century, however, was one in which few intellectual debts were acknowledged. The neglect of the writings of nineteenth century Christadelphian authors by some of the new generation of believers is unfortunate; so are the excesses of others who would pay them alone an honour of which some share is due to others who had paved the way before them. It is hoped that this study will put in perspective the work of many without whose selfless efforts we today would be the poorer. It should be remembered that we do not diminish the teachings or the work of the Lord Jesus by pointing out how much of what he said came straight out of the Old Testament; rather indeed do we give them added richness. So it is with those who have been long respected and honoured among us.

A Noble Tradition

Today the Christadelphian community—"Brothers in Christ"—is the inheritor of a noble tradition, by which elements of the Truth were from century to century hammered out on the anvil of controversy, affliction and even anguish. These pages may help us to appreciate a Bible doctrine that God does not establish truth by the counting of heads, but by the trying of hearts, and also to understand why we as Christadelphians today resist the outstretched hands of broad oecumenical unity, and consider as traitors any among us who sell their birthright for this cause.

There is always an element of danger in appearing in the role of advocate for a misjudged minority, and if there appears in the present work to have been excessive swinging of the pendulum in the opposite direction at any point, that would be meagre compensation for centuries of harsh and bitter judgements. An effort has been made to avoid the use of ethically loaded words such as martyr, and to let those concerned reveal what manner of death, and life, was involved. It is also hoped that the story of the *sufferings* of those recorded here will not be the dominant interest; this is certainly not intended as a Christadelphian version of Foxe's *Book of Martyrs*, but as a sober appraisal of *work* done well.

When Jesus described his apostles as the salt of the earth they were then far from having themselves a full and complete understanding of the Gospel. Yet they were sent by Jesus two by two to preach the Kingdom of God. Salt serves as a preservative from corruption, and it seems fitting that the efforts of men to preserve from decay and corruption various elements of the truth through the long years of the Master's absence should be similarly regarded. In the case of those now sleeping it is the prerogative of the Lord, not of ourselves, to determine the degree to which their faith will be counted for righteousness. Many who grasped eagerly only one element of Gospel truth out of the morass of prevailing corruption and proclaimed it upon the housetops have in so doing acted as the salt of the earth in so far as their work aided the preservation of truth and virtue. Some recorded herein perhaps did not have "all the truth"—so the writer has been reminded—but he hopes that no reader of these pages will be so bold as to consider that *he* understands all truth. If one does not know more of the truth at the end of one's pilgrimage than at the beginning or the middle, then he is a poor disciple indeed.

A Desperate Need

All this does not mean that insistence upon a doctrinal basis for faith and fellowship is misguided. Indeed, on the contrary, to uphold Scriptural teaching was the aim of many whose exploits are recreated in these studies. Their success varied, and the process was continuous, dynamic and even painful, needing to be adapted to the changing character of the corruption prevailing. If contention over dogma and statements of faith has produced schism and unChristlike action, it has also promoted intense study of the Word of God and powerful, burning loyalties and convictions—all things this spineless generation of ours desperately needs. If the faith of Christ means anything at all, it is worthy of our highest and our all. *This, more than any other, is the basic message of this book.* Better one who, like Paul, "gave place by subjection, no, not for an hour, that the truth of the gospel might continue with you", than one who, half ashamed of the Gospel of Christ, sells his salty birthright for a mess of contemporary corruption.

Some may consider that Christadelphians have over-defined their faith. These pages do not encourage such a view. The fact that in the next chapter nine elements of early Christian faith are chosen as a basic theme to follow, and measure men by, later in the book does not imply that there are only nine, and no others are worthy of definition, but that *at least* nine are absolutely vital; to have gone into great detail with others would have made the study tedious. Our purpose is *not* to elaborate the whole Gospel, but to trace the transmission of many basic elements of it. Hence the abundance of carefully chosen quotations throughout.

A Source of Controversy

The author's view that Christadelphians are making in this modern age a serious endeavour to uphold the New Testament form of Christianity (and what can any other form be but human speculation?) is not surprising, for we have the shoulders of our predecessors to stand on. One element of the faith especially may be noted: the teaching of the Bible concerning the nature of Jesus Christ. Nothing in Christianity, even in Christadelphian circles, has stirred controversy so frequently or so readily as this. We are "unitarians" in the *correct* sense, that we believe in the unity of Godhead as revealed to Moses and confirmed by Christ, the Son of God. But in the *incorrect* sense, adopted by the denomination of that name in the nineteenth century, of believing that Jesus was not a theophany but a man having no divine origin at all, merely morally superior, we are not. Neither was the John Biddle of our story, though denominational Unitarians in their literature sometimes allege that he was. Actually, he would have been horrified, since far from dishonouring the Lord Jesus, he is reputed to have bowed his head in reverence every time the sacred name of the Saviour passed his lips. No "Unitarian" in the incorrect sense has been included in this brief history.

Because these believers were combating an over-mystical and thoroughly unscriptural trinitarianism, some of them may seem to overstress the humanity of our Lord. This was perhaps inevitable in the circumstances. But none of those referred to, who fought to uphold the true humanity of our Saviour, would have denied, as do so many professing Christians today, that he was the Son of God and the supreme manifestation of the Almighty Creator for our salvation. Detailed elaboration of the Scriptural doctrine of God-manifestation and a reasoned reconciliation of the divine and the human in a historically manifested Saviour as expounded by later Christadelphian writers is the richest culmination of the story told in the chapters which follow.

1

THE SOURCE OF THE IDEAL

I believe in God almighty
    And in Christ Jesus, His only Son, our Lord
Who was born of the Holy Spirit and the Virgin Mary
    Who was crucified under Pontius Pilate and was buried
And the third day rose from the dead
    Who ascended into heaven
And sitteth on the right hand of the Father
    Whence he cometh to judge the living and the dead;
And in the Holy Spirit
    The holy church
The remission of sins
    The resurrection of the flesh
The life everlasting.

The earliest preserved form of the "Apostles' Creed", 340 A.D., now often known as the "Old Roman Creed"

THE purpose of this book is to tell how a number of little-known individuals, groups and religious communities strove to preserve or revive the original Christianity of apostolic times. Their story has interest not only because most of the men and women are little known, but because they were also extremely virtuous—many of them outstandingly so for the age in which they lived. They were attempting to maintain a standard of virtue which was ethically far superior to even the religious leaders of their own times. These men and communities were not only rejected by their own generation, but have also been grossly misjudged by scholars of subsequent ones. In faith and outlook they were far closer to the early springing shoots of first-century Christianity and the penetrating spiritual challenge of Jesus himself than much that has passed for the religion of the Nazarene in the last nineteen centuries.

It is necessary first of all to discover what it was that these people considered important to conserve or revive. Among the religious tenets and ethical principles of early Christianity—before Greek philosophical concepts gradually overlaid and superseded Jewish, especially Old Testament, modes of thought—nine of particular importance for this study will now be mentioned briefly. Each of them became at some time in the centuries and in the countries covered by this work a key issue; each was considered a point on which conscience could not yield. To each of them worthy men were sufficiently committed in their faith and their search for what they considered ultimate Christian truth that they could not abjure it without abandoning their inner integrity.

The Authority of the Scriptures

When the author of Acts commended the Jews of Berea for "receiving the word with all eagerness, examining the Scriptures daily" to test the teaching of Paul, he was describing an attitude typical of the early Christian church. It was a Bible-based fellowship—in the first instance the Jewish Old Testament, but gradually including their own apostolic writings. The earliest Christians held with conviction that God had through the Old Testament promised and detailed in advance the whole life and ministry of Jesus of Nazareth, and that the same inspiration of the Holy Spirit subsequently revealed the requirements for the spiritual life. They discounted purely subjective mysticism and would have been much more at home in the simple Bible class of Andreas Castelberger described in chapter 3 than anywhere else in Christendom at that time.

Believers' Baptism

The earliest Christian churches which archaeology has discovered possessed not a font but a baptistry. One at Emmaus is ten feet long, three feet wide and five feet deep with a flight of steps to enable both baptizer and baptized to enter the water. The ground-plan of the earliest churches, moreover, is modelled on that of the large Roman house, the baptistry being a development of the domestic impluvium. This certainly takes us back to the "house-churches" of the first and second centuries when, as *The Pastor of Hermas* informs us, every new member was inducted into the faith by descending into the water to "arise living". In the first age of the church only adults who entered it consciously and voluntarily were baptized. The recurring symbolism in early Christian writings of death and life in association with baptism reflects both the intensity of meaning with which they invested the rite and also the manner of its performance. As will later appear, those scholars who came to make believers' baptism a vital issue in the 16th century, were familiar not only with the Scriptural background but with these early patristic writings also.

The Future Reign of Christ on Earth

"The most striking fact of pre-Nicene Christianity is millenarianism or advent hope, and personal rule of Christ on earth." This comment of the historian Schaff is amply borne out by first and second century writers. "There will be a millennium after the resurrection from the dead", Papias is reported as saying, "when the personal reign of Christ will be established in the earth." Papias, who died in 163 A.D., had known intimately some who had known Jesus personally, and Eusebius emphasises the apostolic origin of this millennial hope. The writings of Tertullian (162-240) abound with references to the millennium and the coming stone that would smite the image of Daniel's prophecy. In fact, he makes quite a remarkable prediction stating that on the basis of Scripture he expected an apostate church with temporal power to grow up in Rome, rising from the fragmented ruins of imperial Rome. Hippolytus (died 236) wrote similarly of a revived Roman Empire under a new guise and governing by Roman law. This particular interpretation was to assume great importance in the 16th and the 19th centuries among the groups considered later in our study.

Immortality

The hope of future immortality was undoubtedly a powerful evangelising force in early Christianity. There was no assumption of personal immortality, the prospect of eternal life being bound up with acceptance of a risen Christ, who was considered the first-fruits of a later harvest "at his coming". The Report (1945) of the Commission appointed by the Archbishops of Canterbury and York, *Towards the Conversion of England,* stated: "The central theme of the New Testament is eternal life, not for anybody and everybody, but for believers in Christ arisen from the dead. The idea of the inherent indestructibility of the human soul (or consciousness) owes its origin to Greek not to Bible sources.'' Irenaeus (130-202) calls those heretics who maintain the glorification of the saints immediately after death. In Justin's (100-165) *Dialogue with Trypho the Jew* he states:

> "For if you have conversed with some that are indeed called Christians and do not maintain these opinions, but even dare to blaspheme the God of Abraham, and the God of Isaac, and the God of Jacob, and say that there is no resurrection of the dead, that the souls, as soon as they leave the body, are received up into heaven, take care that you do not look upon these. But I and all those Christians, that are really orthodox in every respect, do know that there will be a resurrection of the body and a thousand years in Jerusalem, when it is built again, and adorned, as Ezekiel, and Esaias, and the rest of the prophets declare."

This passage was later to be of considerable embarrassment to Calvin, who found that others would not abandon Justin's viewpoint as easily as he did when he found it expedient to do so. The Greek view of immortality, introduced soon after the apostolic age—Justin himself is by no means entirely consistent—came to prevail as orthodox, largely through the enormous influence of Origen. His voluminous writings—six thousand different works, taken down by the seven shorthand writers who in rotation were in constant attendance upon him from dawn till nightfall and transcribed by a similar number of copyists—as Froom has said, "blow hot and cold on the resurrection" and tend to replace the primitive biblicism by allegorisation and philosophy.

Hell

The second Letter to the Thessalonians, the second Letter of Peter and the Epistle of Barnabas (*c.* 150), and other early writings which contrast eternal life and perishing or destruction, indicate that the concept of the eternal fiery tortures of the damned as pictured in medieval churches was a later interpretation or addition. The importance of this for the present study will be apparent later.

The Godhead and the Person and Work of Christ

A great deal will be said about this later. But there is much evidence to support the view of Fagginer Auer of Harvard:

> "Fourth-century trinitarianism did not reflect accurately early Christian teaching regarding the nature of God; it was, on the contrary, a deviation from this teaching. It developed against constant unitarian opposition and was never wholly victorious. The dogma of the Trinity owes its existence to abstract speculation on the part of a small minority of scholars. In Tertullian's day, he said that the ordinary rank and file of Christians think of Christ as man."

The fact that the leading 16th-century reformers at first abandoned and encouraged others to abandon trinitarianism—Luther confessed that "nothing to support the dogma can be pointed out in Scripture"—but later reverted to it, led to a complex trial of conscience as will be pointed out later.

As always happens in controversy, extremes beget extremes, and some have felt that a denial of belief in the trinity is tantamount to a rejection of the uniqueness and divine Sonship of Jesus Christ. This is far from being the case. The early church never ceased to stress, nor do their past and present day followers, that Jesus was and is the Son of God, the unique revelation and mediator of God to man, now made higher than the heavens, glorious in power.

The Ethic of Love

Of tremendous importance throughout the period covered by this study was the ethical challenge implicit in the teaching of Christ on love. The issue over the use of force by Christians, especially in the resistance of evil, or abused power, is a major theme. The fact that Zwingli, for example, can be portrayed with Bible in one hand and massive broadsword in the other, as he is in his Zürich statue, indicates the compromise that was and is possible in this matter. The fact that a church could claim the name Christian did not prevent it from engaging in bloody and revengeful persecutions of those whose consciences would not permit them to retaliate.

For the first and second century church this issue was not a particularly live one, since its members formed a tiny minority in the empire and were never in possession of power. Not until barbarian invasions did any question of conscription arise. But there is no doubt that the principles were understood, as the following, written one hundred years after the apostolic age, indicates:

> "How shall he (the Christian) wage war, nay, how shall he even be a soldier in peacetime, without the sword which the Lord has taken away? For although soldiers had come to John and received the form of their rule, although even a centurion had believed, the Lord afterwards, in disarming Peter, ungirded every soldier."

> "Is it right to occupy oneself with the sword, when the Lord proclaims that he who uses the sword shall perish by the sword? And shall the son of peace, for whom it will be unfitting even to go to law, be engaged in a battle? And shall he, who is not the avenger even of his own wrongs, administer chains and imprisonment and torture and executions? The very act of transferring one's name from the camp of light to the camp of darkness is a transgression."[1]

When full military conscription was introduced towards the end of the third century, there were Christians who were beheaded for refusing to accept the military badge. In the same way, to those who are the subjects of these studies the incompatibility of the doctrine of Christian love and the use of carnal force even in self-defence, was a cardinal tenet of faith.

The Ecclesia

The concept of the ecclesia or assembly of believers was an important element in the vitality of the early Christians. Preserving some aspects of Jewish synagogue worship and transmuting them for a wider situation, they kept as their keynote: "One is your master and you are all brethren." The French scholar Auguste Sabatier remarks that:

> "We find no trace of a division of (the original) Christians into clergy and laity. All (members) formed the elect people, and conversely, this people was collectively a people of priests

---

[1] Cited from C. J. Cadoux, *The Early Church and the World,* by J. B. Norris, in *The Christian and War,* p.18. The latter pamphlet is published by *The Christadelphian* Office.

and prophets. There were no passive members. The most humble had their share of activity and were by no means the least necessary."

This spiritual egalitarian structure was at one and the same time both ethically and socially powerful and also fragile, subject to fairly easy coercion by dominant leaders. This principle of "brethren in Christ" is a fundamental link through the broad sweep in time and place covered by this study. Time and again individuals and groups sought to revisualise and recreate the simple community of the Upper Room as the ideal of Christian fellowship, a tight-knit union of kindred minds transformed by the word of God, owning allegiance only to one Master.

The Table of the Lord

The eucharistic meal, or "breaking of bread" as it came to be known among the groups to be considered in this study, began originally as a simple "remembrance", with theories of the mass or eucharistic sacrifice developing gradually over the first two centuries. Much allegorisation was employed by patristic writers which confirms the central nature of the ceremony from earliest times. Those who later viewed the "breaking of bread" as a memorial rather than a sacrifice did so believing that this was its original form, and also that it was more in keeping with a Scriptural view of the Saviour. The tremendous unifying power of this "table fellowship" in maintaining the spirit of witness and stubborn loyalty among those now to be considered is one of the outstanding facts of history.

2

THE VAUDOIS OF THE ALPS

"He that will not swear, or speak evil, or lie, or commit injustice or theft, or give himself up to dissoluteness, or take vengeance on his enemies, is called Vaudois and the cry is 'Death to him'."

IN this poem, "La Nobla Leyczon", of 1100 A.D., we are introduced to the controversial and puzzling religious fraternity of the Vaudois or Waldenses. Traditionally the Waldenses have been considered as originating in the work of "Peter" Waldo, the merchant of Lyons who gave up a prosperous business career to become a "poor preacher". Yet the "Nobla Leyczon" precedes the birth of Waldo by thirty or forty years, and in libraries of Geneva and Cambridge are documents far earlier than Waldo, dating from early in the 12th century, mentioning the Vaudois, and giving details from their sermons.

It is not possible to ascertain with certainty the beliefs and practice of all the scattered Vaudois groups in the Middle Ages and after. As the religious historian Froom puts it: "Much of their doctrine we must piece together from accounts of their enemies." Yet some definitive points seem to emerge, the first of which is that while in the 14th century they were found only in a number of remote mountain valleys in the Alps, originally they had been spread more widely in southern Europe.

A Link with Early Christianity

It became the custom of later writers on the Vaudois, like Newman and Froom, to develop the theory of a continuous "succession" of evangelical and Biblical Christianity, unperverted by Romish "antichrist", from the apostolic age through them to the 16th-century Reformation. Though in the form presented by these apologists sound evidence is often lacking, and there are important missing links, yet the theory has been, in the writer's opinion, too radically dismissed by some modern scholars. It seems clear that the Vaudois' attitude to Christianity was based on an essentially pious yet commonsense approach to the Bible.

"We believe that there is one God alone who is Spirit, creator of all things, Father of all, who is over all, whom we adore in spirit and truth, and to whom alone we give the glory for our life, clothing, health, sickness, prosperity and adversity, author of every good; and we fear Him for He searches the hearts.

"We believe that Jesus Christ is the Son in the image of the Father, in whom dwelt all the fulness of the godhead bodily, through whom we recognise the Father, who is our mediator and advocate, and besides whom there is no name given to men by whom we can be saved; through whose Name we invoke the Father.

"We deny that children who have not reached the age of intelligence can be saved by baptism. We deny that another person's faith can profit those who cannot use their own, since the Lord says 'whosoever shall have believed and shall have been baptized shall be saved'. Sacred shrines for prayer are unnecessary to Christians, since God when invoked hears as well in a market as in a temple, before an altar as before a manger and hearkens to those who deserve it.

"We affirm that sacrifices, prayers, alms and good works done for dead believers by the living are of no avail to aid any one of the dead in any manner.

"We believe that God is mocked by ecclesiastical chanting because He who is delighted solely by pious affections cannot be called to one's aid by high-pitched sounds or soothed by musical modulations."

Here we have a vital link between first-century Christianity and the faith of the Brethren in Christ and the Polish Brethren to be considered later. In the 12th century a formal development of doctrine and practice would have been impossible and inconceivable.

THE PROTESTERS

Even if such a complete body of Bible teaching had existed, it would have had to have been believed and practised in total secrecy. It is even less likely that any evidence of it would ever have been preserved. The papal bondage was so total in those Dark Ages that the endeavours we now know that the Vaudois bravely made to cast off the Romish shackles are such as to merit our appreciation, indeed our admiration.

There is no evidence that a single creed or statement of faith united all Vaudois. Some were evidently broadly evangelical in outlook without overtly abandoning all the papal dogmas; others went much further and proposed a radical return to a scriptural faith involving literally dozens of fundamental changes in doctrine and practice to conform more closely to the Bible.

Forty-five kilometres west of Turin, near Pinerolo, is an Italian alpine village called Torre Pellice. There are two ancient cemeteries there. The Roman Catholic graveyard has an inscription from the Vulgate of Job 3:19, but the entrance to that of the Vaudois has the words of Paul: "The dead in Christ shall rise" (1 Thess. 4:16). The Roman Catholic historian Thuanus, quoted by John Thomas in *Eureka,* confirms that in general the Vaudois believed the Scriptural doctrines of the mortality of the soul and the resurrection. There is much documentary evidence in Switzerland that the Brethren in Christ derived their convictions on these same issues (and maybe others) not only from the Bible directly but also indirectly from the Vaudois. There is one clue of considerable interest in the fact that several surnames characteristic of the Vaudois in the 15th century and earlier—Meier, Treier, Rolet, Huser, Buchar—are perpetuated for generations among the various groups of Brethren from the 16th century onwards. Other evidence points unmistakably to the conclusion that the movements considered in the following chapters had spiritual and even organic roots reaching back through the centuries to simple Vaudois teachers hammering out on the anvils of conscience and tribulation a Biblical and deeply ethical faith. One realises with astonishment that the plain, robust confessions quoted above are contemporaneous with the darkest period of orthodox medieval scholasticism.

"Peter" Waldo

As for Waldo himself, Giovanni Scuderi has shown that the name Pierre (Peter) is not historical, and that *Valdo,* that is, "the man from Vaud" (a canton in Switzerland) was his first name or nickname.

He made the first translation of the Bible into a popular language (Romaunt) since Jerome's Vulgate. The "gospel" (rather than the Roman catechism) was taught under his guidance, and he encouraged the committal to memory of Bible passages rather than the Missal. This practice inevitably led thinking people to question Catholic dogma and subsequently develop systematically out of the Word the doctrines of saving truth. Waldo specifically identified the Papacy as the Antichrist of New Testament prophecy. Groups such as the Vicenza Society in Italy which definitely "repudiated . . . human inventions" and "taught the truth" in the 16th century were undoubtedly influenced by Waldo and the Vaudois.

Waldo died in Bohemia. He was interred on a hilltop in southern Czechoslovakia which is still called Waldhaus, although today's Marxist population has no idea why. Before the days of the Iron Curtain and the rule of the Party, small groups of Bible lovers used to gather annually on this hilltop to pay their respects to a brave pioneer of Bible truth.

Teachers among the Vaudois were not full-time paid pastors: "Some were artisans, the greater number surgeons or physicians; and all were versed in the cultivation of the soil and the nurture of flocks." Being laymen, though ordained for God, there was no rule of celibacy. They received voluntary gifts from the church members to aid them in their work and travels. Of the community's freewill offerings, it is said a third were given to the poor, a third for missions and the remainder to aiding the "barbas" or "uncles" as their spiritual shepherds were affectionately called in studious observance of Jesus' instruction to call none "Father" on earth. High on a col of the Italian Alps west of Pinerolo was their "seminary", Pra del Tor, where the precious hand-written copies of the New Testament were learnt by heart for transmission beneath tree and rock to other eager listeners. David of Augsburg—a fanatical enemy—refers to their great devotion to the study of the Scriptures, while even Pope Innocent VIII admits their great sanctity, at the same time promising "remission of all sins" to such as should kill any of the Vaudois, together with the more mercenary offer of all their confiscated property.

Persecution

The Vaudois, through their love of the Scripture, brought much of its teaching, beauty and truth to light and, moreover, committed these to faithful people in Italy, Switzerland, Poland and elsewhere.

However, it was only with immense sacrifice that this was done. As John Thomas says of them in *Eureka:* "Multitudes died praising God, and in the confident hope of resurrection to eternal life." Martini, in her study of Waldo, quotes Pierre de Vaux-Cernay's account of Count Simon de Montfort's crusade against the castle of Montréal where many Vaudois from the town of Lavaur were sheltering: "The lady of the castle who was an execrable heretic was, on the count's order, thrown into a well which was then filled up with rocks; then the pilgrims (crusaders) gathered together all the innumerable heretics who had crowded into the castle and with extreme joy burned them all alive."

For centuries troops harried the Alpine valleys in their hunt for the outlawed Vaudois. In 1393, Val-Louise was depopulated completely and hundreds of infants suffocated in their cradles. At this date there were adherents scattered over a wide area from Geneva on the north to Arles on the south and from Avignon on the west as far as Venice on the east. But by the 15th century the greater number who remained were cooped up in the most inaccessible Alpine fastnesses. There were, however, in the lowlands many cells which persisted stubbornly.

No doubt in an endeavour to obtain protection from the incessant pressure of persecution two of the Vaudois leaders sought alliance with the Swiss national reformers and sections of the community merged into the general reformation movement. Today the "Valdensian" church in Italy is indistinguishable from the generality of evangelical Protestant sects. There were many others, however, who found a more amenable spiritual home within the community of Brethren, presently to be considered.

The Vaudois, handicapped by their unacceptable views on the nature of man, God, the church and the future, saw only in the instruction of their families any opportunity for perpetuation. To this end they prepared a *Catechism for the Instruction of Youth*. Most significantly it began:

Q. If one should demand of you, who you are, what would you answer?

A. A creature of God, *reasonable* and *mortal*.

Both words were highly significant. The first was by implication an assertion that their understanding of Christianity was based on common sense exegesis, on the exercise of a person's reasoning faculties, not on blind conformity to authoritarian ecclesiastical decrees. The second speaks for itself; its consequence will unfold in due course.

"Peter" Waldo

3

STIRRINGS IN SWITZERLAND

IN the ten years 1522 to 1532 the wave of the Protestant Reformation rolled over Europe. It reached to every part of Christendom, affecting not only those countries which became officially "Protestant", but stirring deep eddies and currents in lands whose governments were most loyally Roman Catholic, such as Spain, Italy and Austria. In some countries there was a clean break. It should be remembered that the first *official* Protestant state was the canton of Zürich in Switzerland, whose council adopted a state church "according to the word of God" in 1523. At that time, although Luther was preaching almost unmolested in parts of Germany, he was still an excommunicated and outlawed heretic in an officially Roman Catholic empire. Not until 1525 did Philip of Hesse, in return for Luther's sanction of his bigamy, form a league of German states to protect the Lutheran church. By 1532 some Swiss cantons, some German states, Sweden and England had seceded from Rome. Elsewhere longings for change proved to be widely diffused and intractable, escaping here and there like suppressed steam from a boiling pot.

In part the Protestant movement was politically motivated, coinciding with a rising tide of nationalism, and marking the death throes of medievalism. In part also it was social, for the burghers and artisan class, seeking a new social frontier, provided much support and inspiration for it. But in part it was the outcome of a new biblicism, a desire to approach the Scriptures direct, through the original tongues and the national languages instead of through the cloudy prism of the Latin Vulgate and medieval theologians.

Many men and women were no longer content to leave their eternal salvation in the hands of immoral friars, monks and discredited penance-vendors. Many clerics themselves, dissatisfied with their position, abandoned their corrupt orders, married and entered workaday society, thus adding to the ferment of thought and discussion. There were ideas abroad, from the universities to groups gathered in the homes of intelligent craftsmen in the towns, of rebuilding the Christian church anew on its original foundations, laid bare in Holy Writ.

Such a group met in a house in Zürich under the guidance of Andreas Castelberger, a figure well-known in the city since he was a cripple and walked on crutches. Regular Bible study meetings with free discussion began not later than 1522, the letters of Paul being the chief topic. In 1523, they met in the home of Felix Manz, a young and learned Biblical and linguistic scholar. They read the Bible together, Manz reading in the original tongues and then translating for the benefit of the less accomplished. They discussed the ideal pattern of the church and aimed through study and discussion to build up the original Gospel. Many groups like this one came independently to similar conclusions, some of which coincided with those which characterised the earlier dissenting bodies mentioned in the previous chapter.

Independence from Rome

The Castelberger-Manz group worked at first in co-operation with the Swiss evangelical reformer Huldrich Zwingli, who was encouraging the Zürich Council to declare its independence from Rome. The Council undoubtedly favoured this, but was rather alarmed at the thoroughness of the reformation proposed by some of the group. On July 7, 1522, Conrad Grebel, Claus Hottinger, Heinrich Eberli and Bartlime (Bartholomew) Pur were summoned before the Council and "forbidden to speak any more against the monks in the pulpits and were required to cease disputing and speaking about these things."

But the group of Bible students continued to meet and to become involved in the reforming movement. In January 1523 Zwingli made his position clear, stating that the new church must be built upon sound Scriptural principles; it must even accept the call to be a suffering church if needful; it was not to be established by force. "In wordly things judges are necessary, but in matters concerning divine wisdom and truth I will accept no one as witness and judge except the living Scriptures and the spirit of God which speaks out of the Scriptures." Manz, Conrad Grebel and Castelberger and their friends supported Zwingli wholeheartedly in this and urged him to use his great influence speedily to remove all traces of Roman Catholic ritual including the Mass, infant christening, worship of images, the *Ave Maria* and invocation of the saints, replacing these things by New Testament beliefs and practices.

In 1523, Zürich officially became evangelical and on October 26 to 28 a great three-day disputation was held before the council, mainly to consider the speed and extent of reform. Zwingli told his friends beforehand that the word of God would be his sole arbiter and that if the Council adopted any course contrary to that he would not accept it, but would continue to work for a true reformation. He also plainly professed repudiation of armed force, and agreed with the Manz group on the importance of believers' baptism.

Hübmaier, the "Unwearied Hearer"

Zwingli, of course, played a leading part in the discussions, but another notable participant was a forty-two year old evangelical preacher from Waldshut, who had formerly been a university vice-rector, Dr. Balthasar Hübmaier. Born in the village of Frieberg near Augsburg, he graduated as Master from the university of Freiburg, studying under the Dr. Eck who later, as the champion of the Roman Catholics, challenged Luther's progress in Germany. Eck commented on the young Balthasar that he was "a diligent reader, an unwearied hearer". He accepted an appointment at the university of Ingolstadt, where he took his doctorate and subsequently became vice-rector. After five years in Regensburg he moved to Waldshut, a town on the German bank of the Rhine. Waldshut is not far from Basel where he met the great Erasmus ("he speaks freely but writes cautiously" was Hübmaier's comment) and became disturbed in mind concerning the truth of his Roman Catholic faith. He plunged into assiduous study of the Scriptures, which led to a revolution in his thinking. After giving a course of lectures in Regensburg on the Gospel of Luke, he visited Zwingli in Zürich, and Grebel's brother-in-law, von Watt, in St. Gallen. Discussions with them centred on the importance of baptism, Hübmaier insisting that no trace could be found of infant christening in the Scriptures; in form and spirit it was foreign to the personal commitment demanded of believers in the early church.

The October disputation referred to was about to take place and Hübmaier was encouraged to participate. Some of his speeches were highlights of the debate; from one on the second day, for example, we have the following:

> "For the Scripture is the sole light and is a true lantern, by whose light all the fictions of the human mind may be discovered and all darkness dispelled. Errors should be examined and corrected by the sole rule of the word of God."

For him it was logical for a Christian to call himself such only if he followed Christ, whose claims and commands were preserved only in the Scriptures. It was vital that all should know as clearly as possible what these were. As he urged on the third day:

> "It is ridiculous to recite Latin words to a German who knows nothing of the Latin language. What else is this than to hide the Lord whom we ought to proclaim? Paul wishes so to speak in the church as to be understood by all and he would rather speak five words to be understood than thousands in an unknown tongue."

Typical of Hübmaier's attitude until the day of his death was his final appeal:

> "These, brethren, are my opinions which I have learned from the Holy Scriptures. If there is any error in them, I pray and beseech you, by Jesus Christ our only Saviour and the day of his last judgement, to condescend to set me right through the Holy Scriptures in a fraternal and Christian manner. I can err, for I am a man, but I cannot be a heretic, for I am willing to be taught better by anybody. And if anyone will teach me better, I acknowledge that I shall owe him great thanks; I will confess the error, and in accordance with the decision of the divine word I will gladly and willingly submit. I have spoken. It is yours to judge and set me right."

There was one in the audience that day who was to prove 18 months later that Hübmaier was true to his word.

Unfortunately there were many who did not consider that Zwingli was true to his, and indeed felt deeply betrayed. He capitulated to the Council on the most significant issues: "My lords will decide whatever regulations are to be adopted in the future."

Claiming that the Reformation must be upheld by arms or it would fail, he abandoned his original "peace principles" and preached a stirring war sermon. Talk of a "suffering church" ceased, and it became clear that infant christening was to be firmly upheld. The church in Zürich must be a state church to which all from birth must belong, not a brotherhood of believers. Simon Stumpf, a member of the Grebel-Manz circle, was horrified at the decision: "I will ask Christ for his spirit, and I will preach and act against it." In the subsequent history of the Zwinglian reformation self-interest now played a very great part.

A Thorough Reformation

Hübmaier returned to Waldshut, and threw himself into a thorough reformation of the entire religious life of the community. Pictures and images were removed from the church and tapers from the altar. Costly vestments, chalices and jewelled ornaments were sold. His marriage to Elizabeth Hügline was the occasion for a great feast provided by the townspeople in their honour.

Nailing theses to church doors was a practice by no means confined to Luther. It was in fact the 16th century equivalent of an advertisement in the press. The following are selected from a number drawn up by Hübmaier to mark the beginnings of his 1524 reform in Waldshut. His characteristic practical style is already evident.

> "—Faith is the knowledge of the mercy of God, which He manifested to us through the giving of His only-begotten Son. Thereby are overthrown all sham Christians.
> —This faith cannot remain dead, but must manifest itself towards God in thanksgiving, and towards our fellowmen in works of brotherly love. Thereby are destroyed all rituals, tapers, holy water.
> —Only those works are good which God has commanded, and only those are evil which He has forbidden: thereby fall fish, flesh, cowls, plates.
> —The mass is no sacrifice, but a memorial of the death of Christ. Hence it may be offered as a sacrifice neither for the dead nor for the living. Thereby fall masses for souls and the like.
> —As Christ alone died for our sins and we are baptized

in his Name, so should we call upon him only as our mediator and intercessor. Thereby fall all pilgrimages.

—All Christian doctrines not planted by God Himself are profitless and self-condemned; here fall to the ground the scholastics and all teachers who in their origin are not from God.

—Whoso seeks purgatory, the trust of those whose god is the belly, seeks the grave of Moses—it will never be found.

—To promise chastity in the strength of man is nothing else than to fly over the sea without wings.

—Whoso for worldly advantage denies or remains silent concerning the word of God, sells the blessing of God, as Esau sold his birthright, and will also be denied by Christ.''

Two Different Interpretations

In June 1524, the Peasants' Revolt broke out in Germany. It was primarily a social upheaval, but it had many religious overtones. Like many another social struggle, historical interpretations are deeply subjective and a picture free from bias is difficult to achieve. In the two republics of Germany today diametrically different interpretations are taught: West German schoolbooks stress the atrocities of the peasants, while Engels' version, which is the only valid one in East Germany, portrays Luther as the arch villain and is principally concerned to vilify the atrocities of the Lutherans.

An important figure in the revolt was Thomas Müntzer. A zealous advocate of radical Protestant reformation, Müntzer is a puzzling figure. Sometimes misleadingly described as an "anabaptist"[1], his avowed aims at first appeared deceptively like those of the Grebelian group in Zürich, his position in relation to Luther being not dissimilar to theirs in relation to Zwingli.

But the parting of the ways came early: on July 13, 1524, Müntzer gave a fiery sermon in the castle of Allstedt in Saxony before an audience of princes, the import of which was clear and unmistakable. The rule of the saints must be set up by violent revolution, and the ungodly destroyed:

"What should be done with the wicked who hinder the gospel? Get them out of the way and eliminate them. Perform

---

[1] The Anabaptists (re-baptists) rejected infant christening and taught adult baptism only.

a righteous judgement at God's command! Let not the evil-doers live longer who make us turn away from God. For the godless person has no right to live when he is in the way of the pious. The godless have no right to live except as the elect wish to grant it to them."

Grebel was deeply disturbed. In September 1524, he wrote a letter to Müntzer deploring this turn of affairs:

"The gospel and its adherents are not to be protected by the sword, nor are they thus to protect themselves, which as we learn from our brother is thy opinion and practice. True Christian believers are sheep among wolves, sheep for the slaughter; they must be baptized in anguish and affliction, tribulation, persecution, suffering and death; they must be tried with fire, and must attain to the fatherland of eternal rest, not by killing their bodily, but by mortifying their spiritual, enemies."

There was no further contact. Müntzer encouraged the insurrection of the peasants and was himself beheaded in May of the next year. This early link and some other tenuous ones, together with certain common features of theology, caused both contemporary authorities and later historians to put a false colour upon peaceful "anabaptism" which is still reflected in some present-day encyclopaedias.

The Baptism Controversy

The question of baptism continued to be an irritant in Zürich. It should be appreciated that the controversy was far deeper than the simple doctrinal issue as to the form and significance of Scriptural baptism. For infant christening was seen as vital to the existence of a national or state church on reformed principles which would simply replace *en masse* the previous Roman Catholic all-embracing theocracy. Believers' baptism was seen as vital to the establishment of a truly evangelical, confessional faith where the keynote was personal commitment. The leading reformers, Zwingli, Luther and others, gave lip-service to the latter but inconsistently upheld the former, when necessary by force. To many sincere and pious people this was intolerably double-minded and a clash became inevitable.

Two discussions on baptism were held on successive Tuesdays in November 1524 before the Zürich Council. Zwingli defended infant christening while Grebel and Hätzer urged its abolition and advocated believers' baptism. The discussion—as was invariably the case—was to be ostensibly on the basis of Scripture.

But Grebel subsequently wrote:

> "We had no chance to speak, and there was no chance for the Scripture to be heard; for when one of us wanted to say the truth in the matter they overwhelmed us and choked the speech in our throats, whereas they themselves should have brought forth Scripture and truth. Zwingli overwhelmed me with so much talking that I was unable to answer on account of his long speeches."

Zwingli, of course, had another view of the meetings. He considered his opponents bigoted, unamenable to reason and carried away with self-conceit.

Manz and Grebel were disheartened and perplexed by the result of the November discussions, and Manz prepared a petition offering "thorough proof that infant baptism is not scriptural". The short but impressive document was condemned by Zwingli and the Council as "inimical to the welfare of the state" and the whole movement to establish a believers' church was ruled as "seditious". Grebel swiftly denied the charge:

> "I never took part in sedition and never talked or spoke in any way anything which would lead to it, as all those with whom I have ever had anything to do will testify of me."

Grebel knew that he and his friends were now in a highly perilous situation, their movement, despite all their efforts, being represented in a treasonable colour. It was at this time, a week before the Christmas of 1524, that Grebel wrote a short letter to his brother-in-law von Watt, who was Zwingli's aide at St. Gallen. It is worth quoting as it reveals important facts about the relationship between the group around Grebel, which was to become a month later an independent religious community, and the Zwinglian reformation. It also indicates Grebel's own awareness of the danger of their position.

> "My dear doctor and brother-in-law,
>
> The thing which you asked me to do I could not perform. The truth will not be bound to the occasion, so do please accept

this in good part. I am begging you to do so. Others who have come to understand the divine truth about baptism do not wish to have their children baptized. They have been warned by my lords, but still stand firm. I hope that God will apply the remedy of patience.

If the booklets are printed, and I live to be able to do so, I shall send them to you. Do pray to God for the advancement of His will and our piety, or rather my own.

Greet for me my sister and all the pupils and beginners in the word of God and the godly life that they (if they so wish) may also pray for us in these perilous times. God knows why, why they are so perilous.

Your sincere brother-in-law,
Conrad.

P.S. I wish rather that we were both unanimously brethren in the truth of Christ.''

4
YEAR OF DECISION—1525

THE year 1525 was of exceptional significance in the religious and historical movements under consideration. It saw the birth of the community of the Brethren in Christ (Brüder in Christo) in Switzerland, and, despite severe attempts at repression, its extension over a considerable area. This chapter surveys the rapid succession of events and some of the chief characters in the drama, leaving for later consideration the religious and ethical principles involved.

New Year 1525 came in with an atmosphere of ominous threat for the little circle of Conrad Grebel and Felix Manz in Zürich. Their views had been unwarrantably but conveniently branded as seditious and a religious controversy was becoming obscured by political overtones. Yet the friends still hoped to avoid a head-on collision with Zwingli and the civic authorities, as Manz's appeal indicated.

In January, 1525, the Zürich authorities invited Grebel, Manz and their friends to yet another public disputation in the city hall. The topic was to be baptism; the basis, as before, the Scriptures. But the very tone of the invitation indicated that the council had already made up its mind; it implied that its purpose was to convert the erring, not to weigh evidence. The "baptism" group never had a chance. Within the next few days the council issued decrees forbidding the opponents of infant christening to preach or even to meet together, banishing non-citizens attached to the group and renewing the order for all parents to christen all children or go into exile within eight days.

The non-citizens were put on oath to leave Zürich within eight days. This meant that the group around Grebel and Manz which had been steadily growing in number and cohesion would now be broken up by the departure of at least five of its most active members, Röubli the pastor of Witikon—who of course would lose his livelihood—Brötli, Hätzer, Cajakob and Castelberger, the cripple who had earlier played the key role. It was a moment of crisis for the group. They had striven for the New Testament practice of adult baptism to be officially recognised in place of the "Romish rite" of christening. They had begun the struggle by the negative protest of refusing to present children for christening; now, outlawed, their convictions pressed hard upon their own spirits. The need for positive response from themselves grew powerfully as the full impact of their situation was borne upon them. The decision of the Zürich Council on January 21, 1525, forbidding all those in favour of adult baptism to meet together was the spark that kindled a fire which was to burn in fervent hearts across half a continent.

Brüder in Christo

On the evening of this fateful winter Saturday, about twenty men gathered in the home of Felix Manz in Zürich. They talked over the situation, and their own needs before God. Let a contemporary account speak of what followed:

> "As they were together, anxiety came on them and pressed upon their hearts. So they began to bend their knees before Almighty God in heaven . . . ; they prayed that He would grant them to do His divine will, and that He would reveal His mercy to them. For flesh and blood and human forwardness did not drive them, since they well knew what they would have to bear and suffer on account of it. After the prayer George Cajakob (Blaurock) . . . entreated that Conrad Grebel should baptize him with the true Christian baptism upon his faith and knowledge. After this had taken place, the others likewise desired of George that he should baptize them, which also he did upon their request. And so they together dedicated themselves in the high fear of God to the Name of the Lord. Each confirmed the other in the service of the gospel and began to teach and hold the faith."

They linked themselves into a brotherhood of faith: Brüder in Christo, Brethren in Christ. It was sealed by a solemn but intimate "breaking of bread", either the same evening or the next day, Sunday.

YEAR OF DECISION—1525

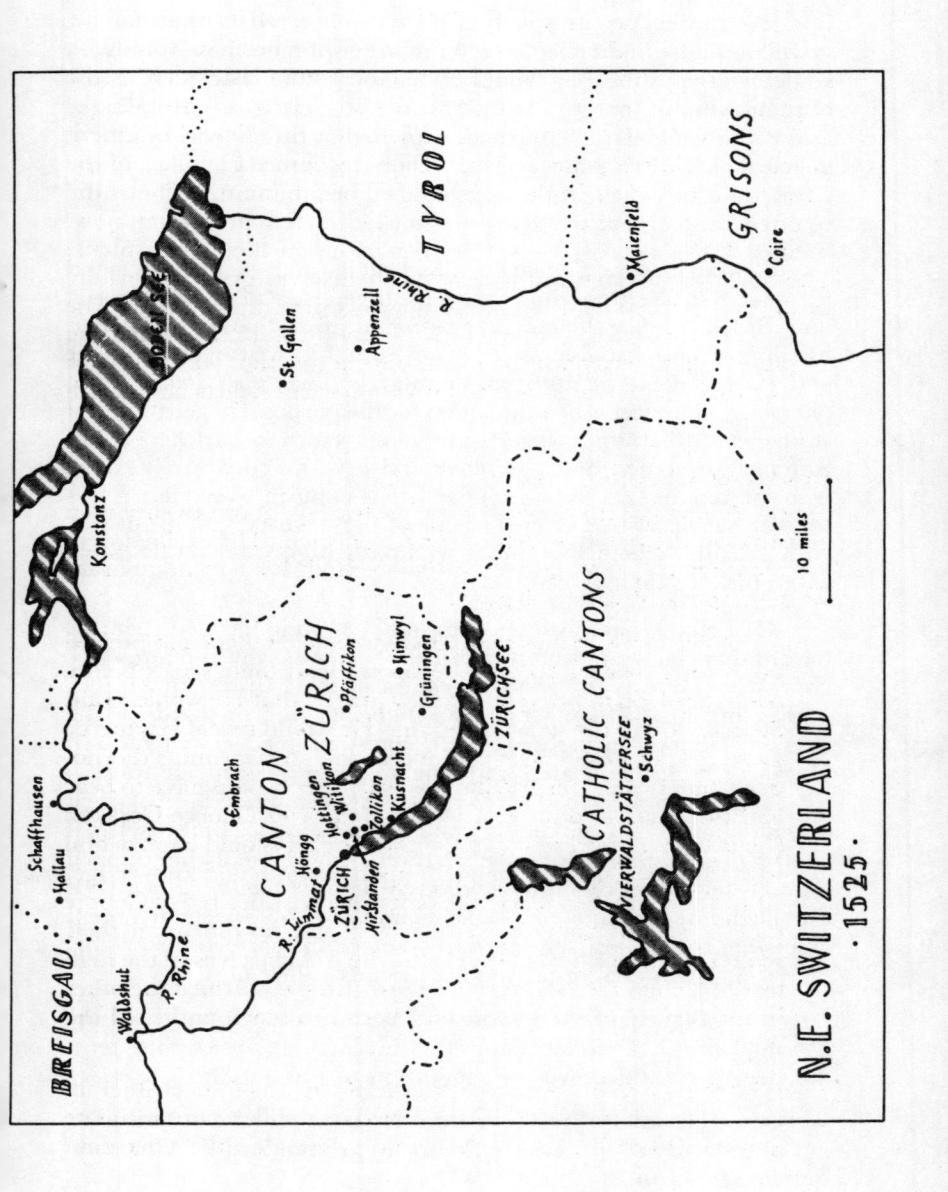

THE PROTESTERS

To appreciate the spiritual power generated in that hour it is well to pause and consider what manner of men these were who so determined that they would obey God rather than men. Most of them were in the prime of life. Cajakob, Manz, Eberli, Hätzer and Brötli were all to be burned, drowned or beheaded within five years of this Zürich meeting, in places hundreds of miles apart. Grebel was to survive little more than eighteen months. They fully realised the peril of the step they took.

Conrad Grebel, 27 years old, had left his native Zürich to spend a somewhat libertine youth at the Universities of Paris, Vienna and Basel. In fact he never graduated. But that he was both intelligent and capable is evident from his writings and later activities. He and his tutor at Vienna, who was also Swiss, made one of the first ascents of a mountain for the purposes of geographical study—Mt. Pilatus in Switzerland. On his return to Zürich a painful romance deepened his experience and it was a converted Grebel who entered the lists on behalf of apostolic baptism. A modern Swiss scholar has described Grebel as one of those earnest, pious people with a scrupulous turn of mind, who put a high value on the Bible as a guide to their lives.

Of Felix Manz, also a young man, no one has ever penned a word that is not a testimony to an altogether worthy and attractive character. He was the son of a canon of the Minster in Zürich, and before their estrangement Zwingli had him in mind for the chair of Hebrew in the projected Protestant academy in Zürich. He was "highly educated and was an accomplished Hebraist". Eberli has been described as "a man of high character and of great popular power". Cajakob, nicknamed Blaurock (Bluecoat) is a controversial figure among the Brethren. Undoubtedly he supplied a great deal of its dynamism, though there is plenty of evidence that he did not dominate it. As an example of how widely divergent assessments of character can be, we can contrast two historians' views of "strong George", as his friends called him:

> "Blaurock was a hothead. Blaurock was dynamic. Many may simply have let themselves be carried away by the temperament and power of suggestion of this pusher."

> "He was entirely free from fanaticism and can be said to have attained to a remarkably high standard of Christian consecration."

Concerning the group as a whole Zwingli's own grudging confession is expressive enough: "Their conduct appears irreproachable, pious, unassuming, attractive; even those who are inclined to be critical will say that their lives are excellent."

Johannes Brötli, originally a Roman Catholic priest, then a Zwinglian, and finally on January 21, 1525, one of the Brethren in Christ, had lived, since relinquishing his pastorship, in Zollikon, a village by the lake of Zürich. With his wife and child he lodged with Fridli Schumacher. On Sunday, the day following the gathering at Manz's home, he talked long and seriously with his landlord, and finally they walked together towards the city. On reaching Hirslanden, Schumacher said to Brötli: "All right then, Hans, you have shown me the truth. I thank you for it and ask you for the sign of baptism." The new brotherhood made its first convert. The same day Grebel officiated at a "breaking of bread" in Zollikon, the new brother being present.

Dr. Fritz Blanke of Zürich University has recently made some interesting comments on these two events:

> "The gripping thing in this scene is its apostolic simplicity. It is difficult to imagine a greater contrast than that between the baptism at Hirslanden and the christenings which at that time were customary in the churches of Zürich. Infants were still christened by Zwingli with blowing, driving out the devil, crossing, moistening with saliva, and anointing with oil. At Hirslanden all these accessories were lacking, as they had been lacking from baptism in early Christianity. The difference between the observance of the Lord's Supper in Zollikon and the manner in which Zwingli and his pastors, in that same January 1525 celebrated the Lord's Supper, is so great that it cannot be bridged. On the altars in the Grossmünster, in the parish church in Zollikon, we still find at that time the monstrance with the host, before it the pastor in chasuble, celebrating the Mass in Latin (omitting the sacrifice part), giving the congregation the wafer but not the cup. But here in the farmers' parlours in Zollikon, laymen break ordinary bread and distribute it along with the wine to all participants—a revolution in the history of the Lord's Supper."

On Wednesday evening, a Zollikon farmer, Ruedi Thomann, with his son-in-law Marx Bosshard, invited two of the expelled non-citizens, Röubli and Brötli to a farewell supper before they left, at his home. After supper Manz and Blaurock arrived from Zürich, and three other farmers from the Zollikon area also appeared. Whether by intention or spontaneously, a Bible study class began. It was much like many others previously held by these earnest Bible students; but there was one difference—it was held under ban of law. The evening had profoundly different effects upon the visiting farmers. Two of them, Jacob Hottinger and Brubbach, were deeply stirred by the meeting. Brubbach in fact "wept aloud, saying he was a great sinner, and desiring the others to pray for him". Both were baptized, Jacob Hottinger becoming an important leader of the Brethren in Zollikon and a thorn in the side of the authorities for some years. One farmer, however, "broke out in sweat" as he expressed it, "and would have run out of the door" rather than join in these unorthodox and forbidden activities. Manz and Blaurock stayed the night with Thomann, and during the night Bosshard, the host's son-in-law, recalls how the things he had heard "kept attacking him". He spent much of that night asking God to give him correct insight and the faith to follow the right. It was no easy struggle to decide to join an outlawed movement. By morning his Gethsemane was over and he sought for Blaurock to fulfil his desire.

Meanwhile, the leaders of the Brethren were dispersing over the country. Grebel, who was under no legal obligation to leave, seems to have decided to go to Schaffhausen, while Röubli went to Waldshut to stay with Hübmaier, and Brötli to Hallay. They did not remain idle. Among Grebel's converts in Schaffhausen, two proved outstanding figures in later work: Martin Lingg and Wolfgang Uollimann, who had known Blaurock intimately for some time. Uollimann was baptized by Grebel near to the famous falls at Schaffhausen. Röubli's stay in Waldshut resulted in April in the baptism of Balthasar Hübmaier. The font in the Waldshut church was "thrown into the Rhine as a papal relic".

Arrest and Imprisonment

Meanwhile in Zollikon the week which began eventfully on January 22 ended on the following Sunday with a disturbance in the parish church which involved Blaurock and the parish priest Billeter. Blaurock seems to have been there not to worship but to criticise, and he had to be rebuked by the deputy bailiff, who was present in the church.

It soon became apparent to the civic authorities that their mandates were not being obeyed, and that the fire was far from extinguished. On January 30 Blaurock, Manz and twenty-five Zollikon citizens were arrested and remanded in custody in Zürich. Blaurock and Manz were imprisoned in the Wellenberg tower which contemporary prints in the local museum show to have been in the middle of the Limmat River near its meeting with the lake. The rest were confined in a former monastery which had been cleared of its hermit occupants by Zwingli a few weeks before.

Zwingli endeavoured to divide the Zollikon converts from their leaders and so quickly reconvert them without resort to compulsion. He went personally to the hearing and put forward his main argument for infant sprinkling. It was that nowhere in the Bible is there any mention of anyone being baptized twice. The Brethren referred him to Acts 19. Zwingli, however, insisted that the men referred to in this chapter were only instructed by John the Baptist; only Paul had conferred water baptism on them. Dr. Blanke rightly comments: "This tortured interpretation was not convincing." In fact it would appear that Zwingli found these peasant farmers better informed in the Scriptures than he anticipated, and that during the hearing he promised by Easter to abandon Catholic usages for more Scriptural procedures. Rudolf Rutschmann spoke in his own name and also for the others that since he was

> "a servant, slave and obeyer of God, I will also do what God tells me. Therefore I will not give way to anyone, nor will I be turned from it by any worldly power. Otherwise I will be respectful and obedient to my honourable masters of Zürich in everything which is not against the will of God".

The Zollikon brethren were released on the understanding that they met only in groups of three or four for Bible study and that there was to be no propaganda.

On February 17 George Blaurock wrote from his cell a letter to the council explaining his previous behaviour. It is a powerful document enshrining a concept of Christianity undoubtedly envisaged by Christ but obscured by the national and ecclesiastical organisations of the 16th century:

> "Christ in sending out his disciples commanded them to go and teach *all peoples,* promising remission of sins through

the power given by God his Father to all who would call upon his Name. For an external sign he commanded them to baptize. As I have taught, some have come to me weeping and begging to be baptized. I have not felt at liberty to refuse, but after instructing them further as did the apostles in Acts 2, I have baptized them. In order that they might always keep in remembrance the death of Christ and his poured out blood, I have instructed them how Jesus instituted the Supper. Together we have broken bread and drunk wine in commemoration of the fact that we were all redeemed by the one body of Christ and washed by the one blood of Christ, that we all might be brothers and sisters of each other in Christ our Lord. In this I feel confident that I have done the will of God.''

Being a non-citizen, Blaurock had overstayed the eight day limit; he was released on February 24, presumably exiled, while Felix Manz remained incarcerated in the Wellenberg tower for a further period.

Blaurock did not immediately leave the canton, however; in fact he went to stay with Eberli at his baker's shop on Rennweg. There they shared a fraternal meal with other brethren. The next day he visited Zollikon and baptized five wives and two daughters of brethren there (presumably domestic instruction was not propaganda). Then he left the area for the Grisons, his native canton, where he was joined by Manz some time later.

The Brethren in Zollikon did not remain inactive as might have been expected in view of their imprisonment and the departure of their leaders. During March they increased in number considerably, with new members from Küsnacht, Höngg and other quite widely separated districts. Most significantly, however, they developed at least four characteristics of an independent church organisation: baptism, breaking of bread, preaching and exclusion of fellowship.

This period was short lived. On March 16 nineteen Zollikon members were arrested and cross-questioned one by one. Dr. Blanke comments that their answers show that they ''were not spiritualists who depended upon personal illumination, but they were biblicists, who found their guidance in the Bible, and the fullest possible compliance with it. These men from Zollikon and Zürich wanted to be considered responsible Christians and Bible readers." The farm labourer Gredig referred the lordly Zwingli to Mark 16 : 16 and Matthew 28 : 19 in explanation of his behaviour. After more serious threats most of the prisoners were again released on the strictest understanding that no further proselytising was to be done. The council later followed this up by ordering the dissenters to give up their private meetings and attend the state church in Zollikon. The reply of the farmer Jacob Hottinger to the prelates of Zürich crystallised the position of the Brethren in Christ. It is not given, he urged, to any government to dispose over God's Word with wordly means of force; is not after all the Word of God free? He begged the council not to compel him to attend church, but to allow him to practise in law-abiding peace his faith in the way his conscience demanded. Zwingli admitted to a friend: "We have accomplished nothing. Some have desisted, not because they have changed their mind, but because they have changed their nerve."

Revival in St. Gallen

Like a pent-up flood which, suppressed at one point, bursts out at another, the activities of the brethren found new direction. Forty miles east of Zürich is the city of St. Gallen, on the river Sitter. Its leading religious leader was von Watt, Conrad Grebel's brother-in-law and former university tutor.

St. Gallen was fertile ground. In this centre of an area where Roman Catholic religious orders had formerly acquired vast wealth and influence, anti-Roman feeling ran high. There was a latent desire to retain as little as possible of old Romanist traditions. Here came first Johannes Kessler, a graduate of Basel and Wittenberg, who gave up his professional career to become a saddler. Kessler held meetings for the expounding of the Scriptures, first in a private home, but later in the hall of one of the guilds. This work paved the way for that of Uollimann who went further than Kessler dared and held regular well-publicised meetings in the Weavers' Hall. These meetings attracted much attention, which increased even more when Eberli came from Zürich and Grebel followed Uollimann from Schaffhausen. The climax came on April 9, the Sunday before Easter, when Grebel led a long procession of candidates to the Sitter River for baptism. At other times vats or tubs were used, and the brotherhood grew rapidly. The campaign was also extended to the neighbouring canton of Appenzell, where it was outstandingly successful, so that for a time in a few villages the Brethren in Christ outnumbered the adherents of the state church. "The highest praise is bestowed", an historian has written, "on the purity and simplicity of the lives of these people, even by their enemies. Considering the intense excitement, it is remarkable that so little occurred that could in any sense be regarded as fanatical."

Von Watt set his face implacably against the movement. The last letter of Grebel which has been preserved was an appeal to his brother-in-law not to associate with Zwingli's bloodthirsty party through fear of persecution or by the thought that he might lose money or position, but rather "to obey the divine truth and trust alone in God". It was in vain. Uollimann was ordered to appear before the St. Gallen council on April 25. He gave a creditable account of baptism from a Scriptural and historical point of view. He agreed, however, to the council's request for temporary suspension of activities. This request was unfortunately misjudged as leniency; actually the council only wanted time to make adequate preparations for a more effective destruction, and so sought Zwingli's advice.

Zwingli urged St. Gallen to take immediate action against the brethren. He published a booklet on infant baptism, and sent copies with a letter to von Watt. Grebel's letter and Zwingli's were read to the council. Exception was taken to the former, and Zwingli's booklet was ordered to be read in all churches. It is one of Zwingli's poorest writings, a rambling and unconvincing work. When it was being read, Uollimann interrupted with, "You may have Zwingli's word; we will have God's Word", and with that he and his fellow-members left the church. Von Watt also prepared a tract on infant baptism, and the Brethren were required to refute it. This they essayed to do, but the council rejected their reply and imposed on them banishment and fines. Eberli agreed to leave St. Gallen in the interests of peace, but he was betrayed to the Roman Catholics and burnt alive in the market place at Schwyz.

An Appeal to Scripture and Reason

Hübmaier, though distant at Waldshut, threw in his glove during the St. Gallen campaign. His leaflet, first circulated during February before his own baptism and entitled *An Open Appeal,* issued its plain but polite challenges:

"Whosoever wills" (a deliberate echo of the opening words of the Athanasian creed), "let him show that one ought to baptize young children, and let him do this with plain, clear, simple Scriptures relating to baptism without addition".

After contrasting the two forms of baptism he concludes:

"Now let a Bible be opened as the right, orderly and truthful judge between these two propositions; let it be read with prayerful, humble spirit, and then this disagreement will be decided according to the word of God and finally settled. Then shall I be well content, for I shall always give God the glory, and permit His word to be the sole arbiter—to Him will I surrender, to Him have I devoted myself and my teaching. The truth is immortal."

Hübmaier was honest enough with himself, but he was certainly over-optimistic of the fairness and honesty of others.

In July Hübmaier wrote *The Sum of a Perfect Christian Life*. It was in the form of a letter to old friends in Ingolstadt and Regensburg. Among other matters, he urges them to view the Eucharist in a way radically different from even the most "protestant" of contemporary reformers:

"Plainly the bread is not the body of Christ, but a memorial of the great truth that his blood was poured out on the cross, for remission of sins. We are not to forget that Christ died for us. Thus Paul writes to the Corinthians, 'For as often as you eat this bread—notice he says bread—and drink this cup—notice it is wine that is drunk—you do show the Lord's death till he come'. He is not there, then, but he will come at the judgement, in great majesty and glory, visibly, as the lightning cometh out of the east and shineth even to the west."

No tortured theological interpretations, but a "common-sense" approach to the New Testament and to Christian foundations. Its appeal to many whom much 16th-century theology must have left cold is obvious. In its simplicity and reversion to plain Biblical patterns the movement which was generated in 1525 by the lake of Zürich was deliberately reminiscent of that by the shores of another lake in Galilee fifteen centuries before.

During the summer Grebel, Manz and Blaurock met for successful preaching activitiy in the vicinity of Grüningen, south-east of Zürich and within its jurisdiction. Amazingly, from June to October their campaign proceeded without serious molestation. It effected a real and genuine reformation within the community: "drinking and carousing" ceased, and local authorities noted the transformation in some of their citizens with no little astonishment. Trouble arose, however, at a meeting at Hinwyl on October 8 where Blaurock utilised the local church for preaching. Magistrate Berger turned him out and a meeting was held in a field outside. This attracted such a large and dangerously enthusiastic crowd that troops were sent for, whereupon the audience developed an ugly mood in attempting to defend the Brethren. They were restrained, however, by Grebel and Blaurock who allowed themselves to be arrested. Manz escaped, but was discovered and arrested three weeks later. Also involved in the round-up were Lingg and Michael Sattler, an eager convert from south-west Germany of whom more will be told later. Non-citizens such as these two were banished, the rest—both men and women—were brought to trial in Zürich.

"A Fair Disputation"

There were some members of the Zürich Council who felt that Zwingli's attitude to the Brethren was domineering and overpowering. It was to satisfy their tender consciences that "a fair disputation" was arranged in the great council chamber of the city hall. Zwingli, von Watt from St. Gallen and Grossmann were to present the official policy and Grebel, Manz, Blaurock and Hübmaier were to present the case for the Brethren in Christ. The encounter took place from November 6 to 8, lasting the full three days. Hübmaier, through illness, did not come from Waldshut as anticipated, and the audience in the council chamber contained so many of the Brethren that the disputation was transferred to a smaller room in the Great Minster, which was of course Zwingli's home ground. (Plate I).

It was not in any sense a fair disputation, but a trial in disguise. As one historian comments, the testimony of the prosecution was "woefully weak". Zwingli personally and enthusiastically advocated the summary execution of all the accused, which included several women. He referred to a comment of the sheriff of Grüningen that "these baptists" made his head grey with their words and proceedings.

Following the disputation severe repressive measures were

passed by council and court. On November 18 Grebel, Manz, Blaurock, Manz's wife Anna, Anna Wiederkehr, Elizabeth and Margareta Hottinger, and about fourteen other men and women were sentenced "to lie in the tower on a diet of bread, water and apple sauce, with no one permitted to visit them, as long as seems good to God and my lords" (see below). Presumably the divine Name is intended as a euphemism for Zwingli! Hübmaier wrote later of the episode in characteristic style:

> "...over twenty men, widows, pregnant wives, and maidens were cast miserably into dark towers, sentenced never again to see either sun or moon as long as they lived, to end their days on bread and water, and thus in the dark towers to remain together, the living and the dead, until none remained alive—there to die, to stink, and to rot. Some among them did not eat a mouthful of bread in three days, just so that others might have to eat."

In prison Grebel strengthened the prisoners by "reading the Scripture and admonishing". It is said that Anna Manz and the Hottinger sisters were "wonderful examples" to the rest of the company. One source comments that Felix Manz "managed to have candles smuggled into the tower" and that a "Bible school" was conducted in the gloom. Heinrich Eberli, who was a baker, even managed to arrange for the prisoners to have bread and wine for the Lord's memorial.

Meanwhile in Waldshut the sick Hübmaier was having trouble. On December 5 Austrian troops stormed into the town and the brief reformation was over. Mass was again celebrated in the church—as it has continued to the present day. Hübmaier and his wife had to flee. Unaccountably—perhaps because he relied overmuch on his previous friendship with Zwingli—they chose to go to Zürich. He arrived there with his family ragged, wretched and ill with the winter cold and exhaustion. With most of the influential Brethren in prison, he found himself in a sorry situation. Zwingli immediately had him arrested. It was in this atmosphere of apparent defeat that the eventful year of 1525 drew to its close.

THE PROTESTERS

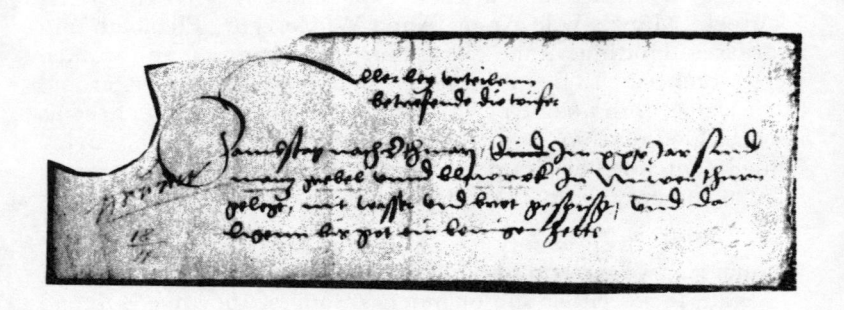

Record of imprisonment in the New Tower, Zürich, following the Court Order of November 18, 1525.

5

DEBATES AND DUNGEONS

THE first Zürich trial of Balthasar Hübmaier took place on January 13, 1526. He was very ill, a condition aggravated by several weeks of confinement. Accounts of the trial vary according to the standpoint of the writer. One account affirms that Hübmaier gave a masterly account of himself and the Word of God, confuting Zwingli out of his own mouth and writings. Zwingli, however, claims that he rendered Hübmaier "mute as a fish". Without question, Hübmaier showed that before coming to his present power Zwingli had in fact stated that there was no clear evidence in Scripture for infant sprinkling; he had witnesses who could testify that they heard Zwingli say that baptism of believers was more Scriptural. Such arguments as we know Hübmaier used were devastating to Zwingli's case, and so thorough was his answer that in addition to Bible testimony he showed historically from papal documents of the sixth century how infant sprinkling had generally superseded adult immersion.

Dialogue

We get some idea of the arguments from Hübmaier's *Ein Gesprech*, a document of his later Mikulov period. The following dialogue there occurs:

Zwingli: You reject infant baptism that you may set up rebaptism.

Hübmaier: You have not produced a single passage to prove infant baptism is baptism. You should remember what you once said, that truth is clearly revealed in the word of God. If now infant baptism is a truth, show us the Scripture in which it is found.

Zwingli: If everyone adopts such views as he pleases, and does not ask the church concerning them, error will increase.

Hübmaier: We should consult the Scriptures, not the church. The church is built upon the word, not the word upon the church.

Zwingli: The thief on the cross believed, and on the same day was with Christ in paradise; yet he was not baptized with outward baptism.

Hübmaier: A man who has the excuse of the thief on the cross will have the favour of God. But when this excuse is lacking the word of Christ holds true that "he that believes and is baptized shall be saved".

Zwingli: Matthew 3 says that "all Judaea" went out to John and were baptized. Here one may say that if the whole multitude went out, we should expect that there were children who went out also.

Hübmaier: Might not one also say that we should expect that Annas, Caiaphas, Pilate and Herod went out and were baptized? It matters not what we think or expect. We must be governed by the Scriptures. I appeal to the Scriptures. Let them decide.

Hübmaier's appeal to the Scriptures was no mere thrust in a verbal battle: it was a genuine approach and was the most reasonable course. For Zwingli frequently and loudly proclaimed that the very basis of his revolt from Rome (and hence his personal position) depended on loyalty to the Scriptures, not to the Roman church. Hübmaier was turning the screw where it hurt the most. It was for this reason that Zwingli was prepared to spend time arguing over the Scriptures with those whose influence he sought to destroy. It was more than disconcerting to find his own particular platform used against himself.

On this particular occasion Hübmaier was at a low ebb; he was ordered to recant, and under severe pressure, reluctantly agreed to do so. He was ordered to read the recantation publicly in the Fraumünster (Minster of our Lady), the great church which still stands on the right bank of the Limmat in Zürich. The moment came, but instead of reading the public recantation he rose and tearing it up, began to address the great assembly on the true Scriptural baptism—to the consternation of all. He was—needless to say—violently interrupted and frogmarched to prison. His wife was also imprisoned without a hearing. They were to be kept on bread and water, like the others, without light until "they should die together, perishing and rotting by the stench". (Plate II)

Balthasar Hübmaier. From an old woodcut.

A Moving Document

It was from this dark hour that there was born one of the most moving documents to survive from the 16th century: Hübmaier's *Prison Confession*. Written as an exercise in self-encouragement, it takes the form of a commentary on the Apostles' Creed. Its feeling is so intense and its spiritual tone so high that it is worth quoting at some length. It also reveals almost incidentally how radically the Brethren's Christian thinking had departed already from that of the new national protestant churches. There is no doctrinaire over-emphasis such as that upon justification with the Lutherans or divine election with the Calvinists. Its chief virtue, like that of its author, is a plain and appealing simplicity. In view of the circumstances in which it was composed the second paragraph quoted below is, to say the least, remarkable:

"I believe and confess, my Lord Jesus Christ, that you were conceived by the Holy Spirit, without any human seed, born from Mary. I believe and trust that in your living, indestructible word and in the spirit I may be born again and see the Kingdom of God.

"I believe and confess also that you suffered under Pontius Pilate, were crucified, dead and buried in order that you might redeem and ransom me from eternal death, by the pouring out of your blood in which your greatest and highest love to us poor men is recognised. For you have changed for us your heavy cross into a light yoke, your bitter sufferings into imperishable joys and your death in the midst of anger into eternal life. Therefore I will praise and thank you, my gracious Lord Jesus Christ, for ever and ever.

"I believe also and confess, my Lord Jesus Christ, that after those forty days in which you walked the earth for a testimony of your joyous resurrection, you ascended into heaven. There you sit, mighty and strong to help all believers who set their trust, comfort and hope in you, and cry to you in all their needs. There is no need to pray to you in any special place, for you are at the right hand of your heavenly Father, as the holy Stephen saw you and prayed to you. It is vain to seek another advocate.

"I believe and confess also that thence you will come to judge the living and the dead on the day of the last judgement, which will be to all godly men a specially longed for and joyous day. Then will be ended our fleshly, sinful and godless life. Then will each one receive the reward of his work; those who have done good will enter into eternal life, but those that have done evil into everlasting fire. O my Lord Jesus Christ, shorten the days and come down to us! Yet give us grace and strength so to direct our lives in the meantime that we may be worthy to inherit the Kingdom.

"I believe also and confess a worldwide brotherhood of

many pious and believing people, who unitedly confess one Lord, one God, one faith and one baptism; assembled, maintained and ruled on earth by the only living and divine word. O my God, grant that I and all who believe in Christ may be found in this church; may we believe, teach and hold all that you have commanded us by your word, and root out all things which you have not planted; that we may not be led into error by any views of men, institutions, or doctrines of old Fathers, popes, cardinals, universities or old customs. O my Lord Jesus Christ, establish again the two bands, namely, water-baptism and the Supper, with which you have externally girded and bound your Bride. For unless these two shall be again established it will never be well with your church.

"I believe also and confess a resurrection of the flesh, though it may be eaten by worms, drowned, frozen or burned. Yea, though my temporal honour, goods, body and life be taken from me, yet will I, at the day of the joyous resurrection, first truly receive the real honour which avails before God, goods that pass not away, a body incapable of suffering, made clear and immortal, and eternal life. O my Mediator, Lord Jesus Christ, strengthen and hold me in your Faith!

"I believe that you will endow your faithful and elect after this suffering life with a sure, clear and joyous beholding of your divine countenance, and satisfy them in eternal rest, eternal peace and eternal salvation, which joy, delight and bliss no man can express or conceive.

"O holy God, O mighty God, O immortal God, this is my faith which I confess with heart and mouth and have witnessed before the church in water-baptism. Faithfully, graciously keep me in that until my end, I pray. And though I be driven from it by human fear and terror, by tyranny, pangs, sword, fire or water, yet hereby I cry to You, O my merciful Father, raise me up again by the grace of Your holy spirit and let me not depart in death without this faith. This I pray You from the depth of my heart, through Jesus Christ, Your best-beloved Son, our Lord and Saviour. Amen."

There is significance in the fact that this poignant personal confession is based upon the Apostles' Creed; it reflects the aim of the Brethren in Christ to imitate and renew the original

Christianity of the apostolic age, before the accretions of later credal traditions. All the implications of this were not yet fully realised, but the trend was already clearly established.

A Severe Sentence

On March 7, 1526, the prisoners in the Water Tower were brought to a retrial, undoubtedly with the intention of passing an even more severe sentence. Execution was advocated by some, but the accused were eventually returned to their confinement under formal sentence of life imprisonment. This, however, in the conditions existing in the notorious Water Tower, undoubtedly meant a comparatively speedy death.

Under pressure from Zwingli, the Zürich government finally made adult baptism a capital offence. An old Roman law of Justinian was revived which made "repeating of baptism" and denial of the Trinity a crime punishable by death. The Brethren were labelled "Anabaptists" (re-baptizers) so that the authorities could bring them under this law, though they consistently rejected the term as being untrue and misleading in their case. It is amazing that protestant Europe of four hundred years ago should have utilised a law of Imperial Rome in order to destroy those who most fully adopted its own avowed principles. This was legally possible by the artificial concept of the "Holy Roman Empire" which was viewed as the direct successor of Imperial Rome, so that an unrepealed law of the latter could still be viewed as in force. Switzerland was still *de jure,* but not *de facto,* within the limits of the Holy Roman Empire.

For the prisoners in the Wellenberg life imprisonment lasted fourteen days. On April 5, a cell window was found to be unlocked, an unexpected occurrence which caused much heartsearching and some discussion. Should they accept it as a sign of a providential release like that of Peter in Acts or should they consider the temptation to escape as one to be resisted, and remain where they were. Grebel, Manz and Blaurock at first favoured the latter. But the condition of some, with swollen limbs and emaciated face, and the convenient presence of a rope, convinced the majority that they should assume that it was the former. The correctness of their assumption appeared to be confirmed when, upon descending through the window to the ground, they found the drawbridge down, permitting them to cross the Limmat to the shore. There was some discussion as to where they should go then. One of them ventured: "Let's go and preach to the Red Indians across the sea!"

They scattered over the country, turning up in odd places, but never willing to cease their work. Two weeks afterwards Manz baptized a woman at Embrach. Blaurock appeared in Grüningen, St. Gallen, Basel. Grebel and Manz preached in Appenzell and in the Grisons. Everywhere the common people found their Bibles, not long translated into their mother tongue, and the teachings of the Brethren to "agree wonderfully", and adherents increased throughout eastern Switzerland.

Plague was epidemic in Coire while Manz and Grebel were there. Exhausted and weakened from their recent imprisonment, Grebel contracted it. Feverish and weary, he travelled down the Rhine valley and sought a haven of rest at his sister Barbara's home in Maienfeld. In August, 1526, five months after the escape, Grebel died there at the age of 28.

It is a sorry measure of the vindictiveness of Huldrich Zwingli that, cheated out of the chance to get even with Conrad Grebel, he had his old father Jacob arrested on a trumped up charge and publicly beheaded. Jacob was a respected member of the city council, a loyal supporter of Zwingli's own Reformation, and in no way personally connected with the Brethren. But Conrad's young wife Barbara and their infant family lived with Jacob and depended on him for survival. Grebel's biographer John Ruth has commented that this "disgraceful affair" was nothing but "Zwingli's frustrated revenge on Conrad". As James 4 : 1-2 reminds us, what will proud and selfish men not do in their lust for power?

Debate and Repression

In Basel the irrepressible Blaurock and other Brethren engaged in a disputation before the council with Zwingli's friends. The Brethren insisted on Scriptural proof, but the "Reformers" were content to quote Origen and Augustine. Blaurock made a ringing response: "What have we to do with your doctors, the church fathers and the councils? They were men as we are, and as subject to blindness as we are."

An old argument fired at every dissenting minority raised its hoary head in this as in so many other debates: how can so many sincere and intelligent people be wrong? But the Brethren's answer was always that statistical counts were irrelevant.

"Baptism, we all agree, is a ceremony of the New Testament. Therefore we demand a plain passage with which you support infant baptism out of the New Testament. The word, the *word,* the WORD! Why will you like the night owl hate the light and refuse to come to the sun?"

Both sides considered themselves victorious in the Basel disputation. But the "Reformers" had the power, and repressive measures were enacted. Blaurock once again took the road, back to Grüningen, to a congregation to which he always seemed particularly attached. It proved later to be particularly resistant to destruction.

During 1526, despite every setback, the Brethren in Christ extended their influence and established conventicles of believers over a wide area of Switzerland, southern Germany and Moravia. A conference was held at Augsburg during that year and early in 1527 another was held at Schleitheim near Schaffhausen. Hübmaier went to Moravia in July, 1526. It is said that there were a hundred organised groups of believers by the end of 1526 in Switzerland alone. But along with this growth was a steady hardening of the attitude of the authorities, both Romanist and Protestant.

In January 1527 Felix Manz and Blaurock were arrested, the former for the last time. Manz appeared on a capital charge and the following verdict and sentence are illuminating as to the real issues at stake:

"He has administered baptism in a way contrary to Christian rule; in spite of all the admonitions he could not be made to repent. He and his followers have severed themselves from the Church and they have constituted themselves an independent sect under cover of a Christian gathering. Such teachings are contrary to the general custom of Christianity and lead to scandal.

"Therefore we commend that his hands be tied together and put over his knees, a stick inserted between his arms and legs and that he be thrown from a boat into the Limmat at a designated spot."

Blaurock was to be "beaten on the naked back through the streets until the blood should flow."

On January 25 Manz was drowned in the Limmat river in the manner prescribed. It was according to due process of law, but it was a tragic waste of the young life of a "zealous and godly man". Viewed objectively, the sentence on Blaurock was curiously lenient. Undoubtedly the more hotblooded of the two, he had been repeatedly banished and just as repeatedly he had returned in defiance of the order and continued the work. But again he was banished, and his first journey was only to Grüningen, still within the Zürich cantonal jurisdiction. Blaurock went on from there to the Tyrol, leaving Switzerland for good. We shall meet him again when considering developments in the Tyrol. His Grüningen brethren and sisters suffered grievously a few months later and many of them were drowned. This method of execution was intended as a mockery of their baptist practices: Zwingli laconically called it "their third baptism".

The sentence upon Manz crystallised the real issue: the Brethren's activities, though entirely peaceful and conducive to the uplift of the human spirit, were classed as subversive of Church and State. It was really the familiar modern situation of a non-revolutionary, law-abiding but proselytising minority within a monolithic totalitarian state. Vedder comments that the Brethren's "doctrines were too scriptural, too spiritual, too incompatible with those that were forced upon unwilling people by men actuated by ambition and greed". A rather extreme judgement perhaps, but not very far from the truth.

6

BALTHASAR HÜBMAIER IN MORAVIA

IN July 1526 Hübmaier left Zürich for the last time, travelling more than 400 miles to the town of Mikulov in Moravia, three miles north of the Austrian frontier. The reason for the choice was the knowledge that the realm of Louis, king of Bohemia, Moravia and Hungary was noted for its tolerance of protestant minorities. In an area where the Moravian Church *(Unitas Fratrum* or Hussites) had made a deep impact already upon religious and moral thinking, fruitful ground would certainly exist for Hübmaier to cultivate.

The immediate cause of Hübmaier's departure from Zürich has been the subject of unjust slanders against his integrity. As has been mentioned already, he was not highly endued with natural courage, but it has been alleged that he left Zürich to save face after an abject recantation. Recantation there undoubtedly was, and Hübmaier wrote grievingly afterwards: "O God, pardon my weakness. It is good for me (as David says) that Thou hast humbled me." But certain letters of Zwingli cast lurid light upon the circumstances in which it was made. He boasts that he "allured" Hübmaier into recantation by torture. In a letter to a friend Zwingli describes Hübmaier as stubborn and states that he did not recant freely. In a gloating style excessive even for Zwingli, he writes that, seeing that Hübmaier was clearly "a sport of demons", he extracted a recantation from him while he was "stretched upon the rack". That this was so is confirmed by the sinister words in his final condemnation in Vienna in 1528: "He was racked also at Zürich on account of the second baptism, and *compelled* to testify who had led him into such baptism, and . . . made a public recantation." Clearly Zwingli was not only interested in a recantation through the rack, but wanted some names as well. It would have been folly for Hübmaier to remain in Zürich any longer.

Reformers' Cruel Persecution

From the comparative safety of Mikulov, Hübmaier could look back upon his Zürich trials with more objectivity. "Faith is a work of God, and not of the heretic's tower, in which one sees neither sun nor moon, and lives on nothing but water and bread. But God be praised who delivered me from this den of lions, where dead and living men lay side by side and perished."

He marvelled at the inconsistency of men who, claiming to be reformers of the Christian faith and preachers of the religion of Jesus, yet used the foulest of means to eliminate those who peaceably endeavoured to be most loyal to it. In one of his finest and most eloquent passages Hübmaier cries from the heart for love and patience and against the brutalities and cruelties perpetrated in the name of Jesus:

> "Christ did not come to butcher, to murder, to burn, but that men might have life and that more abundantly. So long as a man lives, we should pray and hope for his repentance. A Turk or a heretic is to be overcome not with sword or fire but by patience and weeping. We are therefore to wait patiently for the judgement of God. Every Christian has a sword against the godless, that is the word of God; but not a sword against evil-doers. True faith thrives by conflict; the more it is opposed the greater it becomes. When Jehoiakim destroyed the book of Jeremiah, Baruch wrote a better one. The truth is immortal."

The Moravian period in Hübmaier's life was a fruitful one. He was protected by the local lord. He became the much-loved spiritual guide and leader of a growing community of like-minded souls in and around Mikulov. That his own sincerity and magnetic spirituality burned deep into the hearts of many there was evidenced later by the tenacity with which his fellow-Brethren in Moravia clung to the principles they shared, despite the most ferocious persecution ever meted out to a helpless religious community. Many others besides Hübmaier found a temporary haven of refuge in Moravia during 1526, and a steady stream of refugees from Switzerland, the Tyrol, Italy and Germany swelled the ranks of the Brethren in that country.

Some of these, fresh from cruel persecutions, were neither so patient nor so well-grounded in the principles of Christ as Hübmaier. A particularly acute thorn in the flesh was Hans Hetz, who had been associated with Thomas Müntzer before the latter became involved in the Peasant's War in Germany. Hetz, a bookbinder, began to preach on arrival that the Second Coming of Christ would take place at Whitsun 1528, whereupon he would lead his saints to victory. There was even talk of making some practical preparations to that end. However, after creating rather an anxious period for Hübmaier, Hetz returned to Germany where he was killed trying to escape from an Augsburg prison.

Appeal to the Scriptures

But it was not only in his evangelical and pastoral work that Hübmaier was fruitful. During his brief period of freedom writings poured from his pen, writings as overflowing as his earlier works with a reverent love of God's word, alive and vibrant with a passionate spiritual power. Neglected as they were and are, the few unbiased scholars in more recent times who have paid any attention to them have recognised their quality and worth, and have appreciated them as one of the great highlights of the Reformation period, richer in spirit and more honest in exegesis than the works of the more famous "reformers". Contrasting them with Zwingli's unconvincing sophistries, the Swiss scholar Usteri comments that "Hübmaier's exegesis is substantially in accord with modern scientific methods". Vedder has said: "His continual enquiry, as each point is discussed, is *what do the Scriptures* say about this? There are few writers in the history of the church who have searched the Scriptures with a greater zeal to discover their teaching, or have come to the study with a more open mind, or have bent fewer texts from their plain meaning to support a favourite theory."

In a day when dogmas were battlegrounds for wordy controversies, Hübmaier's treatment of the fundamental doctrines of the Christian faith shone with uncommon brilliance. For him no Bible doctrine could be a sterile tenet to be cloaked in verbiage and highly-spun by worldly logic; for him it was a conviction that changed a man or woman's entire being. Water baptism, for example,

". . . is an external and public testimony of the inward baptism of the spirit, set forth by receiving water. By this not only are sins confessed, but also faith in their pardon, by the death and resurrection of our Lord Jesus Christ, is declared before all men. Hereby also the recipient is externally marked, inscribed and incorporated into the fellowship of the churches, according to the ordinance of Christ. Publicly and orally he vows to God by the strength of God the Father, the Son and the Holy Spirit, that he will henceforth believe and live according to the divine word; also in case he should be negligent, that he will receive brotherly admonition, according to the order of Christ in Matthew 18 . . . . It is a pledge and promise which the baptized makes to Christ, our invincible leader and head, that he will contend manfully under his flag and banner in Christian faith until death.''

Hübmaier was convinced that, despite the profound nature of the subject, Christian theology was needlessly complicated by men more interested in displaying their erudition than in explaining the verities of God, for among the Brethren he had witnessed humble artisans become mighty in the Scriptures. In his *Simple Explanation* he wrote:

> "The humblest believer is able to understand the Scriptures, so much so at any rate as is necessary to salvation, and it is his duty to acquire his understanding by his own study of the word, not to take it at secondhand from anybody."

There was rarely need for the seeker to grope for an answer. One golden rule that he enunciated was that Scripture can be interpreted only by Scripture, and he uses a compelling figure:

> "If we put beside obscure or brief passages other passages on the same subject, and bind them all together like wax candles, and light them all at once, then the clear and pure splendour of the Scriptures must shine forth."

Like a thread his emphasis on the Bible as the source and fountain of all we know of Christ and Christianity runs through his Mikulov works. The protestant reformers talked much of the Bible, but continued to cling to traditions, usages and accretions that have no place in it. They claimed to make the Scriptures the standard, but in practice maintained rigid church authority. Hübmaier would have none of this:

> "We should inquire of the Scriptures, and not of the church, for God will have from us only His law, His will, not our wrong heads or what seems good to us. God is more concerned with obedience to His will than with all our self-invented church usages."

Theologians, he contended, split hairs over abstract concepts, yet let great practical demonstrations of obedience such as the baptism of faith and non-retaliation go unhonoured. "But it is just the way of human wisdom to hold as of least weight that which God highly regards or commands." There was logic in his insistence that the church is built upon the word, not the word upon the church. A hymn he composed on 1 Peter 1 : 25 reflects Hübmaier's Biblical approach and that of the Brethren in general:

> "Ah, blind man, now hear the word;
> Make sure your state and calling;
> Believe the Scripture is the power
> By which we're kept from falling.
> Your valued lore at once give o'er,
> Renounce your vain endeavour;
> This shows the way, no longer stray;
> *God's word stands sure for ever.*"

The last verse of this hymn is interesting, anticipating as it does wide development and breathing a conviction that if Peter was right, then neither hidebound tradition nor brute force would completely stifle truth:

> "Praise God, praise God in unity,
> Ye Christian people sweetly,
> That He His word has spread abroad—
> His word, His work completely.
> No human hand can Him withstand,
> No name how high soever;
> And sing we then our glad Amen!
> *God's word stands sure for ever.*"

Death by Fire and Water

Mikulov offered Hübmaier refuge for barely a year. As a haven of freedom Moravia proved a fateful choice, for 1526, the very year of his migration, saw dynastic changes in the country. Louis, who had inherited Bohemia, Moravia and Hungary from his father Vladislav, was killed fighting the Turks on his eastern frontier. The succession fell to Ferdinand, archduke of Austria, who had married Anne, Louis' sister. As a Habsburg he was a stout defender of the Roman Catholic faith. In July 1527, Hübmaier and his wife, Elizabeth, were arrested in Mikulov and taken south to Austria.

Archbishop Fabri of Vienna made a futile endeavour to convert them; they had long conversations and Hübmaier was humble enough to admit that he might well be mistaken on many things, but there were some commands of the Lord which he felt in all sincerity that he could not compromise. The bishop confessed failure and Hübmaier was brought to trial. The outcome was inevitable:

"The aforesaid Dr. Balthasar confesses that he does not at all believe in the sacrament of the altar nor in infant baptism. Therefore Dr. Balthasar, on account of this crime and condemned heresy, is condemned to the fire."

On March 10, 1528, he was led forth to death, Elizabeth "exhorting him to fortitude". An enemy eye-witness said that he remained to the last "fixed like an immovable rock in his heresy". He was urged to confess to a priest, but he steadfastly refused. There was no thought of compromise now, no hope of mercy. The whole sadistic atmosphere of the public burning sickened his deeply sensitive spirit, the morbid curiosity of the crowd providing an additional wound. But there was no bitterness or regret. "O dear brothers", he said as he was tied to the stake, "if I have injured any, in word or deed, may he forgive me for the sake of my merciful God. I will forgive all that have done me harm." With those who rubbed salt and gunpowder into his beard he jested: "O salt me well, salt me well", and as his clothes were removed from him, he muttered: "My Lord, they took your clothes off, too." His last words were his Lord's: "Into your hands I commit my spirit."

It was the senseless slaughter at the height of his powers of one of the gentlest and noblest spirits of his age or of any age. Here was no revolutionary, no obsessed and dogmatic fanatic, but a man whose sensitive and eager conscience only wanted to pave paths of peace and truth for the spirit of man. "Learned, eloquent, free from fanaticism, and without rancour in debate", says a modern scholar of him, "he returned revilings with appeals and insulted no one. He wrote few angry words in a world where most pens were dipped in vitriol."

On March 13 his devoted Elizabeth, described by a court official as "hardened in the same heresy even more constant than her husband", had a great stone tied to her neck and was thrown into the water of the Danube.

Three years before the Vienna crowds flocked to just another victim "roasted at the stake" and knew not what they did, Hübmaier had written a work entitled *Concerning Heretics and Those That Burn Them*. It was an impassioned plea for liberty of conscience, for love rather than hate, for controversy to be conducted in the spirit of Christ:

> "Those who are heretics one should overcome with holy knowledge, not angrily but softly, with a spiritual fire and a zeal of love. The greatest deception of the people is a zeal for God that is unscripturally channelled, for conviction of the right and sincerity are deadly arrows where they are not led and directed by the Scriptures. It is a small thing to burn innocent people, *but to point out an error and disprove it by Scripture, that is art.*"

7

THE FIERY TRIAL

IN describing the campaign at Grüningen mention was made of Michael Sattler, who by the court order of November 18, 1525, was expelled from Zürich as a non-citizen. Thirty-five years old at this time, Sattler had been born of artisan background in the small town of Staufen, in the Rhine valley at the foot of the Black Forest. As an earnest and talented youth, Michael came under the influence of the Benedictines in the city of Freiburg eight miles from his home. He eagerly acquired considerable knowledge of Hebrew, Greek and, of course, Latin. Entering the monastery of St. Peter's in Freiburg as a novice, he rose to the rank of prior. This occurred at a time when evangelical preaching was increasing in the area, and Sattler was encouraged in consequence to make deeper study of the Scriptures. He was also spurred to view critically his ecclesiastical environment. He did not like what he saw.

Later, referring to this formative period in his life, Sattler tells how he "beheld the pomp, pride, usury and great whoredom of the monks and priests". He was unable to reconcile his position as a "spiritual lord" with Jesus' ideal of the disciple as meek and lowly in heart, serving not being served, transforming men by example not dominating them by carnal weapons. The immoral celibacy of the priesthood, which winked at pleasure but accepted no responsibilities, sickened him, and he married. He made a good choice—"a talented clever little woman" we are told—for she proved to be a great help and source of strength to him in his later work and trials. From his later writings it is clear that one field of New Testament study which compelled his attention was the doctrine of the church, the way the "ecclesia of Christ" should be constituted and directed. He saw little similarity between either the worldly, tyrannical Roman church or the newly emerging

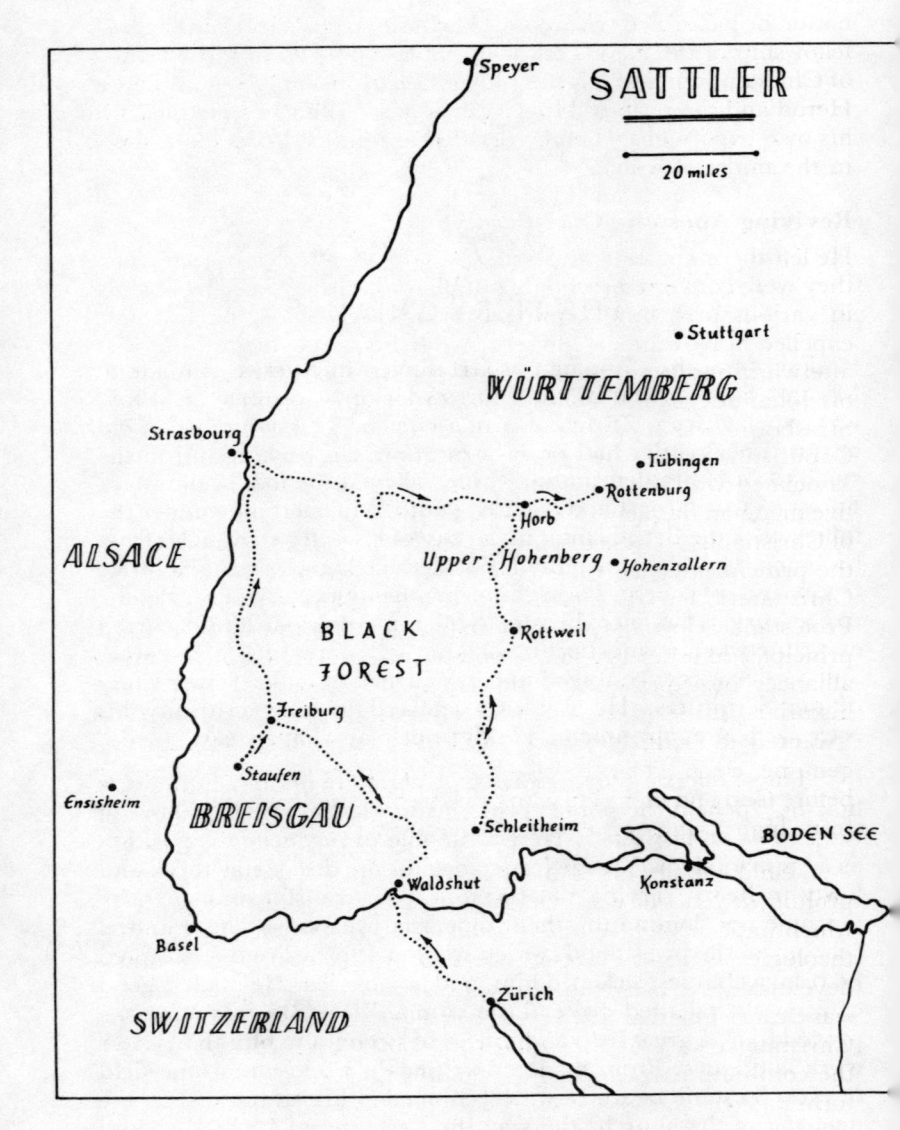

Travels of Michael Sattler

national Reformed churches, and the simplicity and earnest fellowship of the New Testament Christians. To him the leaders of Christendom had left the side of Christ for a place with Pilate, Herod and the scribes. How right he was in this revealed itself in his own experience when he decided to join his Lord as "a sheep in the midst of wolves".

Reviving Apostolic Christianity

He left the monastery and with his wife travelled to Zürich where they were converted through Röubli to the Brethren. He engaged in various preaching ventures during 1525 before being finally expelled in November. He returned to his home district, but soon afterwards moved to Strasbourg, where he made the acquaintance of Johannes Denck who was associated with the Brethren. Strasbourg was a mainly Protestant city, and the two reformers Capito and Bucer were working there. Ludwig Hätzer, also associated with the Brethren, joined Sattler and Denck, and the five men had frequent discussions on the Bible and the reformation of Christianity. These discussions led Sattler to define more clearly the principles which he felt were essential to a revived apostolic Christianity. He was increasingly dismayed at the way the leading Protestant reformers seemed inclined to compromise Biblical principles in order to achieve power, and especially uneasy about alliances of expediency with temporal authorities. A modern historian has expressed Sattler's rapidly crystallising aim: he "wanted to build a church of Christ, pure, God-fearing, and genuine, cleansed by the blood of Christ to be holy and blameless before God and men. He clung to humble simplicity and withdrew from high flying spirits and theologians".

Unlike some other prominent Brethren, Sattler was not a prolific writer, but what he did write has a directness and clarity which indicates a love of essentials and a distaste for highly-spun theological exegesis. His contribution to the literature and development of the Brethren was practical and administrative. It was clear to him that there could be no genuine imitation of original Christianity without a spiritual and ethical power to move and fire the communities of believers. It was while at Strasbourg that he formulated some of the essential principles which he sought to commend to his growing brotherhood.

"Christians are citizens of heaven, not of the world."

"The spiritual are Christ's; the carnal belong to death and the wrath of God."

"Christians are quite at rest and confident in their Father in heaven, without any external wordly armour."

This last item of faith is revealing of Sattler's attitude. For him, the Brethren's tenet of non-resistance was not a negative thing. It was the outcome of a positive confidence in the highest Power. And Sattler also saw the implications of an international fellowship in Christ. Involvement in national and local strife was impossible for one owing higher loyalties and owning wider ties in the family of Christ. The titles of his surviving writings indicate his practical bent and organising interests: *Concerning Evil Overseers, Concerning Divorce, The Hearing of False Prophets, Two Kinds of Obedience,* and others. His work in setting the highest standards for the Brethren to live up to has been described as being carried out with "unfeigned warmth and devotion". There is no doubt of the tremendous affection in which he and his wife were held by his fellow-brethren; this despite the fact that he moved among them for scarcely eighteen months.

During 1526 Sattler and his wife, at the suggestion of Röubli, moved to Horb, today an appealing little town in a lovely setting among the hills of Württemberg. The aim was to envangelise the whole Hohenberg region, which from 1520 to 1534 was part of the Austrian Habsburg lands and therefore officially Romanist. It is a measure of his sincerity and leadership that not only did viable and fervent communities endure after less than a year of his guidance, but that he endeared himself to the populace at large over a wide area of southern Germany.

In the midwinter of early 1527 Sattler journeyed south to Schleitheim in the Swiss Confederation. In this old Roman town below the vineyards of the Staufenberg north-west of Schaffhausen in Switzerland, representatives of groups of Brethren gathered for a conference on a number of important topics of common interest. Sattler was invited to preside and his influence is apparent in the articles drawn up at the conference. These regarded the church as made up of local units of baptized believers. Each of the units was to elect its own serving brethren or "shepherds" according to Scriptural principles and be bound together through the Lord's Supper. Baptism, excommunication, separation from the world, oaths and non-resistance were other articles. The following is article seven:

> "The secular government acts according to the flesh, the Christian according to the spirit. The secular authority has its abode in this world, the Christian's authority is in heaven. The fights and war-weapons of the civil power are carnal and can only attain the flesh; the arms of the Christian are spiritual and are directed against the wiles of the devil. Men of this world are armed with iron, but the Christian is armed with the armour of God, that is with truth, justice, faith and the word of God. In short, the members of the body of Christ must have the disposition of Christ, lest there should come a division in the body which would be fatal to it."

Arrest and Trial

This conference was held on February 24, 1527. Less than a week later, back in Horb, Sattler and his wife, Röubli's wife and several other members of the congregation there were arrested by the Austrian troopers. It is clear that the latter had been seeking a pretext to put a stop to such a radical reformation in Catholic territory as the Brethren were accomplishing. The Roman Catholic hierarchy saw the movement, peaceful as it was, as a threat to their influence, power and privileges. It was the crucifixion of Christ all over again; the Brethren viewed it so. Formal, vested religion was ranged against the faith of the heart, coercion against conscience; "he that was born after the flesh was persecuting him that was born after the spirit" (Galatians 4 : 29). Sattler was convinced that it could not be otherwise. At Binsdorf, where he had been taken, and yearning for his beloved flock in Horb, he wrote them a deeply moving letter. A precious document of the human spirit, it reveals a triumphant faith, unmarred by the glorification of martyrdom which characterised certain periods of early Christian history. The Austrian Imperial authorities were determined to make a *cause célèbre* of the trial and spared no pains in the preparations, which took several months. Considerable effort was made to create an atmosphere of legality. However, unforeseen hindrances arose.

The unimportant town of Rottenburg was chosen for the trial, and Tübingen University, at that time Roman Catholic, was asked to send two lawyers, as it was believed they would ensure a more severe sentence. But the request was refused on the grounds that if the death sentence was passed the lawyers would be disqualified for the priesthood, since technically they could not be consecrated if they acted as prosecutors in a criminal court. Matters dragged on, and meanwhile appeals for mercy were being increasingly made by many influential people. For the authorities it became even more necessary to simulate legality; but they remained absolutely determined that Sattler at all costs must suffer the ultimate penalty. Only after three appeals, accompanied with much pressure, did Tübingen eventually send two laymen, who were not doctors of law at all. The chief prosecuting counsel were two lawyers from the provincial government—Jodokus Gundersheim and Eberhard Hofmann, the town clerk of Ensisheim in Alsace. A bench of twenty-four judges was summoned, presided over by Count Joachim of Hohenzollern.

The trial was skilfully prepared, chiefly by Hofmann. Joachim was jittery about the local support for the prisoners and they were escorted to Rottenburg by a squad of twenty-six cavalry and fifty-six foot soldiers. From the four surviving accounts of the trial, a picture emerges of the characters in the drama almost as vivid as that of the trial in the Gospels. Count Joachim, not a particularly vindictive ruler but anxious to appear a good defender of Catholic orthodoxy in his part of the Imperial dominions; his wife, secretly horrified by the whole proceedings; the twenty-four judges, not all equally callous perhaps, but determined to maintain their privileges and unaware of the fundamental ethical nature of the whole case; the sympathetic sergeant-at-arms; and Hofmann, undoubtedly the archfiend of the piece, bloodthirsty, fanatical, a vicious bigot of evil reputation and ferocious temper.

The trial of Michael Sattler opened with pomp on Friday, May 17, 1527. Imagine the scene: on a long dais the twenty-four judges represented the overpowering weight of Imperial authority; below them, the testy Hofmann, armed, scans his brief, and the prisoners—Sattler and his wife, nine other men and eight other women—crowd the dock, flanked by guards with halberds. The odds were heavily against the accused.

It has been stated in the principal modern reconstruction of the trial that Jacob Halbmayer was Sattler's defence counsel and that he appeared only at the beginning and end of the trial. This is, however, a misinterpretation of Halbmayer's office, for as mayor of Rottenburg he carried the courtesy title "attorney for the defence of his lord", meaning, of course, His Imperial Majesty. Actually, the prisoners had no defence counsel. Sattler had informed Halbmayer that "the way of law was forbidden them by God's word". He had no desire to be acquitted by the oratory and skill of a man of the world. Actually, Halbmayer leaned over backwards to prove himself zealous in his office.

There were seven charges against all the prisoners and two specifically against Sattler. These were read on the first day, after which Sattler made a plea questioning the competency of the court, since the issues were basically religious and matters of personal conscience. The accused had committed no breach of the peace. Heresy was supposed to be tried by ecclesiastical courts at Konstanz. This plea was, of course, dismissed, since the Austrian judiciary considered itself defender of the Roman faith as well as guardian of the peace. The charges placed the Brethren on the same level as Turks, called their beliefs a secret revolt, an unchristian attack on the "Faith". The Roman Catholic church alone was valid on Austrian soil. A panegyric in praise of the Roman church was included, recounting its splendours and its miracles, which it was alleged Sattler was undermining. Rejection of trans-substantiation, infant baptism, and extreme unction constituted a heinous crime. The accused were charged with despising the Mother of God and refusing to swear by the Holy Trinity. The expression "breaking of bread", peculiar to the Brethren, was through the doctrine of trans-substantiation construed into a charge that they were guilty of breaking Christ! The two charges made against Sattler alone were firstly abandoning the monastic order and marrying, and, secondly, refusal to fight the Turks if they invaded.

A Remarkable Answer

On the second day Sattler requested that the charges be re-read as they were so many and he did not have them in writing. Hofmann objected with the jibe that there was no need; the Holy Ghost should tell the prisoners. However, he grudgingly agreed and they were re-read. A contemporary chronicle continues—

> "Thereupon Michael Sattler requested permission to confer with his brethren and sisters, which was granted him. Having conferred with them for a little while, he began and

undauntedly answered as follows . . ."

The answer that follows is remarkable. "He began, unafraid, skilfully but modestly, to discuss each article in turn." He refers throughout to his judges as "ministers of God". A wonderful, radiant dignity seems to pervade his defence, even when reported through the pen of von Graveneck, sergeant-at-arms of the court, whose account of the trial is preserved in the old town of Wolfenbuttel in north Germany.

He began by pointing out that Austrian law only forbade adherence to the "Lutheran delusion", and of this they were not guilty. "I am not aware that we have acted contrary to the gospel and the word of God. I appeal to the words of Christ." He denied certain points in the charges and admitted others, such as disbelief in trans-substantiation and infant baptism. On the charge of insulting the Mother of God and the saints, Sattler spoke with disarming frankness, carefully choosing his words and terms so as to make his beliefs clear:

> "We have not insulted the mother of God and the saints. For the mother of Christ is to be blessed among all women because unto her was accorded the favour of giving birth to the Saviour of the whole world. But that she is acting as mediator and advocate—of this the Scriptures know nothing. She is not yet elevated, but like all men, is awaiting the judgement. Christ is our mediator. As regards the saints, we say that we who live and believe are saints, which I prove by the epistles of Paul, where he always writes 'to the beloved saints' . . ."

On the two personal counts he spoke quietly of his own experiences: of his disgust at the conduct of the monks, their show, deception, covetousness and great fornication in seducing this man's wife, daughter, maid irresponsibly. Finally, in an eloquent and challenging peroration, he denied that in word or deed the Brethren had ever opposed the Government:

> "In conclusion, ministers of God, I urge you to consider the purpose for which God has appointed you, to punish the evil and to defend and protect the pious. Since we have not acted contrary to God and the gospel, you will find that neither I nor my brethren and sisters have offended in word or deed

against any authority. Ministers of God, send for the most learned men and for the sacred books of the Bible in whatsoever language they may be and let them dispute with us in the word of God. If they prove to us that we err and are in the wrong, we will gladly desist and recant and also willingly suffer the sentence and punishment for that of which we have been accused. We are ready to be taught from the Scriptures."

After a violent reaction from the prosecutor Hofmann, who drew his sword and waved it violently in the air, the judges retired to an anteroom and remained there for an hour and a half. During this time, with Hofmann's encouragement, Sattler and his friends were "set at nought". Insults and mockery not usually offered to the worst criminals were flung at them by the soldiers. The Brethren remained silent and this incensed the soldiers more.

Unmitigated Savagery

The judges returned with a verdict of guilty and a sentence of horrifying and unmitigated savagery. "Michael Sattler shall be committed to the executioner, who shall convey him to the square and first cut out his tongue. Then he shall forge him fast to a wagon and thereon with glowing iron tongs twice tear pieces from his body, then on the way to the site of execution five times more in the same manner, and then burn his body to powder as an arch-heretic."

There was a moment of emotion. The prisoner's wife turned to her husband and, drawing him to her, embraced him in the sight of the entire crowd. It moved at least one member of the audience.

Sattler was remanded in custody for a further three days. Said a friend in a letter: "What fear, what conflict and struggle flesh and spirit must have undergone cannot be imagined."

There is a spot on the Tübingen road, about a mile out of Rottenburg, where men, following such dim light as they had, in the name of perverted justice, removed from their midst one more worthy than themselves. The cutting out of the tongue was bungled, allowing Michael to pray for his persecutors. As he was lashed to the ladder he spoke with concern to Halbmayer, urging him to have no part in the deed lest he also be condemned. The mayor answered defiantly that Sattler should concern himself only with God.

His last public words, uttered with difficulty, were a prayer for God's help to testify to the truth. The ladder was thrown on to the fire. As the fire burned through the ropes that bound his hands, he raised two fingers of his hand in a victory sign, a pre-arranged signal to his friends that he had been steadfast. He was thirty-seven. (Plate III)

The Countess of Hohenzollern, the wife of Joachim, tried to persuade Sattler's wife of the folly of persisting in her belief. She promised that if the condemned woman gave up her faith she could come and live with her at the castle. But she declared that she would rather be true to her Lord and her husband. Eight days later she was thrown into the Neckar river and drowned.

The grim proceedings provoked a wave of revulsion through Württemberg, and there was much conscience-searching by many people, as evidenced by some contemporary publications and letters. But the religious and civil leaders had their way, and bigotry and fear prevailed.

The Brethren and their sympathisers were not slow to notice the striking comparisons between the Rottenburg trial and that of Jesus himself; the attempts to preserve outward legality, the determination to secure a capital verdict, the demeanour of the accused, the viciousness and envy of the prosecutors, the weakness of the judge, the insultings and revilings, the helplessness of the populace who had been taught by the accused themselves not to resist force with force, the resignation and heroism of the condemned. There were others less sympathetic who were able to see them too and to draw their own conclusions.

The trial had more significance than was realised, for it brought into focus a major human ethical dilemma—whether religion should be a compulsion of government and the party in power or a compulsion of the heart and conscience. It was also a test of another conflict: whether lives based on loyalty to the spirit of the Christian Gospel by an international communion can be permitted to co-exist alongside national laws and policies based on expediency. It is a conflict by no means resolved even today.

Four hundred and thirty years after the prayers of Michael Sattler were stifled by the sulphurous smoke of the faggots, a small plaque was unveiled in the evangelical church in Rottenburg to one of whom the world was not worthy.

8

SCATTERED ABROAD

By the end of the year 1527 little communities of Brethren in Christ were scattered through the central and northern cantons of the Swiss Confederation, and also in Moravia, the Tyrol, and southwest Germany. Yet almost all of the original leaders of the movement—barely two years old—were either dead, in prison or in exile. Especially was this true of Switzerland. Egli, a Swiss historian with no marked sympathy for what the Brethren stood for, had to comment when surveying the stubborn staying-power of the community which they founded: "What extraordinary men these leaders must have been."

The Brethren preached at street corners and even in taverns, according to official reports from the canton of Bern. The death penalty, however, introduced in 1527 as has been mentioned by invoking the ancient code of Justinian, was frequently enforced against both sexes. In Protestant cantons it was generally effected by drowning. The Bern government passed measures in 1527 to "eradicate these weeds" and a special police force called *Täufer-Jaeger*—"Baptist hunters"—was enrolled.

The Zürich decision was confirmed in 1529 when, at an Imperial meeting at Speyer in Germany, Catholic and Protestant authorities came together for the first and only time in order to agree upon the infliction of the death penalty upon all "rebaptizers", whether peaceful or otherwise in all territories of the Holy Roman Empire. This Mandate required that "rebaptizers and rebaptized, all and each, male and female, of intelligent age, be judged and brought to death without antecedent inquisition of the spiritual judges". Following this savage edict, efforts were intensified throughout Europe to destroy the movement. Mere identification

THE PROTESTERS

Edict of Ferdinand, 1528, promulgating the death penalty for the Brethren in Christ.

with the Brethren was enough. In Basel a man appearing on trial earnestly appealed that his life might be spared, pointing out that so long as he had lived in wickedness no one had molested him, but since he had become interested in virtue and religion he had received nothing but persecution. Generally in the Swiss cantons a public disputation was held before enforcing the edicts for suppression. In Aargau, at Zofingen, Martin Weniger engaged in a debate with the Zwinglian ministers Megander and Haller which lasted nine days, but the result was the usual one.

Inhuman Persecution

At one stage there were as many as seventy small congregations of Brethren in Zürich canton alone, but most were extinguished within a few years. Many of the members who survived travelled to Moravia, Poland and Germany. So severe were the repressive measures that the Zürich religious leaders had to deal with protests from among their own ranks at the treatment meted out to peaceful citizens:

> "There are those who tell us that the magistrates ought not to punish in body or in estate those who mislead others, or are misled by others; since first, the apostles did not do so, and second, faith cannot be given or taken away by force."

But these objections were deemed to be trifling and so they concluded:

> "Let those who will recant be pardoned. Those who relapse should be punished as evil doers in accordance with divine, secular, and imperial edicts."

In 1527 George Blaurock left Switzerland for the Tyrol. This was a Habsburg domain directly governed from Catholic Vienna. Undoubtedly what drew him to this hornet's nest was the knowledge that fields there were white to harvest. For two years, in extremely difficult circumstances, he and others evangelised the length of the Isarco valley. By the time the 1529 Mandate was promulgated, many vigorous communities of Brethren had come into being throughout the Tyrol. Studies have shown them to have comprised a full cross-section of Austrian society, but with a predominance of craftsmen and artisans. This was probably typical of every country in which communities were established.

The Mandate of 1529 was carried out in the Tyrol with

THE PROTESTERS

unremitting thoroughness. Blaurock was burnt at the stake on August 26; hundreds were arrested and a visitor to the country reported that he saw "stakes burning all along the Inn valley":

> "Some they have executed by hanging, some they have tortured with inhuman tyranny, and afterwards choked with cords at the stake. Some they roasted and burned alive. Some they have killed with the sword and given them to the fowls of the air to devour. Some they have cast to the fishes. Others wander about here and there, in want, homelessness and affliction. They must flee with their wives and little children from one country to another, from one city to another. They are hated, abused, slandered, and lied about by all men."

The last phrase was not quite true. If it had not been for kind, sympathetic farmers and burghers the carnage would have been even worse than it was, for some were enabled to escape. But even so, by 1530 over a thousand men and women had been killed in the Habsburg lands alone.

From the Swiss cantons, the Tyrol and Roman Catholic Germany many refugees made their way to the comparative safety of Moravia and Poland. Although Moravia became part of the Habsburg dominions in 1526, there were parts of the country where friendly local princes offered a measure of protection and even encouragement. One of these was the Liechtenstein family, one branch of which at the present day rules a small independent principality adjoining Switzerland. Owning large estates in the Moravian highlands, they found that the Brethren made hard-working and conscientious tenants.

However, the little spell of comparative prosperity and peace was short-lived. It was followed by one of the most inhuman persecutions of pious and peaceful folk in all history. It was inspired by Dominicans who were urging Ferdinand, the Austrian Emperor, to take more active measures for the suppresssion of heresy in his wide domain. So was passed the terrible edict of 1535, which envisaged the complete extirpation of all dissent against Roman Catholicism, and was principally directed against the Brethren.

A Noble Appeal

The first response of the Brethren was to convey a petition to the Imperial government in Vienna. This moving document is so astonishing in its restraint and so free from any bitterness of spirit in the face of implacable hatred that part of it is worth quoting at some length:

> "We Brethren, who love God and His word, banished from many countries for the Name of God and for the cause of divine truth, beg you to know, honoured ruler of Moravia, that your officers have come to us and delivered your message. Already we have given a verbal answer, and now reply in writing—that we have forsaken the world, an unholy life and all iniquity. We believe in Almighty God, and in His Son our Lord Jesus Christ, to whom we have devoted our entire selves, our life and all that we possess, to keep his commandments, and to forsake all unrighteousness and sin.

Title-page of the *Brüderliche Vereynigung,* a Statement of Faith in seven parts, drawn up in 1527 by Michael Sattler. It contained also "a brief but true notice of how . . . he witnessed with his blood".

> "We have injured no one, we have occupied ourselves in heavy toil, as all men can testify. We are driven by force from our possessions and our homes. We are now in woods and under the open canopy of heaven; we know not any place where we may securely live; nor can we dare to remain here any longer for hunger and fear. If we turn to the territories of this or that sovereign, everywhere we find an enemy. If we go forward, we fall into the hands of tyrants and robbers.

THE PROTESTERS

"With us are many widows and babes in the cradle, whose parents were given to the slaughter and whose property was seized. These widows, orphans and sick children have been committed to our charge by God and He has commanded us to feed, clothe and cherish them and supply all their needs. They cannot journey with us, and unless otherwise provided for, they cannot live for long. We dare not abandon them. We may not overthrow God's law to observe man's law, although it may cost gold and body and life. On their account we cannot leave, but rather than that they should suffer injury we will endure any extremity, even to the shedding of our blood.

"We desire to molest no one; our manner of life, our customs and conversation are known everywhere to all. Sooner than strike our enemy with the hand, much less with the sword as the world does, we would die and surrender life. We carry no weapon, neither spear nor gun, as is clear as the open day. We would that all the world were as we are, and that we could bring and convert all men to the same belief; then should all war and unrighteousness have an end.

"There remains no refuge for us, unless God shows us some special place to which we can flee. Day and night we pray to Him that He will guide our steps to the place where He would have us to dwell. Grant us a brief space: perhaps our heavenly Father will make known to us whither we must go.

"We earnestly intreat you, submissively and with prayers, that you take in good part all these our words. Farewell."

Methodical Massacre

The response of the government to this appeal was to send troops, egged on by fanatical priests, into every communal settlement, into the woods and into every corner of the country in a methodical massacre of incredible ruthlessness. This was not an event in a religious war as was, for example, the massacre of St. Bartholomew in France, where both parties had no compunction concerning the use of arms, but the unprovoked slaughter of hundreds of some of Europe's most valuable, conscientious and good-living citizens. A contemporary record speaks of those times of sorrow:

"Some were torn to pieces on the rack, some were burnt to ashes and powder, some were roasted on pillars, some were torn with red-hot tongs. Some were shut up in houses and burned in masses, some were hanged on trees, some were executed, some plunged in the water, many had gags put into their mouths so that they could not speak and were led away to death. Others were starved and allowed to rot in noisome prisons. Many had holes burned through their backs and were left in this condition. Like owls and bitterns they dared not go abroad by day, but lived and crouched in rocks and caverns, in wild forests, in caves and pits, where they were hunted down with hounds and catchpoles.''

Not until the scientific horrors of Nazism was Europe to witness and suffer such brutal bigotry.

Of the way in which this onslaught was met we have testimony from both friend and foe. After reporting the death of 2,173 of his friends, one friendly writer comments:

"No human being was able to take away out of their hearts what they had experienced. The fire of God burned within them. They would die ten deaths rather than forsake the divine truth.

"They had drunk of the water which flows from God's sanctuary, indeed, of the water of life. Their faith blossomed like a lily, their loyalty as a rose, their piety and candour as the flower of the garden of God. The things of this world they counted only as shadows. They were so drawn unto God that they knew nothing, sought nothing, desired nothing, loved nothing but God alone."

The Lutheran pastor Faber, a bitter enemy, was amazed at the attitude of the Brethren. He wrote:

"They behold the glittering sword with undaunted hearts, they speak and preach to the people with smiling mouths, they sing psalms till the soul goes out, they die with joy as if they were in festive company, they remain strong, confident, steadfast even unto death."

He then goes on to suggest as the only possible explanation that they were dupes, possessed of the devil.

The depopulation of Moravia was so great that the Parliament in Vienna, with the support of the hierarchy, passed a special law permitting men in Moravia the extraordinary privilege of taking

THE PROTESTERS

two wives so that the country could be repopulated.

Those who were able hid in the pine forests of the mountains by day, and by night trekked across eastern Europe seeking a place where they could live and work and worship in peace—first to Hungary, then to the Cluj region of what is now Romania, and finally far into Russia. Some of these communities remained well into the present Soviet era.

Ferdinand I, Holy Roman Emperor

9

TROUBLED TIMES IN LUTHERAN LANDS

IF the Brethren had hoped to find in the Lutheran areas of Europe an attitude more tolerant of their faith and ideals than the Roman Catholics showed at Rottenburg, they were swiftly disillusioned. Martin Luther's own character may be illuminated by reference to his relationship with Caspar Schwenckfeld. The case of this Silesian nobleman is interesting since he was not a convert to the Brethren, but only disagreed with Luther on certain issues, including the communion, urging that certain views held by the Brethren were more in accord with Scripture than Luther's own. Schwenckfeld owed much to Luther and made despairing efforts to maintain communication with one from whom he had learned so much. A "friendly, Christian petition and request" on the part of Schwenckfeld was sent to Luther by a third party, Hermann Riegel. Luther had Riegel arrested and then addressed the following to him:

> "Tell your master, Caspar Schwenckfeld, that I have received from you the booklet and the letter and would to God he would be silent. Formerly he kindled a fire in Silesia against the holy sacrament, which is not yet extinguished and will burn upon him forever. He continues with his creatureliness, and misleads the church, though God gave him no command, nor sent him. And the mad fool, possessed of the devil, does not understand anything; does not know what he is babbling. But if he will not cease, let him leave me unmolested with his booklets which the devil excretes and spews out of him. Tell him this is my last answer: may all those who have part with you, together with you and your blasphemies, be blasted to destruction.
>
> Martin Luther, by his own hand."

THE PROTESTERS

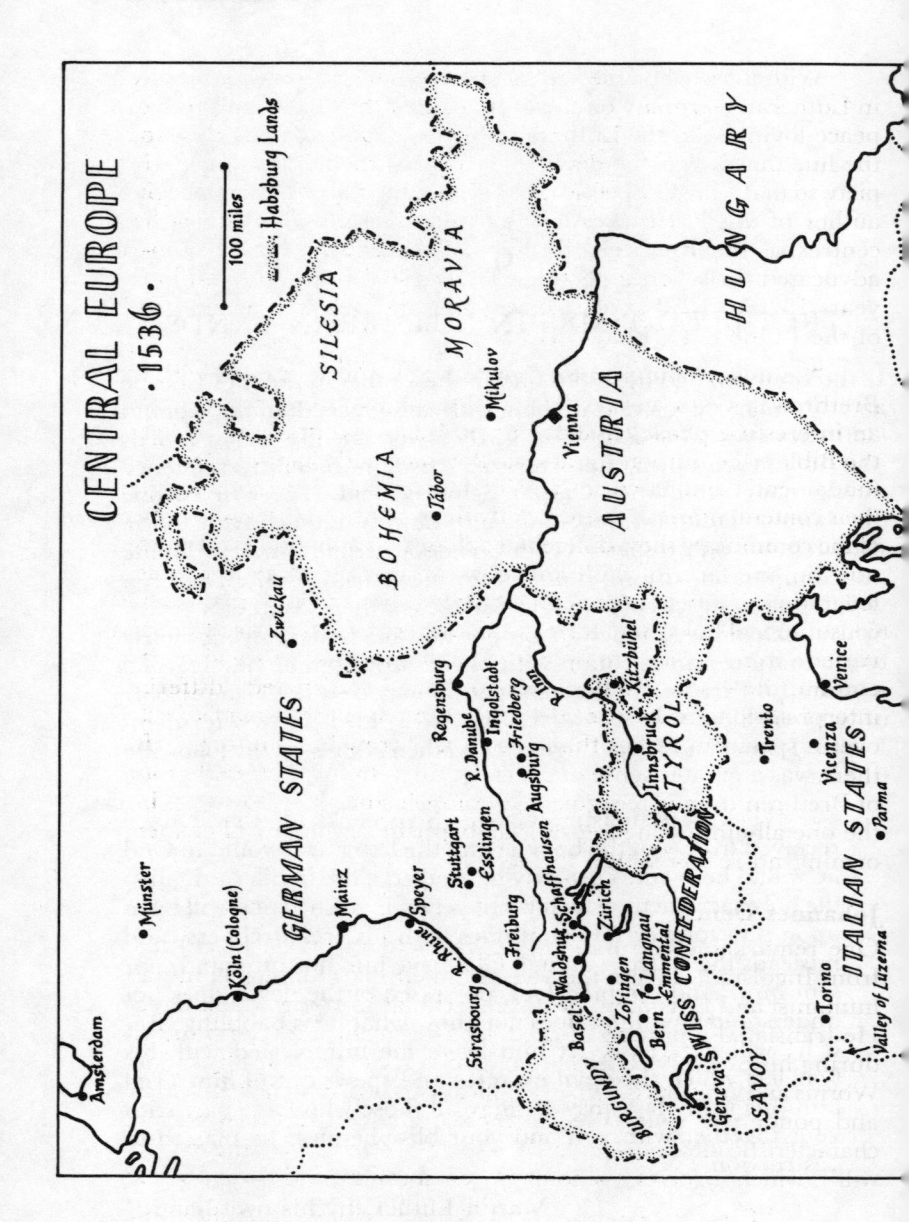

CENTRAL EUROPE
· 1536 ·

----- Habsburg Lands

With those who objected to a heresy-hunt against the Brethren in Lutheran Germany on the grounds that they were a devout and peace-loving folk, the Lutheran leaders, unable to deny this, took the line that it was the devil who inspired them with this kind of piety so that "the Gospel (Lutheranism) may fail". Urban Rhegius, author of this last expression, harried greatly one of the earliest centres of the Brethren, the city of Augsburg. Luther himself advocated the severest penalties for arrested Brethren, and in the years 1526 to 1530 at least three thousand perished at the hands of the Lutherans. (Plate VI).

A number of important figures among or associated with the Brethren in Germany deserve mention. The brotherhood was in an interesting phase, challenging ecclesiastical practice, bringing the Bible to bear upon traditional dogmas, and shaping a far more fundamental and practical New Testament doctrinal structure than their contemporaries. Consequently the writings of various members of the community show different emphases, as attention was focussed now on one facet of faith and now on another. Also as it was a federation of independent congregations with spiritual rather than constitutional links, and not a monolithic organisation, this emphasis varied from place to place. The opportunity—within the community—for free discussion also permitted differing interpretations to be considered, accepted, allowed and rejected over a spectrum rather than within a narrow band of belief. But there was a greater sense of organic unity among scattered groups of Brethren than is recognised by most historians who sweep into the one all-embracing net of "anabaptism" a motley of elements owning no real common loyalty.

Johannes Denck

One remarkable German writer was Johannes Denck, graduate from Ingolstadt during the vice-rectorship of Hübmaier, initially humanist and Erasmian, proficient scholar in Hebrew and Greek. He translated a portion of the Old Testament into German, and during his extensive travels to Nürnberg, St. Gallen, Strasbourg, Worms and Augsburg, wrote prolifically though generally in a heavy and ponderous style. We see there prominently the Brethren's characteristic ideal of *Gelassenheit,* a spirit of active "yielding to God's will", which involves a renouncing of all things worldly and selfish:

"Clearly, all who truly fear God must renounce the world.

And although they have of necessity to use the world, they ought always to be ready for tribulation as sojourners in this world. Whoever lives in security and happiness in the world should take heed lest he be overtaken with her, and his shame exposed. For the Lord is coming. He will come like a thief to require what he gave to us as shepherds, to serve him therewith, and which like thieves we have appropriated for ourselves so that we may have power. Then it will help no one to cry 'Lord, I have preached the gospel': 'Lord, I have heard it preached'. O dear brethren! He always says (Luke 11 : 28), 'Blessed is he who hears the word of God and does it'."

He entered the lists, not altogether successfully, in the ferocious word-battles of his time on the vexed questions of predestination and freewill, the following indicating his reasonable and constructive approach. He charged most of the protagonists—Lutheran and Calvinist—with "sorting out Scripture in fragments and mending the old garment with new patches".

"You may say: 'Yes, Jesus died indeed out of love, but not for all: rather, only for a few'. But since love in him was perfect and since love hates or is envious of none, but includes everyone, even though we were all his enemies, surely he would not wish to exclude anyone. Scripture says that he died for many (Matthew 20 : 28) and yet again, for *all* (I John 2 : 2). But this is not contradictory, since, though the light shines upon all (John 1 : 9), many deny even the Lord that ransomed them."

Denck died of plague in Basel in his mid-thirties.

Ludwig Hätzer

Associated with Denck in his translation work was Ludwig Hätzer, described as "a man of great learning deeply versed in the original languages of the Scriptures". After engaging in the disputations in Zürich along with Hübmaier and Grebel, Hätzer wandered in south Germany. He wrote a work against the Trinity, but this fell into Zwingli's hands before it could be published. His trial and burning at Konstanz in 1529 was a matter of some notoriety as he was accused not of heresy but of polygamy and immorality. This was later enlarged upon until a nonsensical story was circulated that he had had twenty-four wives. A document of the Brethren, however, whose practice was to excommunicate for immorality, refers to his being "condemned for the gospel and witnessing in knightly fashion for the truth with his blood".

Martin Cellarius

Another brilliant German scholar and linguist—he was able to speak fluent Chaldee for example—was Martin Cellarius. Educated at Wittenberg and at one stage a personal friend of Luther, he was one of the most fair-minded and peace loving men of his age in Germany. Deputed to represent the Lutherans at a debate with Stubner and Storck of the Brethren, he admitted to being convinced of their position and became a convert. In 1536 he had to flee Germany and under a false name lived in Basel, where he taught philosophy.

Denck, Hätzer and Cellarius are linked in a particularly significant way. The French historian Leclerc comments that quite early anti-Trinitarian tendencies came to the fore among the Brethren. "Their principle of being strictly guided by Scripture led them to criticise the Trinitarian formulas accepted in the church." From Denck we have the following:

> "God is the fountain of all created things; the Holy Spirit is the power of God; Jesus Christ is the Word of God begotten of God by the Spirit."

Hätzer taught similarly that "the Father alone was the true God; that Christ was inferior to the Father and of a different essence; that there were not three persons in the Godhead."

These German writers had wide influence, especially upon Brethren who under pressure of persecution moved eastwards and in turn affected Polish and Hungarian dissenting movements. The nature of the Godhead proved to be a cause of dissension and division among the Brethren. At Strasbourg in the 1550s a conference suggested a unifying formula, but the "confusion of tongues among the Brethren" ultimately caused the movement to pursue diverging paths, as a later chapter indicates.

Melchior Hofmann

A much more controversial figure than any of the above was Melchior Hofmann. A convert to the Brethren from the Lutherans at Strasbourg, his short career was colourful and his writings passionately charged and full of highly-wrought Scriptural imagery.

He carried this somewhat mystical presentation of the Brethren's faith to the Netherlands, where social and political conditions favoured radical religious reform. Described as a man of peace who taught quiet confidence and non-violence, Hofmann encouraged the Brethren to a burning missionary zeal and an eager anticipation of the imminent return of Jesus Christ.

> "The King of Kings commands his servants that they should be his emissaries and teach all people, yea, all peoples, pagans, tribes, tongues and nations, just as it happened in the time of the apostles, until their noise went out into all lands, and their word unto the ends of the World. Just as the Lord Christ himself calls them 'Come unto me, all you who are tired and burdened, I will refresh you'. All those who hear this, and do not stop up their ears but rather attend with alertness, will inherit their salvation and will not despise it."

Accepting the word of life means surrendering and yielding to the Lord,

> "that they should purify themselves and bind themselves to the Lord Jesus Christ publicly, through baptism, the true sign of the Covenant. This to the end that ever thereafter they should remain obedient to, and follow the will and pleasure of, the Father, the Son, and the Holy Spirit, and that their own will, life, desire, spirit and passion be wholly slain and that henceforth they live solely from the wisdom of God and the eternal word of life."

In an age when the religious were more concerned to justify themselves as the elect than to blaze such a missionary trail, the theological basis of Hofmann's exhortation—namely the freedom of men to accept or reject the Gospel preached—was seriously suspect. So too was the idea that salvation depended upon a faithful walk in Christ. In their trials and persecutions Hofmann encouraged his fellow-pilgrims to be steadfast, and hope in the promise of the Kingdom:

> "They who now remain steadfast in the doctrine and school of Christ unto the end, through struggle and victory, and who remain unwavering and are not overcome, the same shall be saved. For as one believes and is enlightened and receives the Lord, so is salvation and the inheritance of the

Kingdom of God *promised;* and if one pilgrimages toward the land of promise, one will *gain possession* of the inheritance. For they who believe in the name of Jesus Christ, to them he gives in the first place the power to become the children of God. The Lord Christ Jesus will give all victors the crown of life. He will make them into a pillar in his temple, whom no suffering will befall, nor the second death. They will also sit with him on his throne and rule over the nations."

Hopes of Christ's Appearing

As persecution was intensified in the lands of the Rhine, adventist hopes and apocalyptic expectations intensified also. Hofmann suggested 1533 as the year of Christ's appearing. In fact that year only brought him imprisonment in Strasbourg; he remained there for ten years until his death. It is said that he frequently invited his friends to the prison so that he could encourage them and warn them against the spirit of fanaticism that was stirring in some areas of north-west Europe.

For the relentless persecution from both Protestants and Roman Catholics, the years of living under the constant shadow of death, was producing strains and tensions; unbalanced elements appeared in places and gained a notoriety greater than they deserved.

Outbreaks of militant millennialism occurred in north-west Europe, despite the warnings and pleadings of more stable spirits. Revolutionaries fanned flames of discontent. Fanatical power-seekers utilised widespread interest in apocalyptic expectations, claiming in some cases to be divinely authorised to overthrow the godless. One of them was Jan Matthys, a tall Dutchman with a long black beard. Together with a young follower of his, Jan Bockelszoon, Matthys came to reside in Münster, quickly dominated the town, deposed the bishop, and finally established what amounted to a virtual reign of terror. Claiming to offer an open door to all persecuted "anabaptists", he drew a considerable number of refugees from the Low Countries into the city. He then instituted a communistic system in which surrender of money was made a test of loyalty. Many who found themselves deceived were unable to leave. The city was finally captured by the Roman Catholic army and Bockelszoon was displayed in a cage like a performing bear.

THE PROTESTERS

The Münster episode, together with less flamboyant uprisings in Groningen, Amsterdam, and Minden, had important repercussions. Although there was no similarity in spirit between the militant "anabaptism" of Münster and the simple piety of the Brethren, the possession of certain common doctrines and practices, and certain other links such as the writings of Campanus, led the innocent to be involved in the general condemnation of the guilty. Severer penalties were invoked upon all those who practised believers' baptism, and "anabaptism" of whatever colour became a word of odium invariably associated with Münster. Despite the fact that force and revolution and the whole attitude of the Münster revolutionaries were uncompromisingly repudiated by the great majority of the Brethren, the episode was an acute embarrassment to those with nobler aims, and the state religious authorities found in it a convenient means to destroy the influence of those whom they looked upon as thorns in their path.

Within the fellowship of the Brethren there were repercussions too. Emphasis upon the imminent return of Jesus to establish the Kingdom of the saints, having risen in some places almost to fever pitch in the early 1530s, subsided somewhat and was given generally less prominence, but rose again in the turbulent years of the mid-seventeenth century. Much attention was focused on the "ban", that is the Scriptural procedure of withdrawal of fellowship for departure in faith or morals from "the faith". Efforts were made to tighten the bonds that bound the loose international movement together, but inevitably this led to a considerable amount of fragmentation. Menno Simons, a Netherlander, engaged in many discussions on this question of church discipline.

> "A church without the practice of a genuine apostolic excommunication would be like a town without ramparts or barriers, a field without enclosure, a house without doors or walls. It would stand open to all lies, all godless mockery, all idolatry and every insolent transgression, to every moral laxity and adultery, as happens in all the large sects of this world that call themselves, however wrongly, churches of Christ. To me it is a typical feature of, and an honour and way of prosperity for, a true church to teach with the necessary discretion the true apostolic excommunication and to put it into practice with care and an alert charity, according to the instructions of the divine Scripture."

For Simons the brotherhood of believers in Christ could never be content with merely outward forms or a legalistic attitude to membership:

> "Christians must crucify the flesh and its desires and lusts, prune the heart, mouth and the whole body with the knife of the divine word of all unclean thoughts, unbecoming words and actions."

The highest love must be extended to all, even to enemies. No other community is worthy to be the "purchased possession" of the King of Kings.

William Tyndale

William Tyndale, the great English Bible translator, was (at the very least) strongly influenced by both Vaudois and the Brethren in Christ, particularly during his years as a fugitive on the Continent. His deep committal to believer's baptism, the second coming of Christ and the mortality of man—among many other Scriptural doctrines unacceptable to his contemporaries—led him to break with Luther, a fact not mentioned by any of his popular biographers. Although his zeal for Bible translation and his missionary outlook have led contemporary evangelicals to honour his name ("Tyndale Bible Translators", "Tyndale Press") his beliefs would be no more acceptable to most modern evangelicals than is the faith of present day Christadelphians. Tyndale House, of Wheaton, Illinois, is one of the leading religious publishing houses in the world, and prints a veritable snow-storm of paper propagating "heaven or hell" and other very orthodox but unscriptural doctrines. Indeed, it is not an exaggeration to say that almost the only affinity between Tyndale and the institutions that would use his name today is a shared reverence for the Bible.

A monument commemorating his birth at North Nibley in Gloucestershire is in fact an error, for it seems much more likely that he hailed from the other side of the Severn. His birthdate is often given as somewhere between 1491 and 1494 but this is probably several years too late. An Oxford undergraduate at 16, and a priest at 24, after nine years in university, he started having serious doubts about Roman Catholic doctrines and consequently the seemliness of his profession by the time he was 30. Most biographers state or take for granted that Tyndale went to

Cambridge to study under the great Erasmus, who was visiting lecturer there from 1509 to 1514, or at least heard him lecture while he was there. In fact, it seems that Tyndale only moved from Oxford to Cambridge in 1519, five years after Erasmus had left.

Tyndale was a compelling open-air speaker, by all contemporary accounts, and folk on many village greens in the English West Country listened enraptured to his poetic diction, immersed in Biblical idiom. Typical of his written works is his *A Pathway into the Holy Scripture,* a document of great interest, and published in 1525, the same year that the Swiss Brethren were organised in Zürich. He carefully outlines the hope of the Christian as depending on faith and understanding of the revealed Word, not on obedience to church decrees. Eternal life is not inherent, but will be bestowed at the second coming of Christ in glory. In an even earlier work, *Exposition upon Certain Words in Holy Scripture,* he explains the Scriptural meaning and significance of "hell", distinguishing carefully between *sheol, hades* and *gehenna,* the last a place of destruction into which the rejected will be consigned "at the general judgement".

Sir Thomas More, Henry VIII's Romanist Chancellor, vigorously attacked Tyndale's works and what has been described as a literary war followed. More scorned belief in the return of Christ, asserting that the faithful should not have to wait aeons for their reward, but enter bliss with their last breath. To which Tyndale replied:

> "Christ and his apostles taught no other; but warned to look for Christ's coming again every hour; which coming again because ye believe will never be, therefore ye have feigned that other merchandise."

And again,

> "I marvel that Paul had not comforted the Thessalonians with the doctrine, if he had wist it, that the souls of their dead had been in joy; as he did with the resurrection, that their dead should rise again. If the souls be in heaven in as great glory as the angels, after your doctrine, show me what cause should be of the resurrection?"

In 1529 or 1530, as a direct result of his translation work, he came face to face, intimately and in the original tongues, with God's

Way, with pristine Bible teaching unadulterated by traditions, and he came to realise that not only was Roman Catholic Christendom hopelessly astray but the newly-arisen Protestant Reformers *were very little better!*

From 1529, when he left Britain, until his arrest in 1535, Tyndale was a fugitive. He used an assumed name, or perhaps several. More called him "our heretick exile who is everywhere and nowhere". This fact poses great difficulties for tracing all of his movements, and even more for identifying his friends. We know that he lived for a time in Cologne and later in Worms. In 1526 a young preacher Jakob Kautz formed a community of the Brethren in Christ in Worms which lasted through the 1530s before it was extinguished by persecution or went underground. Worms was at that time a small city, barely a twentieth the size of Cologne. All printers would be known to each other, especially those interested in the Bible. It is hardly conceivable that Tyndale and Kautz did not know of each other's work. It is tempting to suggest that while in Worms Tyndale was converted to the Brethren in Christ. No evidence of this has been found—it would of course have had to be in secret anyway. Yet time and again in Tyndale's later writings—the ones the evangelicals ignore, that is—there are unmistakable echoes of Balthasar Hübmaier, Conrad Grebel and other writers among the Brethren in Christ. Indeed, some passages, were they translated into German, would then be even closer in style as well as content. More significantly, the doctrines are those of the Brethren and not those of the Lutherans or the evangelicals of today!

In the 1530s copyright laws were unheard of, and in view of a rising demand for vernacular Bibles, even illegal ones, pirate editions of Tyndale's translations appeared without his consent. In one of these the printer took the liberty of changing Tyndale's translation "resurrection" into "life after death". This led to Tyndale issuing, at his mortal peril, the following interesting document:

> "Concerning the resurrection, *I protest before God and our Saviour Jesus Christ,* and before the universal congregation that believe in him, that I believe according to the open and manifest Scriptures . . . that we shall all both good and bad rise both flesh and body and appear together before the judgement seat of Christ, to receive every man according to his deeds. And

that the bodies of all who believe and continue in the true faith of Christ shall be endowed with immortality and glory as is the body of Christ.

"And *I protest before God and our Saviour Christ,* and all who believe in him, that I hold of the souls that are departed in the faith of Christ and the love of God to be in no worse case than the soul of Christ was from the time that he delivered his spirit into the hands of the Father until the resurrection of his body in glory and immortality. I confess openly that I am not persuaded that they be already in the full glory that Christ is in, or that the elect angels of God are in. *Neither is it any article of my faith:* for if it were so, *I see not but then the preaching of the resurrection of the flesh were a thing in vain.*"

A Literal Resurrection

An American historian has this comment: "Tyndale believed the first resurrection to be literal, and looked for God's Kingdom to be established by Christ's second coming for which he longed." One of his more honest biographers states that on the subject of the Breaking of Bread, Tyndale "rejects both Romanist and Lutheran interpretations" and follows rather the views of a "third unnamed party". There can really be little doubt as to the identity of the third unnamed party. His words betray him:

"That thing that is there done in that supper, as the breaking and dealing and eating of the bread, and the whole like action of the wine, signifies, represents and puts into our hearts by the spirit of faith this commemoration, joyful remembrance and so to give thanks for that inestimable benefit of our redemption wherein we see with the eye of our faith presently his body broken and his blood shed for our sins."

The same source suggests itself for Tyndale's own stated view of baptism:

"The plunging into the water signifies that we die and are buried with Christ, as concerning the old life of sin, which is Adam. And the pulling out again signifies that we rise again with Christ in a new life."

In 1530 only one of the Brethren in Christ would have dared to write such things. But there is still other evidence of an association with the Brethren in Christ, and perhaps other elements of the "underground Reformation". Tyndale's popular biographers, even those who refer to or list his works by title, normally make no reference to any of the following, some of which speak for themselves:

The Disclosing of the Man of Sin.

The Revelation of Antichrist.

De ecclesia adversus.

A Book concerning the Church.

A Godly Disputation betwen a Christian Shoemaker and a Popish Priest.

Wiclif's Wicket.

The following two quotations surely need no comment from a Christadelphian—but, remember, this is 1530!

> "The apostles were clear-eyed and espied antichrist at once, and put him to flight, and weeded out the doctrine quickly. But when charity waxed cold, and the preachers began to seek themselves, and to admit glory and honour and riches, then antichrist disguised himself after the fashion of a true apostle, and preached Christ wilily, bringing in now this tradition and now that, to darken the doctrine of Christ; and set up innumerable ceremonies, and sacraments and imagery . . . the Bishop of Rome made a law of his own, to rule the church by, and put Christ's out of the way."

> "Seeing John took for a sign of the last day that he saw antichrist begin, how nigh ought we to think that it is, who, after eight hundred years reigning in prosperity, see it decay again, and his falsehood to be disclosed, and him to be slain with the spirit of the mouth of Christ."

Tyndale in fact traced accurately the development of the Papacy, and emphasised that the decree of the Byzantine Emperor Phocas establishing Boniface III as Papal head was a key event in the history of antichrist and the sweep of divine history. He identified the great Harlot as the apostate church, and the secular arm of the state as the beast or false prophet that do her bidding, in particular the Holy Roman Empire. Tyndale's expositions of Daniel and Revelation were clearly within the tradition which led from the Brethren in Christ through Newton and Bicheno to John Thomas.

In 1526 Cardinal Wolsey preached to an overflowing congregation in old St. Paul's Cathedral (they had been ordered to attend) while outside in the churchyard Bishop Cuthbert Tunstall watched prisoners convicted of reading the Bible shovel one hundred and fifty-eight baskets of Tyndale's New Testaments on to a great bonfire.

But Tyndale set his stamp upon the English Bible. To James I who "authorised" and his Protestant divinity professors who translated the King James' Version, Tyndale's beliefs were "pestiferous" and some of his translations "naughtie". Some of his honest renderings were deliberately changed to ones rather less so. Bishop Gardiner complained that Tyndale's English was "too clear" for a holy book!

Tyndale was hounded around Europe, his Bibles destroyed by the crateload, and he was finally betrayed in Flanders to the Imperial authorities. It has been stated in a major work that in 1534, tricked into believing that Henry VIII had "repealed the law against English Bibles, he set out happily for London. On the way he was captured..." Irrefutable evidence indicates that nothing of the sort happened. Actually, a secret agent gained Tyndale's confidence in the house where he lived incognito in Antwerp, and he was arrested by Charles V's police as he took his "friend" out to lunch. Imprisoned at Vilvoorde castle near Brussels, he was strangled and burnt in the prison courtyard.

The sad fact remains—all the literature of the Bible Societies notwithstanding—that even when Tyndale's dream came true that a "plowman" could *read* the Bible in his English mother tongue, it took two more centuries and much tribulation and persecution before he could *confess belief in its truth freely and unmolested*. It now seems more than likely that Tyndale died at Vilvoorde not because he translated and printed the Bible—for Bibles in English were already legal by then—but because he believed and understood its truth.

10

STRANGERS AND PILGRIMS

TWO features characterised 16th-century Italy: the scandalous behaviour of the Roman Catholic priesthood and the humanist Renaissance. They were not unconnected, since many thinking people, educated and uneducated, became increasingly disenchanted with a corrupt and venal church, seeing in the "new learning" a path to progress and a new window on the world.

In many ways intellectually Italy was more ready for the Reformation than northern Europe, for there was a current of both dissatisfaction and constructive thinking in Italy that ran disturbingly deep. But two factors checked the current and caused it to flow elsewhere. One was the political situation in northern Europe which led to the development of the reformed national churches; the other was the strength and power of the Inquisition in Italy. The Romanist hierarchy had a tremendous hold over the bodies of Italians even if it did not fully hold their minds in thrall. Almost every scholar in Italy who sought to develop an evangelical or Biblical faith had to leave the country—if he could. A typical example was Paolo Ricci.

Paolo Ricci seeks Bible Truth

Paolo Lisio Phileno Ricci was born in the city of Syracuse in Sicily in the year 1500, the son of a shield-maker. He was apparently named Paolo in honour of his home town's most famous visitor, the apostle Paul. "A big man and well formed" according to his contemporaries, he, like many other promising Italian youths, was selected by the order founded by Francis of Assisi and became a friar. It was evident to his superiors that he was potentially a brilliant scholar and admirably suited to an academic career. He progressed rapidly in this, studying theology and philosophy at Naples, then doing graduate work at Padua, at that time the most famous university in Europe.

Ricci reached Padua at a crucial time. The community of the Brethren in Christ had come into being in Switzerland a few years previously, and their activities had just begun to penetrate into northern Italy. It seems that as a man in his late twenties Ricci somehow became involved with them. Friar though he was at this time, he began then a love affair with his Bible that lasted a lifetime. At some stage he must have made the great step of obeying the truth he found, but just when and where we do not know.

Venice was at this time a hotbed of papal espionage, and as a result of this new trend in his life Ricci narrowly escaped (the first time) the clutches of the Inquisition in the Serene Republic before he was out of his twenties. At the age of thirty-eight he was offered a lecturing post at the prestigious university of Bologna.

He found that three of his colleagues in the medical faculty were propounding the idea—on physiological grounds—that both the body and soul of man are mortal. Ricci turned to the Bible and (we are told) "was amazed to find that there were many passages in Scripture" indicating that man is mortal and that not even the saints "had been admitted to paradise".

Risking the wrath of his superiors, Ricci plunged into a ferment of discussion with colleagues and students, who (he wrote later) "were always eager to discuss new and wayward doctrines". By 1540 he was convinced of Bible teaching concerning death, resurrection, eternal life and damnation, as well as other important doctrines, and was zealously though no doubt circumspectly advocating them in his university environment.

But on Ash Wednesday, February 11, 1540 (he mentions the date quite specifically, as if he could never forget it!) Ricci's troubles began. It was on that day that he had an unexpected confrontation with a fanatical, officious and short-tempered ecclesiastical dignitary by the name of Girolamo Seripando. This man, losing a Scriptural argument with Ricci, recalled that he was an "excommunicated apostate" from thirteen years before in Venice, and promptly "proceeded to inform the Dominicans" (the papal inquisitorial spy service). Orders were immediately issued to search for him (as the directive states) "in the church, the assembly, the schools, the square, and throughout the city".

This was, in fact, the second of five occasions when he was arrested by the Inquisition. This particular trial, held in the courtroom of the fearsome prison of Degli Angeli in Ferrara, with pincers, rack, thumbscrews and other various implements of torture arranged as silent reminders of who had the power, began on December 12, 1540. The room is little changed in Ferrara today, and it is not difficult to imagine the scene. And the court proceedings, in the flowery scribal calligraphy characteristic of the time, are still extant, filed in the archives. Therein the various counts against Ricci are described—forty-three of them.

He is charged with asserting, among many other things, that "the souls of the saints and the others justified have not entered heaven"; that none will enter God's kingdom until after the resurrection and judgement; the Bible's hope is "resuscitation" at the resurrection; the souls of the sinful are not suffering purgatory or hell. "All ecclesiastical practices based upon the assumption of a natural immortality are without scriptural warrant." Thus masses, prayers to the virgin (who is asleep anyway) and saints, confession, fasts and the like, indeed the whole sacramental system, are useless. Instead, Ricci contended, all sincere Christians should have the Holy Scriptures "in their hands, studying, meditating, conferring, testing the spirits, and mutually seeking the Truth, day and night".

The evidence is clear that Paolo Ricci was so very powerful and convincing a speaker, and his defence at the trial was so spirited and well argued, that the prosecution was in considerable difficulty. The location of the trial was twice moved and the "jury" of six "consultors" finally tied 3-3 as to whether he should be burnt alive or imprisoned for life. The court decided for the latter, and also formally unfrocked him (although he had actually left his order long before). But his imprisonment only lasted two years when he "escaped".

So in 1542 Paolo Ricci moved north again, this time to Tirano in the Italian Alps, a town within the domain of the Parravicinis of Caspano, a noble family sympathetic to (if not actually members of) the Brethren in Christ. Here he began a new life as a successful teacher and preacher, propagating in this relatively isolated area the typical Christadelphian doctrines which we now take for granted but which were considered both strange and blasphemous by the "church" authorities of that day, both Catholic and Protestant.

If the prosecutors' records are any indication, the most "shocking" were the view that the ignorant wicked, who are not responsible to the judgement, perish and will not be raised at the Last Day; and his teaching on the Atonement—that Christ bore "sinful flesh" inherited from Adam, was subject to temptation and capable of sin, but is our Saviour "precisely because he accomplished what he did" in holiness and righteousness, triumphing over sin in himself and so opening for others the way of redemption and reconciliation with a loving and merciful God. It was noted that Ricci (who at this time conveniently used the *alias* Camillo Renato) "managed to avoid all trinitarian formulas in his correspondence".

Ricci was arrested more than once during this phase of his long life. On one occasion he travelled to a fraternal gathering of the Brethren in Vicenza, not knowing that he was being trailed by the police. At Bergamo, a stop on the way, he was seized, but somehow managed to escape again.

When he died at seventy-five or so, blind and feeble, Paolo Ricci left behind ecclesias of Brethren in the valleys totalling some hundreds of members. These communities perished in the "Sacred Massacre" of 1620 in the Alps, and even one of the Parravicini nobles was burnt alive for refusing to recant. Within forty years the people of the Alpine valleys were again chained to papal superstition.

The Vicenza Society

In the 1540s a group of men, who came to be known as the Vicenza Society after the city in which they met, endeavoured to study the Scriptures and distil from them a faith free from Romanist dogma. There is no doubt they were considerably influenced by the writings and preaching of Brethren in Christ in areas to the north, and indeed felt themselves to be a part of the same thoroughgoing movement of return to the original Gospel and practice of Christianity. Their views on the Godhead were to be of profound significance:

> "There is but one most high God, who created all things by His mighty word, and preserves them by His will and good

providence . . . His only Son, Jesus Christ, was as to his nature a man, but not merely a man, having been conceived of the Holy Spirit by the virgin Mary."

This simple, apostolic view of Jesus Christ, expressed thus in Vicenza, was to be of profound significance, for it was to be a cardinal tenet of faith of a wide fellowship of Brethren over a large part of Europe. One day there was a sudden interruption of the Society's proceedings as soldiers burst into the gathering. Three whom the authorities viewed as ringleaders were arrested; Tervisiani and Francis de Ruega were executed, Chiari was imprisoned. The rest made a hasty departure, as they knew that the tender mercies of the Inquisition, established in a fervour of zeal in 1542, were cruel. They dispersed in fact over Europe: some, including Valentino Gentilis and Darius Sozzini joined Brethren in Moravia; Laelio Sozzini went to Switzerland.

Laelio Sozzini

When Laelio reached Switzerland, Calvin was installed in Geneva and engaged in his celebrated controversy with the Spaniard Miguel Serveto over the doctrine of the Trinity[1]. Laelio joined issue himself with Calvin, sending him lists of questions which only brought an "angry and pettish letter" in reply. Serveto was not an "anabaptist" and his views on the nature of Christ did not coincide with those of Sozzini or the Brethren, but the notoriety of the trial of Serveto in Geneva brought the whole issue very clearly into public light; whether the proof was plain in the Bible or not, the "Reformed" churches meant to uphold the full trinitarian dogma at all costs. The spirit of Calvin is illustrated by his letter to Viret, a henchman of his in Lausanne, stating that he would be satisfied with no atonement for Serveto's criticism of his creed short of the death of his adversary, should the disposal of his life ever be in his power. Calvin never disguised his implacable hatred of Serveto, calling him a dog; when the disposal of his life did come into his power and he had Serveto burned alive, he savagely exults after his execution:

> "Lest idle scoundrels should glory in the insane obstinacy of the man, there appeared in his death a beastly stupidity; whence it might be concluded, that on the subject of religion he never was in earnest."

---

[1] See the series on Servetus in *The Christadelphian,* 1962.

THE PROTESTERS

It is not surprising that Laelio Sozzini did not stay to argue very long with Calvin and went elsewhere.

A Fellowship of Churches

By 1550 there was a fellowship of churches in northern Italy and adjoining areas of Switzerland which the historian Leclerc calls "anabaptist". Their connections with the Brethren in Christ of Germanic Switzerland, the Tyrol, Moravia and especially Poland were close and fraternal. In this year these congregations held a conference in Venice. In a society where tenets of faith were subject to constant free discussion, there were of necessity differing viewpoints on interpretations and also varying emphases. The aim of the conference was, as far as can be ascertained, twofold: to clarify certain points of doctrine and discuss the basic framework of the church's organisation, and also to provide a fraternal atmosphere for a solemn period of devotion and worship. Sixty delegates met together, all congregations sending at least one delegate and some sending two. There was Iseppo of Asola; Celio Curio, who later became known as "the apostle of freedom of conscience", played a prominent role; but perhaps most outstanding was Negri. A former abbot, he had forsaken this position to assist a humble group of Brethren, offering them 1000 ducats a year from his private income in order to further their cause. The congregations themselves paid the travelling expenses of their own delegates, sharing the cost according to their means.

The conference lasted, probably by design, forty days. Each first day of the week during this period the Lord's Supper was celebrated in a solemn but simple form. We are told that "the utmost devoutness seems to have characterised the entire proceedings of the convention". At the close of the forty days a statement was issued listing those points upon which the delegates had deliberated and which they considered were substantiated by their close scrutiny of the Scriptures. Among them were the following:

1. The Scriptures of the Old and New Testaments are to be accepted as our fundamental authority.
2. Christ is man only, but filled with all the power of God.
3. Where Scripture speaks of angels, it sometimes can mean human messengers.

4. There is only one devil, namely human selfishness.
5. By the serpent in Eden, nothing else than this is to be understood.
6. There is no other hell but the grave.
7. If and when the elect die, they slumber till the day of judgement, when they shall be awakened. The souls of the godless and ignorant die with their bodies just as in the case of the beasts.
8. The elect are justified through God's eternal mercy and love.

In addition it was agreed by all the congregations that admission to the fellowship of the church should be by immersion of adult believers.

If the delegates looked for a period of development in Italy following their conference, they were disappointed. "No punishment was deemed serious enough for them", and in the face of swift persecution many of them had to flee or go into hiding. Some went to the Grisons, Switzerland and to the Tyrol, but there conditions were worse, and only those who made their way as far as Poland found in the "ecclesia minor" there a temporary refuge and an opportunity for furthering their faith.

Flight from Italy

One Italian who reached Poland came to wield considerable influence upon the fortunes of the Brethren there and elsewhere, though it was probably less than some historians have claimed. Fausto Sozzini, a relative of Laelio Sozzini mentioned earlier, has been so abused and vilified by both contemporary and succeeding scholars that it is well to record the opinion of George Ashwell, an Anglo-Catholic fellow of Wadham College, Oxford in the seventeenth century, and certainly no sympathiser with Sozzini's cause:

> "Qualities which excite admiration and attract the regard of men were united, so that he charmed, as it were by a kind of fascination, all with whom he conversed and left on the minds of all strong impressions of admiration and love. He so excelled in lofty genius and persuasive character, such was the strength

of his reasoning and the force of his eloquence, so great were his natural endowments and so exemplary was his life, that he appeared formed to captivate the affections of mankind."

Ashwell's purpose in so eulogising Sozzini is to suggest that the Polish Brethren and those influenced by them were mesmerised by Fausto's personality rather than convinced by the Scriptures; we must account the description as therefore an exaggerated one, but the impression remains that he must have been a strikingly attractive personality as compared, for example, with the more famous "reformers". Ashwell considered Sozzini to be "the devil's great snare" and warned people against one who clearly was a Satan masquerading as an angel of light.

With the departure from Italy of leading intellectuals such as Ochino, the Sozzinis and Gentilis, the Biblical reform movement ceased to make headway there and the Inquisition made short shrift of the vestiges that remained. Meanwhile the seed which had thus germinated in central and southern Europe began to put forth healthy and vigorous shoots in the Slavic lands.

One of the Italian emigrés found a home in England; this was Bernardino Ochino, who became associated with and had considerable influence over a community known as the "Strangers' Church" in London. This congregation, whose persistence over several decades is witnessed to by many contemporary documents, owed its origin to small groups of Brethren from various parts of Europe who sought refuge in England. They arrived at least as early as 1534, for in 1535 ten of them were burnt in London as an "occasion of gleeful jollity". Germans and Dutch predominated, with Swiss and Italians and later Poles and Moravians. International in outlook, they consistently sought adherents from among their hosts in London, but were harassed and hindered by prelates and government; their influence was more in the nature of a subtle leavening of English protestantism than by the actual making of large numbers of converts.

Anti-trinitarianism

The anti-trinitarianism of the group was a cause of deep suspicion. Wrote John Assheton in 1548:

"The Holy Ghost is not God but a certain power of the Father. Jesus Christ was conceived by the Holy Spirit of the Virgin Mary but was not the true and living God."

On April 25, 1551, a leading member, George van Parris, a physician originally from Mainz, Germany, was roasted alive at Smithfield after conviction on a charge of denying infant baptism and the Trinity. Other burnings followed spasmodically. We have, for example, the following instructions of Queen Elizabeth to the sheriffs of London in 1575:

"Greeting.

Since it has been made known to us by the Reverend Fathers in Christ the Bishops of London and Rochester and by Inquisitors, that John Peeters and Henry Turwert, Flemings by birth, guilty of enormities like the wicked crime of heresy and the detestable sect of the 'anabaptists', did presumptuously and from a kind of stubbornness, uphold and defend the aforesaid wicked crime of heresy and the detestable sect of the 'anabaptists'; the Bishop of London has now passed that they are heretics condemned to be eliminated from the Lord's flock by the punishment appropriate.

We therefore, being zealous for justice and to root out and extirpate errors of this kind wherever found, command that you cause the said John Peeters and Henry Turwert to be taken to a public open place at West Smithfield to be really burned in that same fire for an example to other men lest they fall into the same crime.

Signed, sealed, etc."

A remarkable confession of faith, written by these two men in a foul London jail in the same year, has been preserved. It vigorously affirms their hope in the promises of God, in the resurrection of those who sleep in death and in the second coming of the Lord Jesus Christ.

Such were the tender mercies of England's Elizabethan age, and such one of the pleasant sports of "Merrie England". The eastern counties, Norfolk and Suffolk, being closest to the Netherlands and centres of the wool and cloth trades, witnessed a considerable number of fiery executions during the 16th century. After a rather notorious trial, an Ipswich tanner, Peter Cole, was roasted before curious crowds at Norwich in 1587. A group of fourteen were burnt at the instigation of Cranmer (who of course, was to expire by the same method himself under Mary I). Turner comments: "What they really suffered for was their pacifism, their personal faith in Christ, their opposition to the lending of money (on usury) and, above all, their religious toleration." Roasting, incidentally, was normally reserved for Brethren who were considered the worst cases; furze was fixed to beard and face—a ceremony known laconically as "trimming the dog's beard" and carried out invariably by officiating clergy. Most of the principal factions burnt each other in their blind bigotry at this period, but the Brethren seem to have been universally detested by the authorities for their lack of a spirit of intolerance and revenge. A Parliamentary Commission was appointed to hunt them out, which seems to indicate that they exercised considerable influence.

A Heinous Heresy!

One of the most heinous heresies of 16th-century Brethren, evident from the *Thirty Dialogues* of Ochino onwards, was—judging by the vituperation it provoked—their belief in the revelation of the love of God in Christ. Contemporary theology, Roman and protestant alike, presented the death of Jesus as a sacrifice to appease the wrath of an offended Deity and so as a means of reconciling a distant God to man. In keeping with their whole attitude to the godly life, the God of the Brethren was a God of love, and the Cross a revelation of that love. On Calvary God *gave;* it was a supreme appeal by a God who "takes no pleasure in the death of the wicked", to men alienated by their own follies, that they might be reconciled to Him through understanding the Word, repentance and baptism, based for example on 2 Corinthians 5 : 19: "God was in Christ, reconciling the world unto himself." In the 16th century such a view of God was self-condemned and cried out for extirpation. Unfortunately there was a blind zeal for a God far removed from the yearning divinity in Hosea or the Father to whom the prodigal returned.

11

PRINCIPLES AND PRACTICE

WHAT were the principles upon which the Brethren in Christ based their faith and life, and for which so many of them died? Whence did the community derive such dynamism and power to survive? The first and foremost, indeed the basic principle underlying all others, was the conscious intention to restore and revive original New Testament Christianity.

Back to the Bible

In this the Brethren were not obsessed by loyalty to an historical past, but were possessed of the firm conviction that no Christianity other than that of Christ was worthy of the name. In a world where foul deeds equally with fair were done in the name of the Nazarene, and where official Christianity usually meant ruthless power, pride, luxury, and corruption, they were convinced that the religion of Jesus and the apostles, truly understood and faithfully obeyed, could be a vital and transforming force. To them the Scriptures, as the most authentic source of knowledge about the Gospel, were obviously a better guide to original Christian truth than councils of bishops and the fossilised tradition of a corrupt medieval church.

The main national Protestant reformers originally took this stand at their first break with Rome, but—as their own writings frankly testify—compromised it and modified it more and more under steady pressure from various quarters, political and ecclesiastical, and through plain self-interest and desire to retain power. Like many before and since, these emergent national religious leaders became convinced of a divine calling to maintain power, even though it meant abandoning their original principles.

The Brethren in Christ perpetuated the initial principles of the Reformation, and would have no compromise for expediency's sake. But they were more than dissenters against Protestantism; they were possessed of a positive independent inspiration through the Bible, newly-translated into the national tongues of Europe, from first-century Christianity. That this was direct, and not merely second-hand through the Reformation as has sometimes been maintained, is apparent in all the relevant historical sources, in their community life and their literature.

This "Back to the Bible" call was characteristic of all the preaching activities of the Brethren. For them it was not the preacher who converted. No convert was acknowledged as such who had not felt the touch of the living Word, not second-hand, but direct, by reading it himself or, if illiterate, having it read to him. "The word of God is eternally true and is a dynamic force which converts sinners; it will sing its own truth into the heart"—so Conrad Grebel expressed it. They believed that it was possible for the humblest believer, if fair minded and sincere, to understand and follow that Word.

Bible Study Groups

One of the fundamental activities of the Brethren was consequently the Bible study class. The Vaudois and Lollards had met as "gathered groups" for memorisation of and meditation upon paraphrases of the Scriptures in their native tongue, but with the growing numbers of printed Bibles in national languages readily available and the increase in Greek and Hebrew studies at universities, these Bible classes took on new power, as in the case of Castelberger's group in Zürich referred to in an earlier chapter. The meeting was opened with prayer. At first there was no singing of hymns, as Grebel for some unaccountable reason discouraged it, but later, under pressure of persecution, this became a vital unifying exercise. Then the Scriptures were read, and often one who was familiar with the original languages would elucidate various points in the chosen passage. "The meaning of the sacred word was then unfolded" by a member of the group. Brethren took turns to lead the class in this way. Finally, there would be opportunity for discussion upon the topic chosen before further devotions concluded the class. Very clearly, this was in its day a novel and radical form of church activity. (Plate IV).

In these simple meetings the Brethren hammered out a framework for their community life and the tenets of their faith. Both will be increasingly apparent in later chapters. In this chapter attention will be focused on those elements which found greatest prominence in the second and third quarters of the 16th century. Others were there only as yet in embryo.

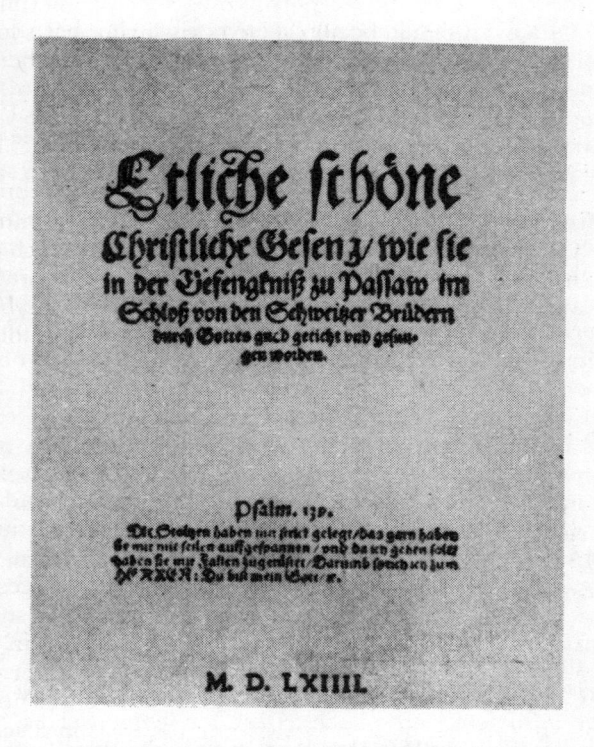

Title-page of the Hymn Book of the Brethren in Christ, 1564.
Many of the hymns were paraphrases of Psalms and other Scriptures.

The Brethren were almost naive in believing that men like Luther, Calvin and Zwingli would be honest and consistent enough to follow and abide by the Scriptures. In the many disputations in the 1520s and 1530s it was frequently recognised that the Brethren had the best of the argument, yet it was not argument but power that won the day. "Not many noble, not many mighty are called."

True Baptism

Many of these disputations concerned the subject of baptism. Scripture and history alike indicated that the christening of infants bore little resemblance to the baptism of fervently repentant believers of apostolic days or to the new birth of water and spirit commended by the Lord to Nicodemus. Grebel defined the Brethren's position:

> "Baptism should be applied to one who has been converted by the word of God, and changed his heart, and henceforth earnestly desires to walk in newness of life. Baptism means a dying of the old man, and a putting on of the new. Christ commanded to baptize those who had been taught, and the apostles baptized no one except those who had been taught."

It was sometimes alleged that there was an over-emphasis on the water aspect of baptism, that baptism was a mere mechanical rite. Hübmaier disposed of the criticism in his inimitable way: "Water is not baptism, else the whole Danube were baptism and the fishermen and boatmen would be daily baptized." Only adult conversion and commitment provide an adequate basis for baptism: "all others would still belong in the world, even though a whole ocean of water had been poured over them". They viewed infant baptism as "an impertinence, the anticipatory doing by others of that which it was alike the privilege and duty of every believer to do for himself". Hence their rooted objection to allow their children to be christened. A tract, disseminated in the region of Neuchâtel in the 1540s, outlining various aspects of the Brethren's faith, expresses their view of baptism:

> "Baptism ought to be given unto such as be taught unto repentance, believing that their sins will be taken away by Jesus Christ, and will walk in his resurrection. Therefore it ought to be ministered unto such as ask for it themselves, and not unto infants, as hitherto has been done in the Pope's kingdom."

Calvin's Resentment

Neuchâtel was in that part of Switzerland which John Calvin considered to be under his spiritual superintendence, so he thought it necessary to publish a rejoinder to this tract. He was no man to cross: like Zwingli, Luther and too many other religious leaders of his day, he could be bitterly cruel. But few could match his flaming and intemperate resentment against any who differed

Council House in Zürich, 1525

Statue of Zwingli.
It is significant that he should be commemorated grasping both Bible and Sword.

The Fraumünster in Zürich

One of the Brethren being burned at the Stake.
The use of the ladder referred to in the burning of Michael Sattler is shown.

A Bible Class held for safety in mid-river

spirit. 1 *Cor.* 15.45.

Qu. By whom shall God judge mankinde?

A. God shall judge the secrets of men by Jesus Christ. *Rom.* 2.16.

He commanded us to preach unto the people, and to testifie that it is he which was ordained of God to be the judge of quick and dead. *Acts* 10. 42.

Qu. What assurance hath God given that he will judge the world by this man?

A. In that he hath raised him from the dead. *Acts* 17.31.

Qu. What shall be the different issue of the good from that of the bad at the resurrection?

A. All that are in the graves shall come forth; they that have done good, to the resurrection of life; and they that have done evil, unto the resurrection of damnation. *Joh.* 5.28, 29.

Qu. Shall not the wicked and unbelieving live for ever, (though in torments) as well as the godly and the faithful? or is eternal life peculiar to the faithful?

A. He that believeth on the Son, hath everlasting life: and he that believeth not

not the Son, shall not see life: but the wrath of God abideth on him. *John* 3.36.

Qu. Though this passage which you have cited seem clearly to prove that eternal life agreeth unto no other men, but the faithful: yet since the contrary opinion is generally held amongst Christians, I would fain know farther of you, whether you have any other places that directly affirm that the wicked dye, and that a second death; are destroyed, and punished with everlasting destruction; are corrupted, burnt-up, devoured, slain, pass away, and perish?

A. The wages of sin is death: but the gift of God is eternal life, *Rom.* 6.33.

If ye live after the flesh, ye shall dye: but if ye through the Spirit mortifie the deeds of the body, ye shall live. *Rom.* 8. 13.

I will give unto him that is athrist, of the fountain of the water of life freely.

But the fearful, and unbelieving, and the abominable, and murtherers, and whoremongers, and sorcerers, and idolaters, and all lyars, shall have their part in the lake which burneth with fire and

K 4

Typical pages of John Biddle's *Twofold Catechism*

Title-Page of Calvin's *Briefe Instruction* in the English

Cages for imprisoning Brethren, Nürnberg. It was

Seventeenth Century Meeting Hall of the
Brethren in Hessen

An early 19th-Century Meeting House in Illinois

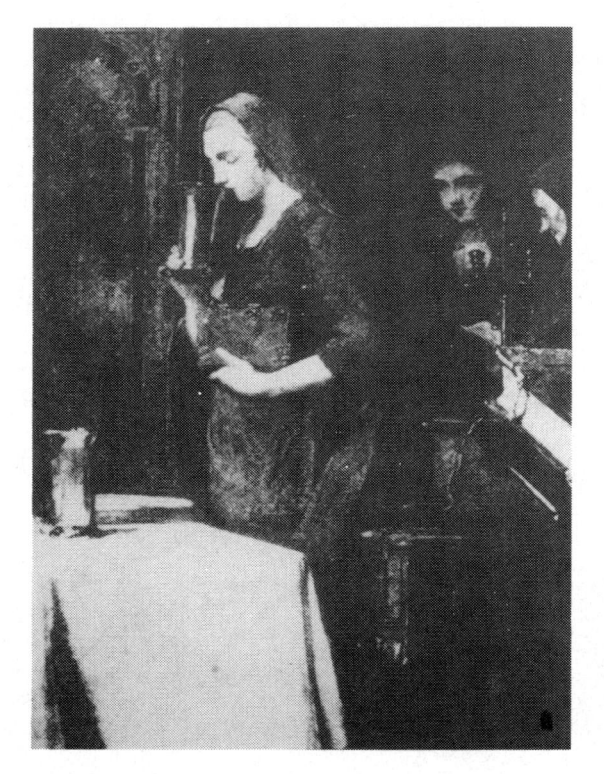

Taking Communion Wine—18th Century.
Note the large chained Bible at right. Comment was frequently made on the modest yet attractive dress of the young sisters.

radically from him. So it was that the *Brieue Instruction pour armer tous bons fidèles contre les erreurs de la secte commune des Anabaptistes* appeared in 1545. Its cover has a flaming sword and the sinister words in Latin: "I have not come to bring peace but a sword." A poorly translated English edition appeared shortly after in London. The cover now has the English coat of arms, an almost naked man and a woman with only one leg. Horns sprout out of the man's head and below is a vignette showing a king with two fierce hounds. It was to be sold "at the new shop by the little conduit in Cheapside". In the title *"erreurs"* in the French becomes "pestiferous errors" in English.

A tone of scurrilous derision runs through the work. The Brethren, described as "occupied with pride and presumption", "through obstinate and deliberate malice shut their eyes because they will not see the light when it is evidently offered to them". Calvin calls them "these poor phantasticals who so mightily vaunt themselves"; their writings are "barren and trifling ... made by ignorant people ... so unlearnedly and foolishly written ... dangerous poison ... a whole sea of false and foolish opinions ... unsettling the simple who have not the judgement to discern". "To write against the false opinions and errors of this bottomless pit would be a thing too long, and such a bottomless pit as I would not well come out of." None the less he attempts it. The main argument is that the Brethren cannot really "have the Word" because they have not helped Calvin who certainly does have it, but "have hindered and disturbed us". Whatever view is "raised against ourselves" is repugnant and bound to be false.

Yet Calvin's refutation of believers' baptism must be admitted as woefully weak. It is impudent slander, he claims, to call infant baptism papist in origin. He wishes to inform the simple that there is no doctor so ancient who does not confess that it is a practice as old as the apostles. (This is, of course, either bad scholarship or dishonesty.) On Mark 16 : 16 an interpretation that would make the belief precede the baptism he calls "a naughtie conclusion". The baptisms recorded in Acts 2 are dismissed as being exceptional because they needed special repentance. He calls attention to the expression in the New Testament "children of God" and asserts that this implies that they must have been baptized as infants.

A century later another Calvinist, the Glaswegian Robert

Baillie, in *Anabaptism, the True Fountaine of . . . Errours . . . Unsealed*, has a quaint jibe at the practice of adult baptism:

> "They esteem sprinkling no baptism at all, they will have the whole body to be plunged over head and ears into the water. This circumstance of plunging they account so necessary and essential to baptism, that the change thereof to sprinkling makes baptism to be null. That such a plunging draws upon some sickness and death, and upon a woman great shame and scandal, while they are stripped and must stand altogether naked in the presence of men and of the whole congregation: these and other inconveniences they do not much regard."

There is actually no evidence from the Brethren's own accounts that naked baptisms were universal or even normal or that men and women were in fact baptized together in this condition.

In the *Brieue Instruction* Calvin attacks another article of faith which will receive more attention in later chapters:

> "They do think that their souls do sleep unto the day of judgement without feeling or knowing anything; that the soul of man is nought else but his life which through sin dies until such time as he be raised up again. Some say it is only the virtue that man has to breathe, to move and to do other actions of life while he is yet alive; some that it sleeps without any sense or understanding until resurrection."

He describes this as "a blind opinion" and adds "everyone can see the consequences of this error". He also notes with disdain the view that hell is the grave. (Plate VI).

Calvin's answer is that "by death we may not simply understand the common death but a death which doth emport rejection". St. Peter, he asserts, proved that the souls of the faithful are immortal when, having asserted that all flesh is grass, he adds that the word of God abides for ever.

A Fellowship of Brethren

It is clear from events described already that the Brethren experienced a great deal of trouble with religious and civil authorities because of their view of the church as a free and voluntary society of the committed, not a state institution. An early work of Grebel's sets the pattern; it is paralleled by many other writers:

> "The church has Christ as its head, and the believers as members. This church is in truth a fellowship of brethren in life and suffering, which is maintained by an outward bond of faith and the inward bond of love. When a member of the body fails to maintain love towards the brethren or does not order his life according to the Gospel, he breaks the bond of fellowship. Brethren who give offence by their sinful conduct and who will not hear the church must be excluded from fellowship."

The church was conceived as consisting of heartfelt believers, all equally "exemplifying within her fellowship the living and dying of the Lord Jesus, a community of saints whose members, though not perfect, yet aspire to perfection and strive mightily". It was a society at once completely lay and completely ordained. Distinctions of clergy and laity had little meaning. Those serving the church in such capacities as preachers and elders "worked with their own hands for their livings"; indeed they "cried down all set stipends for church officers". Each particular congregation elected those whom it considered fit to act as shepherds, and the commission to preach was considered as applying to all members. Latourette, the French historian, makes the comment: "Many were ardently missionary, seeking to win not only professed Christians to their views but also dreaming of carrying the gospel to all mankind." Men such as Calvin and Baillie took great exception to the fact that "each single congregation had supreme and independent power to judge in all ecclesiastical causes, also to proceed to the highest censure of excommunication", and even more to a situation where "any member could question in public the doctrine of the preacher".

Women and Marriage

In contrast to the age, the position of women in the church was extraordinarily emancipated; they always appear to have been treated with affection, chivalry and respect. It is one of the most attractive features of their life and literature. A real spiritual cameraderie between husbands and wives, between brethren and sisters seems to be reflected, so different from the contemporary scene which was a severe man's world. In a century when it was deemed both unwise and unnecessary for women to interest themselves in Biblical studies, Hübmaier could remark that the pious woman Argula of Stauffen knew "more of the divine word than the red-capped ones will ever see and lay hold of". Many wives of prominent Brethren were themselves outstanding characters and Bender estimates that one third of those who suffered death for their faith were women. Women wrote hymns, instructed other women and were encouraged to perform almsdeeds.

Bender notes that among the Brethren marriage was elevated to a more spiritual relationship than was then recognised. Marriage within the faith and strong, loyal families became a firmly established tradition. Although the following comes from a document of a century later, it is expressive of their view from the beginning: "Marriage is instituted of God, and shall be entered into only with those who are members of the same Christian fellowship, who have received the same baptism and who belong to the same church."

Believers in Society

The relationship between this voluntary society and the state has largely been interpreted as one of withdrawal. They avoided prominent civil office, and would not assume the roles of judge, police, or any occupation entailing force; they were convinced that Christians should never participate in national wars. Indeed, as a Swiss chronicler wrote with amazement: "They carry no weapon, neither sword nor dagger, nothing more than a pointless bread knife, saying that these were wolf's clothing which should not be found on the sheep." We have already seen how this tradition of complete abandonment of the use of physical force and violence was emphasised as early as Grebel's correspondence with Müntzer. Despite a continuous history of provocation the great majority of Brethren in every country remained loyal to this self-sacrificing principle. They considered it the natural outcome of obedience to Christ and of membership of an international brotherhood of believers that knew no national boundaries, jealousies or enmities. Going to law and oaths were considered unworthy of Christians, and prohibitions of both figure largely in some confessions of faith.

They themselves, however, were convinced that their attitude was not really negative withdrawal, but positive example. Friends and enemies alike testified to the extraordinary moral and ethical power generated within the brotherhood. One of the most striking features of the documents of the period is the glaring inconsistency between the savage and irrational condemnation of the Brethren by leaders such as Zwingli, Calvin and Luther and the lengthy observations of more objective but yet unsympathetic witnesses. While Zwingli himself calls them "inhuman" and charges them with vice and brutality, a contemporary Roman Catholic observes:

> "No lying, deception, swearing, strife, harsh language, no intemperate eating and drinking, no outward personal display, but rather humility, patience, uprightness, meekness, honesty, temperance, straightforwardness in such measure that one would suppose they had the spirit of God."

And a Zwinglian:

> "Their walk and manner of life is altogether pious, holy and irreproachable."

As the Pharisees taunted Christ with possession by Beelzebul, by the same odd logic the Lutherans attributed this holiness to possession by the devil.

The Brethren in Christ were alone in the Reformation period, and indeed until the late 17th century, in making religious liberty a cardinal point in their creed: to them it was futile to coerce a man to believe. Some of them also spoke against capital punishment, advocating an approach to both education and justice that was not widely adopted until the 20th century.

Community of Goods

One society that grew out of the Brethren in Christ and which still exists—the Hutterite Brethren—came to adopt "community of goods" as an essential tenet of their corporate life, as a result of special developments in Moravia. At the beginning, however, this was not so; Hübmaier when asked about it by Zwingli replied that "one man should have regard to others so that the hungry may be fed, the thirsty receive drink and the naked be clothed; for we are not lords, but stewards. There is certainly no one who says that all things must be common". This was the attitude of most of the Brethren. While the memory of the German Peasants' War was still fresh, governments in Europe were naturally rather nervous on the subject of communism.

With only the Bible and the Apostles' Creed as acceptable

expressions of doctrine, Trinitarian credal formulae, as might have been expected, early came under increasing suspicion. As will be seen later, the nature of the Godhead and of Christ proved to be topics of controversy, but quite early the consequences of reversion to purely Biblical modes of expression and thought became apparent. Claudius Allobrex in Switzerland about 1530 found himself in trouble through his anti-trinitarian teachings, and Spitalmaier in the Tyrol expresses his faith in a way which indicates an increasing abandonment of Athanasian theology:

> "We hold and believe that Christ here on earth became a real, essential man, such as we are, of flesh and blood, a son of Mary, who conceived him, however, without human seed. He was Son of God. He is not God, but a man, an instrument through which God has made known to us His word."

One of the Zwinglian reformers (Microen) complains about this trend and teaching in a letter preserved in the Zürich archives:

> "In addition to the ancient errors respecting paedobaptism, the incarnation of Christ, etc., new ones are rising up every day, with which we have to contend. The chief opponents, however, of the divinity of Jesus Christ are the Arians, who are now beginning to shake our churches with greater violence than ever, as they deny the conception of Christ by the Virgin.
>
> "Their principal arguments may be reduced under three heads: The first is respecting the Unity of God, as declared throughout all the Scriptures both of the Old and New Testaments; and that the doctrine, as well as the name, of the Trinity is a novel invention, as not being mentioned in any passage of Scripture.
>
> "Their next argument is this: the Scripture they say, which everywhere acknowledges one God, admits and professes that this one God is the Father alone (John xvii. 3), who is also called the one God by Paul (1 Cor. viii. 6).
>
> "Lastly, they so pervert the passages which seem to establish the divinity of Christ, as to say that none of them refer intrinsically to Christ himself, but that he has received all from another, namely, from the Father (John v. 19; Matt. xxviii. 18)."

Another Tyrolese, Pilgram Marpeck, who had to abandon his employment as a government mining inspector after his conversion to the Brethren, picks his way through the "minefield" set by his theologian adversaries, and quietly and carefully explains the faith of "those called the Swiss Brethren" (1531):

> "Conceived by the Holy Spirit in Mary, Jesus Christ is the Son of God according to Spirit, Word, and power. The Father was manifested in Him, through the power of His divine essence, with all powers, works, and miracles. He has also shown and demonstrated His true humanity. As the Lord says in John 14 : 10: 'Philip, do you not believe that I am in the Father and the Father is in me? If not, why do you not believe for the sake of the works that I do?' Thus, the Father is manifested in the Son of the true God ...
>
> "Brought forth from the seed and line of David, He was shown to be, in His weakness, a natural, earthly, true man. He was born of the race of man, but without the seed of man or sin. He grew and was brought up by earthly creatures as a truly earthly man. His physical life was sustained by eating and drinking and He died a natural death. Like those who also died a natural death, or who will yet die, He rose again from among the dead through the nature of God, Spirit, and Word, which is the resurrection and the life (as He said to Martha). He was taken up into heaven, and seated Himself at the right hand of His heavenly Father. We wait for His return and for our resurrection from the dead, according to the flesh, to be received through Him. Forgiveness and remission of sins come only through the Lord Jesus Christ."

The further development of this distinctive emphasis upon the unity of the Godhead will be considered in the chapter on the Polish Brethren.

Belief in the second coming of Jesus Christ and the reign of the saints was characteristic of the brotherhood, the intensity of millenary zeal fluctuating from time to time with varying political fortunes. Undoubtedly the apocalypses of Daniel and Revelation were among the books studied both individually and in groups. The symbols in the Apocalypse were variously identified with the Pope, Zwingli and the persecuting emperor Ferdinand. One day

THE PROTESTERS

in the summer of 1525 members from Zollikon marched peacefully through the streets of Zürich in a long procession as a warning of impending judgement.

12

LIGHTSTAND IN POLAND

AFTER the brief survey of some of the fundamental principles and tenets upon which the society of the Brethren in Christ was built up in the early stages of its existence, attention will now be focused upon further historical development. Other important principles arising from this development will be considered in their place.

One day in 1546 or thereabouts a certain Rudolph Martin was browsing through the library of a Polish nobleman in Kraków. Clearly religion was very much an interest of this gentleman, and Martin observed him praying to the Trinity. As he concluded, Martin approached his host. "My Lord", he said, "have you then three Gods?" A lengthy discussion followed, and ultimately Martin succeeded in convincing the nobleman John Tricessius that

> "the Father alone is true God; the Son is not co-eternal with the Father, nor yet omnipotent, nor consubstantial nor equal to Him, but is one with Him in will; and that the Holy Spirit is the power or operating energy of God."

The secretary of the Polish king, one Andrew Modrevius, was also a party to these discussions and was similarly converted to Martin's views.

Emigration to Poland

Rudolph Martin, a colourful figure from among the Brethren in the Netherlands, had emigrated to Poland from his homeland after having fallen out with other Dutch Brethren, particularly Obbe Phillips and Menno Simons, over this very question of the nature of Christ. The controversy led to the definitive development of the Mennonites, followers of Simons, as that wing of the Brethren

THE PROTESTERS

became known which taught the full Deity of Christ. For many years, however, Martin's view continued to be held by many Brethren in the Netherlands.

This is confirmed by many court records of the Inquisition which have been preserved in what is now Belgium (then under Spanish rule). A typical example is the following brief excerpt from the surviving proceedings of the trial of Herman van Flekwijk in Bruges in 1569:

Inquisitor: "What! Don't you believe that Christ is the second person of the Holy Trinity?"

van Flekwijk: "We never call things but as they are called in Scripture... The Scripture speaks of One God, the Son of God, and the Holy Spirit."

Inquisitor: "If you had read the Creed of St. Athanasius, you would have found in it 'God the Father, God the Son, and God the Holy Spirit'."

van Flekwijk: "I am a stranger to the Creed of St. Athanasius. It is sufficient for me to believe in the living God, and that Christ is the Son of the living God, as Peter believed. He is called in the Acts of the Apostles, 'Jesus of Nazareth, whom God raised from the dead'. And Paul calls him 'that man by whom God shall judge the world in righteousness'."

Inquisitor: "If you are content to call Christ the 'Son of God', you do not give him a more eminent title than that which St. Luke gives to Adam ..."

van Flekwijk: "God forbid! We believe that the body of Christ is not earthly, like that of Adam, but that he is a heavenly man, as Paul says ..."

Inquisitor: "But St. John says... 'There are three that bear record in heaven, the Father, the Word, and the Holy Spirit, and these three are one'."

van Flekwijk: "I have often heard that Erasmus, in his Annotations upon that passage, shows that this text is not in the Greek original."

Broer Cornelis (turning to the Secretary and the Clerk of the Inquisition): "Sirs, what think you of this? This

LIGHTSTAND IN POLAND

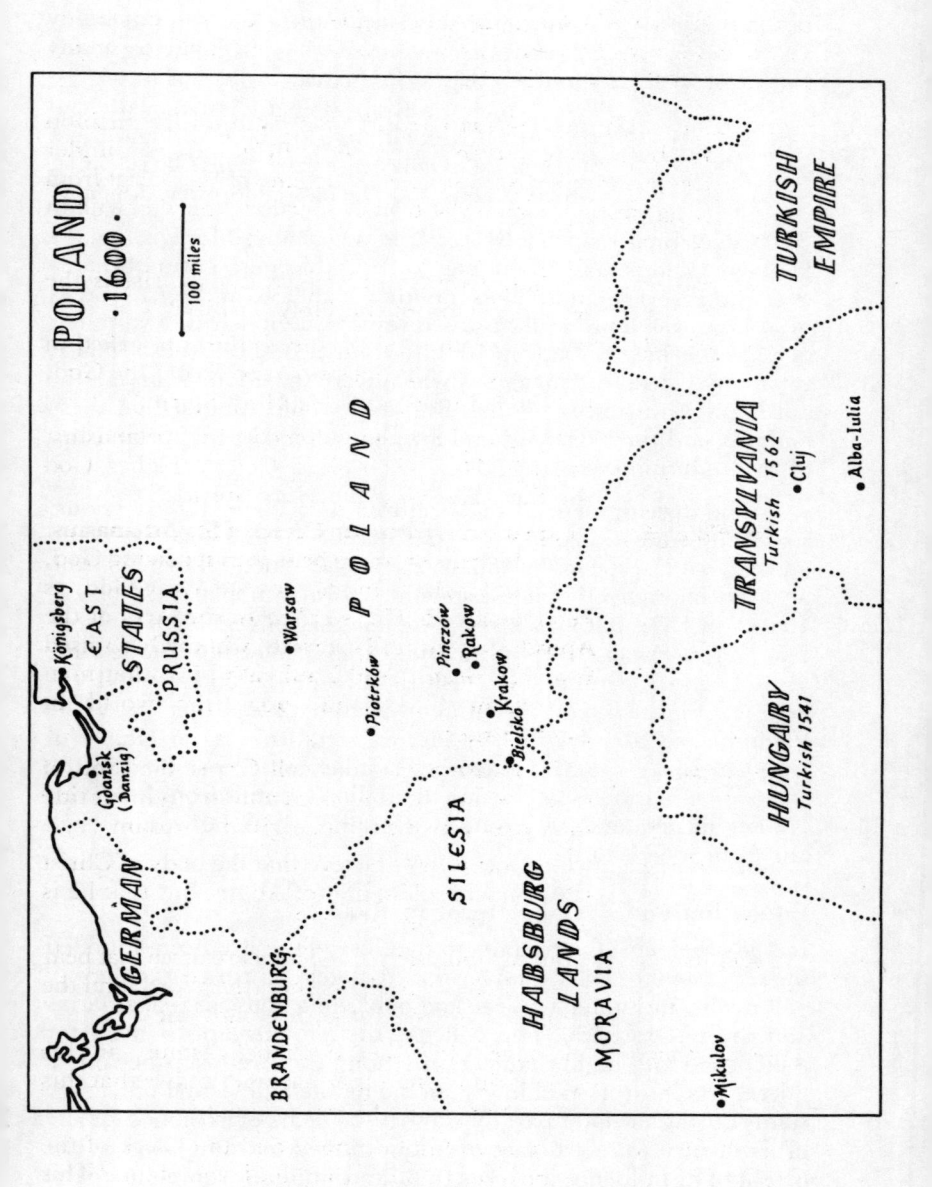

Antitrinitarian whom you see here, and the archheretic Erasmus, reproach us with having added these words, 'Who is over all, God blessed for ever. Amen,' in Rom. ix. 5. Or else they pretend that this doxology ought to be translated thus: 'Of whom, as concerning the flesh, Christ came, who is over all. God be blessed for ever. Amen'."

Other Brethren from Switzerland, Germany, Moravia and the Habsburg lands made their way to Poland as persecution became ever more severe and it became known that King Sigismund II of Poland was quite well disposed towards a non-trinitarian view of Christ, believers' baptism and freedom of Biblical study. In fact, the many Germanic surnames which were to be found among the 16th and 17th-century Polish Brethren would suggest that these emigrés and their descendants formed a considerable proportion of the community.

The development of the Brethren as a distinctive religious, social and educational force of considerable significance in Poland and eastern Europe in the 16th century was influenced by men from a variety of origins. Francis Lismanin, a former monk from Corsica, arrived in 1551, and was instrumental in the conversion of Gregory Paul, a Kraków cleric of wide learning and scholarship. In the same year, Laelio Sozzini made a visit to Poland. In 1558 a synod was held at Pinczów and prominent in the proceedings was the Piedmontese Biandrata, who almost certainly was originally of Vaudois background. To another similar conference held in the same town five years later came the Italian Gentilis from Moravia. He left subsequently to go to Switzerland where he was arrested and beheaded.

Education and Social Reform in Raków

In 1569 Sienienski, a prominent member of the Brethren, founded the settlement of Raków on a wooded plateau north-east of the city of Kraków, including a college and publishing house as well as farms and craft industries. The college, though fulfilling a need for theological and higher education among the Brethren, became a liberal arts institution of international repute and virtual university status during the later part of its thirty-six years of existence. Many of its faculty were scholars of unquestioned learning, and at the height of its influence it drew a thousand students from many parts of Europe, including three hundred from families of European nobility. It became known as the "Sarmatian Athens", but its associated publishing activities gradually aroused the bitter hostility of the Jesuits, as an increasing flood of books inimical to their doctrines came off the Raków press. The still prevailing use of Latin as an international language among scholars ensured a wide dissemination of these publications.

Visitors to Raków and other centres of the Brethren from other parts of Europe expressed surprise at the atmosphere they found and at the spirit of well-being which prevailed. A Scot who spent some time at Raków commented that he felt he had been transported into another world:

"For whereas elsewhere all was full of wars and tumult, there all was quiet, men were calm and moderate in behaviour, although they were spirited in debate and expert in language."

Education was not the only field in which the Brethren in Poland sought to express their Christianity. Gentry who were converted abolished serfdom three hundred years before it was abolished finally in Europe; some sold their estates or performed minor social and economic revolutions on their estates.

In the wide spaces of eastern Europe, settlement was at this period still comparatively sparse and scattered; there were still great forest tracts in the centre and south of Poland, and some of the settlements composed of families of Brethren were of a pioneer nature. Since communications were poor, it is quite surprising how wide an influence in Europe they exerted. The solid, hard-working, conscientious attitude which had commended itself to the Moravian nobility similarly impressed the Polish landowners who encouraged settlement on their lands, and for longer than in any other European country resisted the pressure of Jesuit calumny and opposition. The Jesuits entered Poland in 1564, only a year after the second synod of Pinczów, and for fifty years worked surreptitiously to end toleration and reimpose Roman Catholic domination.

After the Jesuits had achieved their objective of closing the Raków academy and publishing house, thus silencing its vigorous proclamation of Bible truth, the library and archives were hidden away for a time by the Sienienski family. Later, this large and precious collection came into the possession of the Czartoryski

Library of the Jagellonian University in Kraków, where it is still treasured by Polish scholars in a very different manner from which comparable literature of our own is treated in the west.

The Socinians

Fausto Sozzini, exiled from Italy, reached the Cluj region of what is now Romania after various wanderings, and made the acquaintance of Brethren there. Though an ardent advocate of most of their basic tenets Sozzini had an independent attitude in certain respects and never became a member. The principal barrier was the Brethren's insistence upon the necessity of his being baptized, which for some reason Sozzini never accepted. The strain apparent in Cluj intensified when he reached Poland. Officially he was "not permitted to join in communion with the churches or to have any voice in the direction of their affairs", but in fact by his personality and his voluminous writings he won the personal friendship of many of the Brethren and his views commanded considerable respect in private. Posthumously, his influence was probably greater than during his lifetime. That wing of the Brethren which most clearly expressed non-trinitarian views became known to 17th-century and later historians as Socinians, an appellation rejected as completely by themselves as the contemporary designation "anabaptist".

Georg Schomann's Last Will and Testament

Among the documents of the Polish Brethren preserved in the Czartoryski Library, one of the most moving is the "last will and testament" of a Polish teacher, Georg Schomann. It tells at great length of his search for Truth, how he and his wife came to obey it, and their passionate loyalty to it. Here we give just a short extract in which the father exhorts his family to hold fast to the things they have learned. What this testator left for his posterity was a treasure far more precious than the few material possessions listed at the end.

> "Dearest sons, daughters and little grandchildren, I have tried to outline those things from which you can truly judge concerning both our religion and our poverty. Wherefore I ask and admonish you, and call to witness our Lord Jesus Christ, that the ecclesia in which I have lived is "little" indeed, but despite that, in it you may progress more than we have, and to you it is the hope of eternal life. Truly, you have seen and heard that this ecclesia, based on purer principles, appeared

in my generation. The things for which it stands were judged by me to be soundly based. If you want to find out these things for yourselves, there is my second catechism which I compiled from Holy Scripture privately for you. It explains about the Most High God the Father and the Lord Jesus Christ, man, only begotten Son of God our Lord, who are to be worshipped in spirit and in truth; about baptism, the washing of repentance; about prayer; about the teaching of the Word of God; about the exercise of holy discipline, to labour with our fellow-brethren in the Lord's vineyard and with the talent he has given us. So learn it; it will be a guide to the divine principles; to the understanding of pure words; to the true faith. Learn much, for there are those who with foxy frauds will try to separate us and dash us down. But, with God and Christ as your defence, you may stand firm and we hope that you will be helped to persevere even to life's end ... May your understanding of God be that which we have from the prophets of Israel and not after the fashion of the Lutherans and Papists. It is truly a great work we do, to gather people into the ecclesia of the Lord from far and near, from all sects of Christendom, from Gentiles and Jews; so that we may all have an understanding of Truth and live a life of purity ...

"Truly my sons may divide my things, such little as there is to have. But God will be your portion, and your real income will be far, far greater, if you cling to Him with all your hearts."

A "Confession of Faith"

Georg Schomann was not, like some of his contemporaries, a prolific writer, but he was a quiet, dedicated organiser who was greatly beloved by his brothers and sisters throughout Poland. In 1574 Alexander Turobinczyck, a printer in that city, published a small duodecimo work entitled *Confession of Faith of the Congregation Assembled in Poland*. This is considered to be basically Schomann's work. This "curious catechism", as the church historian Mosheim unkindly described it, opens with a challenging preamble:

"The little and afflicted flock in Poland, which is baptized in the name of Jesus of Nazareth, sends greeting to all those who thirst after eternal salvation; praying most earnestly that grace and peace may be shed upon them by the one supreme God and Father, through His only begotten Son, our Lord Jesus

Christ, who was crucified."

The introduction goes on to urge the reader to abandon the doctrine of Babylon and the conduct and conversation of Sodom and to take refuge in the ark of Noah.

The document is remarkable for its clear presentation of the tenets of faith of the community. Its form is a common one, beginning with God, then Jesus, the Holy Spirit, justification, oaths, baptism and so forth. The careful plainness of two of the items needs no comment:

> "Jesus, our mediator before the throne of God is a man, who was formerly promised to the fathers by the prophets, and in later days was born of the seed of David, and whom God, his Father, 'has made Lord and Christ', by whom He created the new world, to the end that, after the supreme God, we should believe in him, adore and invoke him, hear his voice, imitate his example, and find in him rest to our souls."

> "Justification consists in the remission of all our past sins, through the grace and mercy of God, in and by our Lord Jesus Christ, without our merits and works, and in consequence of a lively faith. It also consists in the certain hope of life eternal, in the true and unfeigned amendment of our lives and conversation, through the assistance of the divine spirit, to the glory of God the Father, and the edification of our neighbours."

Similarly baptism is described as being "immersion and subsequent emersion"; and the Lord's supper as a memorial.

The Racovian Catechism

The 1574 *Confession,* short though it was, undoubtedly paved the way for the famous—or notorious, according to one's viewpoint—*Racovian Catechism* drawn up not later than 1605 by Smaltzy, Moskorzowski and Volkel. This large, detailed exposition of the faith of the "Brethren in Poland and Lithuania who confess One God the Father" ran through many editions and several translations and was still being reprinted as late as 1812. Minor alterations were made, but substantially the work remained the same for two hundred years. In many countries, including England, it was completely banned and its possessors punished, often by death.

> THE
> Racovian Catechisme;
>
> *WHEREIN*
>
> You have the substance of the Confession of those Churches, which in the Kingdom of *Poland*, and Great Dukedome of *Lithuania*, and other Provinces appertaining to that Kingdom, do affirm, That no other save the Father of our Lord *Jesus Christ*, is that one God of Israel, and that the man *Jesus* of *Nazareth*, who was born of the Virgin, and no other besides, or before him, is the onely begotten Sonne of GOD.
>
> Printed at *Amsterledam*, for *Brooer Janz*, 1652.

Title-page of the Raków Catechism, 1605 (edition of 1652)

The 1609 edition opened with what, by any Christian standard, is a splendid preface by Joachim Stegman and the most brilliant of the Raków professors, Andrew Wiszowaty, Fausto Sozzini's grandson. It is a compelling plea for what was then a revolutionary approach to Christian teaching and church life. He explains the way in which the Brethren were organised:

> "We all are brethren, to no one of whom is given authority and dominion over the conscience of another. For although some of the brethren may excel others in spirituality, yet in respect to freedom, and the right of sonship, all are equal."

A professed aim of the catechism was that "our equity, gentleness and modesty should be known to all men". Considered especially against the background of its intolerant age, and compared with many contemporary conceits that bore the title of catechism, it certainly can be said to have succeeded in this aim if in no other. Its tone is reasonable, its approach appealing and in keeping with the spirit of Christ. It was this fact, joined with teachings deemed blasphemously heretical, which caused it to become hated by the generality of prelates and theologians.

As always with the Brethren, the first section of the catechism proper deals with the authority of Scripture. The view is developed that any man or woman who comes to the Bible with a truly seeking spirit can without doubt find its true teaching consistently and plainly revealed, despite some doubtful passages. Manifestly, from the confusion that reigns, many do not do so, and a suggestion is offered as to the cause of the multiplicity of interpretations of the Christian Gospel:

> "Although some of them may arise from the obscurity of particular texts, yet the greatest number must be charged to men's own fault. For either they read the Scriptures with negligence, or bring not with them a sincere heart, disengaged from all corrupt desires; or have their minds warped by prejudice; or seek not divine assistance with becoming earnestness."

Section two of the work deals with the way of salvation, explaining with copious references to and quotations from Scripture that man does not possess an immortal soul but is a sinner cursed with sin and consequent mortality. The way to immortality lies in the knowledge of and obedience to the truth of the Gospel. Faith to the Brethren meant far more than the Lutheran concept: it involved an understanding, an intellectual and moral cognisance of a certain "Way", of promises made by God, of "the first principles of the oracles of God"—coupled with an obedient bending of self to the revealed will of God.

The True Divinity of Christ

After a section in which the nature and will of God is considered, there is a long section on the person of Christ. Eight reasons are adduced why Jesus could not be God, one of the most cogent of which is that Jesus is portrayed in the New Testament as ascribing divine words, attributes and works to God, not divine nature to himself. Almost every passage bearing on the topic is discussed, some in a more thoroughly convincing manner than others, but in every case with fairness, in an attempt to arrive at a consistent, unified and harmonious view of the person of the Redeemer. Despite the fact that the full trinitarian deity of Jesus of Nazareth is rejected, yet there is throughout a reverent attitude to the divine Sonship of Christ and a careful insistence that Jesus is more than other men, that he revealed the Father, that in him dwelt the character and powers of God.

The Christ of the Raków catechism is not the simple ethical teacher of later Unitarianism. Although modern Unitarians look upon this work and its authors as in some measure the source of their own religious view, in fact there is little similarity. The Brethren of Raków were not rationalists in the Unitarian sense, but thorough-going Biblicists; they considered that the Jesus of the New Testament was the true Jesus, not the God of very God of the fourth and fifth century ecclesiastical councils. They saw the need for faith in religion, but they saw no sense or point in accepting a view of Deity which was inconsistent with itself and with the apostolic doctrines which all Christians at least in theory professed to follow.

Many passages in John's Gospel which deal with the person and attributes of Christ are considered at length. Typical is the following on John 17 : 5:

> "That a person may have had something, and consequently may have had glory, with the Father before the

world was, without its being concluded that he actually existed, is evident from 2 Timothy 1 : 9 where the apostle says of believers that grace was given to them before the world began. Besides it is here (in John 17) stated that Christ prayed for this glory. Christ beseeches God to give him, in actual possession, with Himself, the glory which he had with Him, in purpose and decrees, before the world was. For it is often said that a person has something with any one, when it is promised, or is destined for him. On this account believers are frequently said by this evangelist to have eternal life. Hence it happens that Christ does not say absolutely that he had had that glory, but that he had had it *with the Father;* as if he had said that he now prayed to have actually conferred upon him that glory which had been laid up for him with the Father of old and before the creation of the world.''

Doctrine and Manner of Life

The later sections of the catechism deal with a wide range of Christian doctrine: baptism, the Supper, faith, freewill, justification, eternal life, the work of the Holy Spirit (two forms, the one continuing for a time only, visible; the other perpetual, invisible), the death of Jesus, resurrection, the future age. The church is seen as a partly visible, partly invisible community of believers:

> "Those who truly confide in Christ and obey him; and are therefore, in the most perfect sense, his body; an assembly or congregation whom, because we cannot infallibly judge the hearts of men, we shall not fully recognise except at the coming of Christ."

The whole aim of Christianity is put forward as the transformation of the moral being; the teachings and beliefs are to be indelibly printed on the mind and the whole of life regulated "conformably to their directions".

In the early 17th century the Brethren were fortunate in possessing both a period of religious freedom in Poland and a number of gifted thinkers, writers and organisers. Johann Krell, Jonas Szlichtyng and Andrew Wiszowaty were prolific writers whose work was collected in the *Library of the Polish Brethren,* published in 1666 in Amsterdam. It is significant that Sozzini's works were not included when the series of eight massive folios was first published.

Two later volumes added writings by Przypkowski and Brenius. Brenius was a keen student of prophecy and his most important work—and, judging by the refutations published, the most unwelcome outside the brotherhood—was entitled *The Glorious Reign of Christ and the Church on this Earth*. It expounded at considerable length the early Christian view that there would be a resurrection of the pious dead to reign on the earth for a thousand years. It postulated the regathering of the twelve tribes of Israel to the land of Israel, Jerusalem and Judaea as the future centre of the kingdom of God, ruled by those faithful who will be blessed with bodily and substantial immortality. The wicked, those wilfully resisting divine favour, will be "punished with everlasting destruction" (2 Thessalonians 1). "The time of the establishment of this kingdom is unknown, but imminent."

Copies of this work circulated in Britain as well as on the Continent, along with contemporary efforts to refute it. Hedworth (see page 151) and Knowles corresponded concerning points in it and implied that it was well known.

Death and Resurrection

Joachim Stegman, for a time principal of the Raków college, and later a preacher at Cluj in Romania, published in 1633 what came to be known as the *Brevis Discussio*, a "Brief Discourse" concerning the prevailing opinion of Calvin and Luther "wherein they hold that the dead live".

Certainly neither Lutherans nor Calvinists had satisfactorily reconciled Scriptural teaching concerning the death state and bodily resurrection with their support, for reasons of expediency, of the late patristic and medieval belief in immediate transfer of departed souls to heaven or hell. Stegman challenges and easily penetrates the illogical position, endeavouring to show its inconsistency. "It will seem absurd, and indeed the thing itself is very absurd; yet they believe it." The document deserves quotation at some length:

> "For they suppose that the souls of men, in that very moment wherein they are parted from their bodies by death, are carried either to heaven and do there feel heavenly joy and possess all kinds of happiness which God has promised to His people; or to hell and are there tormented and excruciated with unquenchable fire. This they attribute to the mere souls

separated from their bodies, even before the resurrection of the men themselves, that is to say while they are yet dead. But these things cannot happen to something which is not alive. That which does not live, does not feel. They neither enjoy pleasure nor endure pain.

"The argument of Christ (Luke 20 : 34) wherein he proves the *future resurrection* of the dead would be fallacious if before the resurrection they felt heavenly joy. For God would be their God although their body should never rise again.

"Likewise the reasoning of the apostle (1 Cor. 15 : 30-32) would be fallacious wherein he proves the resurrection by argument. Certainly this would be false, if the godly, presently after death, did in their souls enjoy celestial happiness, and the wicked feel torment.

"Furthermore, why should Peter defer the salvation of souls to the last day (1 Peter 1 : 5) and Paul the crown of righteousness to the day of judgement (2 Tim. 4 : 8)? To what purpose should the judgement be appointed? How could it be said of the godly of the old covenant that they 'received not the promise' (Heb. 11 : 40) if the soul of every one presently after death, even without the body, felt celestial happiness?

"Is not living, dying, feeling, learning, acting, proper to the whole man, the compound of soul and body? Let the eye be shut, the soul will not see. The very nature of the thing itself refuteth it."

The last paragraph is illustrative of a persistent characteristic of the Brethren's exegesis of Scripture, that its words and concepts are in the generality of cases to be understood in a plain, straightforward sense, not in a highly mystical way. Theology for them was not abstruse and mystifying, but the common-sense unfolding of divine wisdom. God has revealed His purpose in a way amenable to man's rational comprehension, even though the ultimate infinities of things may be far beyond his grasp. "If Christians would shake off their drowsiness and prejudice", Stegman contended, "and set upon a diligent and impartial trial of all religious doctrine by Scripture and reason", they would assuredly become acquainted with the original Christian Gospel.

Persecution and Foreign Invasion

The period of freedom for the Brethren in Poland and Lithuania lasted until the second decade of the 17th century and in a restricted form until after the middle of the century. By this time some three hundred "ecclesias" existed in Poland and Lithuania. The Jesuits, struggling to thwart the protestant reformation and advance their own "counter-reformation", became increasingly influential in the affairs of the Polish state. Many of the priests had an implacable loathing of the Brethren's way of worship and life, and stirred up by every means hatred and hostility towards them. Several tirades, exhorting Roman Catholic peasants to rid their districts of this despicable sect, have survived. The slightest indiscretion on the part of any of the Brethren was seized upon to condemn all. In 1611, Jan Tyshkovych of Bielsko refused to swear in court by the triune God, and was alleged to have thrown down the crucifix offered to him in the dock. He was convicted of blasphemy, his tongue was pierced and his hands and feet cut off. He was then executed in Warsaw on November 16 of that year. Catherine Vogel, an attractive woman of considerable talent, was publicly mutilated in a savagely sadistic fashion in Kraków and finally roasted alive for the crime of "believing in the existence of one God". In 1638 some indiscreet and boisterous young students at the Raków college—not themselves members of the Brethren for the most part—stoned a cross in the vicinity. The parents of the boys and the college authorities made a public apology and offered restitution. But this was unacceptable and the affair was exaggerated out of all proportion and enabled the Jesuits to force the final closure of the college.

The 1650s were a period of great turmoil in Poland. Armies of various factions roamed about the country living by pillage. At one time it was said that nearly two-thirds of a million soldiers— Cossacks, Tartars and Poles—were living off the land, while Austrians and Romanians raided in the south. The nation's economy crumbled and the Polish people were reduced to deep penury and distress. At the instigation of the Jesuits, the Cossacks, aided by many peasants, burned and looted everything they could lay their hands on belonging to the Brethren; many families were killed. In the midst of the turmoil the king of Sweden invaded and drove King Casimir of Poland from the country. He exacted a pledge of obedience from the Poles: this was given first by the

Roman Catholics; the Reformed church followed suit and it was only under duress that the Brethren eventually acknowledged the king of Sweden as their temporal sovereign. Actually they did not wish to be embroiled in any way in the wars of religion which were plaguing Europe and only desired to be left in peace to worship according to their way. However, taking advantage of the Swedish king's absence on quarrels elsewhere, Casimir restored his fortunes and expelled the Swedish forces from Poland. The majority of the population readily abandoned their recent pledge and joined in the rebellion. The Brethren continued to take no active part in the political strife, but this was interpreted as loyalty to a foreign monarch, and severe persecution ensued. The Roman Catholic authorities, now fully in the ascendant, determined on nothing short of complete extermination or expulsion, and encouraged the Diet to extend no toleration whatever to the Brethren.

In 1658 King Casimir proclaimed adherence to or protection of the Polish Brethren a capital offence:

> "In the name of the Lord, Amen. We, Jan Casimir, by the grace of God King of Poland ... Although the public law always forbade the *Nowochrzceńcy* (anabaptist) sect to exist and propagate in Our dominions, yet by some fatal misfortune the said sect, which rejects the pre-eternity of the Son of God, began not long since to spread in Our dominions. We do ordain ... that if anyone of this kind is found who dares or attempts to profess, spread, or preach this sect, or to protect or support it or its advocates, shall without delay be capitally punished ... Yet, desiring to show our clemency, if any such person is found who will not renounce this sect, we allow him three years in order to sell his property, etc. During this time, however, he is forbidden to perform any exercises of this sect or to take part in any public offices, subject to the penalties above ..."

The Polish Parliament followed this up with a formal law of expulsion:

> "The toleration granted to dissenters from the church does not legally extend to the unitarians whom they call anabaptists, this being a new heresy. Therefore all who within such a limited time will not embrace the Roman Catholic religion shall be

banished out of Poland; allowing, however, two years to sell their estates, whether real or personal."

"We refuse to desert"

An anonymous response to this cruel edict by one of the Brethren has been preserved for us among the musty volumes in Duke Humphrey's Library, Oxford:

> "The charge is that we are enemies of the pre-eternity of the Son of God, that we deprive him of this. But we attribute to the Son of God whatever Holy Writ clearly attributes to him. In the most excellent and the fullest way that can be conceived and that can be, he is truly the only begotten Son of God the Father, with a name that is exalted above every name. If we cannot reconcile the pre-eternal generation of both the Father and the Son, if we cannot comprehend how they can both be co-eternal, both begetter and begotten, if these things pass our understanding, if we do not see how they agree, is this a crime to be paid for by death?

> "Our case is one of steadfastness of faith in God, of escape from papal superstition and tyranny, and, in general, the desire for a good conscience (1 Peter 3 : 1). We refuse to desert to the enemy, choosing the command of God rather than the inventions of men, Christ rather than the Pope. Our conscience is good, bound to no wickedness, crime or disgrace, dangerous to no one, friendly to all, proved by an endeavour to lead a blameless life, simply devoted to the One God and the oracles of God."

The brief freedom was ended. Months of anxiety followed, especially as the law was popularly imagined to allow anyone to sequester, loot or freely acquire the property of the Brethren:

> "So, as we go into exile, no sure and safe home presents itself. Shut out of our own land, we find almost the whole world closed against us. We have no way to support ourselves in exile. Our property is left behind. Our money was seized by soldiers or consumed as we led our wandering life. Our estates and farms are left behind ruined, wasted and despoiled, ravaged by fire and sword. The frightful prospect of an unjust exile drove many of the more wealthy to defection. They professed themselves

ready to die, but with wives and children they could not bring themselves to incur the hazard of the most wretched poverty. Those who had the greater abundance deserted Christ; those who had the more courage followed him. For those certainly desert Christ who abandon conscience. *Rather than abandon that, we have determined to give up all else."*

By 1660 the position of many was desperate in the extreme, and Andrew Wiszowaty made a courageous appeal at a religious conference in Roznów. It was a brave act to attend the council at all, since it was a hornet's nest of bitter enemies, but to speak out there for a mitigation of the sentence laid upon his people was an extraordinary act of self-sacrifice. Eyewitnesses record the considerable impression made by the "splendour of his talents and the magnanimity of his spirit". One Roman Catholic priest remarked that if all the devils from hell had been there, they could not have maintained their religion "more ably than this one man had done". The governor of Roznów, who was a fair-minded individual, asked what then would have been the outcome if more of Wiszowaty's calibre had been present and added that it was fortunate that some others he knew were not there. The priest replied that it was certainly a good thing they had not appeared, as he would have been hard pressed to get support for his case. As it was, even the friends of the Jesuits openly spoke of the conference as a defeat for them, and their chagrin led, not to mitigation of the sentence, but to the even more rigorous decree of July 20, 1660.

A great migration began, as the Brethren scattered to Prussia, Silesia, Moravia, Russia. Four hundred moved south to Transylvania to join like-minded friends already there. A considerable number migrated to the Netherlands, a few even reached England. In this they were helped by members of the congregations founded through the influence of John Biddle, the colourful figure who is the subject of a later chapter.

Transylvanian Confession of Faith

Transylvania had been overrun by the Ottoman Turks in 1562 and subsequently owed allegiance to the Porte of Istanbul. It is a sad reflection on Christendom that these pious, deeply moral and dedicated Bible Christians found more peace and rest among the "heathen" Turks than among their fellow-Christians. After an appeal by Ferenc David, one of the most eloquent of the Brethren, in 1568 a session of the Transylvanian parliament passed the first Act offering tolerance and freedom for Bible believers for the first time in at least a thousand years. It was later repealed, but it was a milestone in history. It was in the lovely hills and attractive towns of the Transylvanian Alps that communities of Brethren persisted longer than anywhere else in Europe. The following twelve-point confession of the Transylvanian churches (somewhat summarised) indicates that many of the old ideals remained unimpaired:

"We believe

1. In One Almighty God;

2. In Jesus Christ, Son of God by the virgin Mary;

3. In one Holy Spirit, the power of God;

4. In one holy Christian 'ecclesia';

5. That kings and magistrates are ordained of God;

6. In Holy Baptism in water: by it we are initiated into Christ, become an effective member of the church, and declare our profession in Christ and desire to amend our ways;

7. That the communion of the Supper is a remembrance of Christ;

8. The human race we believe to be 'under sin', but we can be justified by the grace of God. Through that grace we receive remission of sins;

9. Faith involves keeping the commandments of Christ;

10. We look for the glorious advent of our Saviour Christ;

11. We believe in a resurrection of the body, both of the just and the unjust;

12. We believe that the faithful will be granted to be with Christ and to sit down with him wherever his throne will be. There shall be eternal happiness and we shall be ever with the Lord."

The close parallel to the Apostles' Creed will be noticed, a deliberate characteristic of so many of the confessions of the Brethren. It was their constant hope that as this Creed was nominally acknowledged by the major churches, they would be granted recognition as loyal Christians instead of being considered, as was almost always the case, as worse than the heathen.

The work of the Transylvanian Brethren in and around Cluj and Alba-Iulia, in education and craft skills became widely known in eastern Europe, though knowledge of this isolated community became virtually lost to scholars and even to remnants of the Brethren in western Europe until 19th-century Unitarians (in the modern sense) "discovered" them and made contacts with them. By this time some changes in doctrine and practice had occurred, and further changes resulted from these links with the Unitarians and subsequently after World War II from the establishment of a communist government. But, while not now holding to all the tenets of their 16th-century forbears, there are still vigorous churches in Romania today which confess One God in unity and the Son of God, and which not only trace their lineage directly from the Transylvanian Brethren, but revere and honour the memory of their early "pioneers" such as David and Biandrata.

In north-east Germany, chiefly in the farming villages of Brandenburg, around Königsberg in East Prussia, and far into Russia small groups of descendants (literal and spiritual) of exiled Brethren persisted into the 19th century, their way of life and principles still having a less prominent but quietly leavening influence.

13

THE IRREPRESSIBLE HEADMASTER

IN the year 1615 a son was born to a woollen draper in Wotton-under-Edge, a village in the broadcloth district of the West of England. In a variety of ways this boy was a prodigy, not least on account of extraordinary powers of memory. From the time that he began his formal education at the Wotton Free School it was apparent that John Biddle was destined for the highest academic level. His progress being brought to the attention of the local grandee, Lord Berkeley, he was given an exhibition at this school so that he could matriculate. While he was in an upper form, and around fifteen years of age, an anthology of his translations from the Classics into English verse was published. Before he finished at Wotton, it was reported that not only had he surpassed his schoolfellows but "outran his instructors and became tutor to himself".

He went up to Magdalen Hall, Oxford (now Hertford College) at seventeen, and quickly became notorious for his independence of established scholastic authority. Names and dignities never meant very much to him. After graduating he remained as a tutor at Oxford but at twenty-six was elected headmaster of the Crypt Grammar School, Gloucester, in his own West Country. At that time such appointments were frequently made with a view to providing sinecures for the masters to pursue their own scholarship, but in this case Biddle, with characteristic diligence, threw himself into improving the school and became an outstanding head.

His own scholarship, however, did not suffer. Conscientious far beyond the standards of his age, his appointed duties to teach his charges the Christian faith caused him to make a painstaking and assiduous study of the Scriptures. He was no doubt supposed,

THE PROTESTERS

The Crypt School in Gloucester, England. In the Headmaster's room above the archway, John Biddle lived and wrote. The building is virtually unchanged since his time.

since the school was attached to the Cathedral, to teach the children according to the Catechism of the Church of England, but Biddle was no parrot. Influenced, as he later remarked, by "the love of Christ, who is truth and life", he accompanied his studies with fervent prayers for illumination.

For two or three years the young head immersed himself in his studies of the Bible, until his knowledge of it was encyclopaedic. He knew the whole New Testament by heart in English and almost all of it in Greek. When someone commented on the latter, Biddle admitted that he did have a little difficulty in remembering the Greek after the fourth chapter of Revelation. In discussion he was able to give from memory the full context of every New Testament passage quoted, a facility which made him greatly respected—and feared—as a debater.

"The Fathers"

His studies led John Biddle to question traditional views. He disliked the dependence placed by the theologians of his day upon the old church fathers. "The Fathers, the Fathers", he would say, "they are always croaking about the Fathers." He himself is said to have had "a low opinion of their judgements". Biddle raised certain questions and "a long time waited on learned men for a satisfactory answer to these arguments, but received none". The kind of question and the way it was presented showed the trend of his thinking: it was clearly in the direction of the Polish Brethren. Biddle claimed that he had read none of the literature of this community before coming to his own opinions. Considering its fairly wide dissemination at both universities at this period, this would be difficult to credit were it not for the generally scrupulous nature of his conscience.

The Holy Spirit

Prominent among the subjects raised in these early questions was the deity of the Holy Spirit, indeed the whole trinitarian concept of the Godhead. The following comment on 1 John 5 : 7 is typical, indicating his consistent habit of relating any passage to its context and to parallel Bible usage:

> "It would have been hard, if not impossible (had not men been precorrupted) that it should ever come into anyone's head

THE PROTESTERS

> to imagine that this phrase 'are one', did signify 'have one essence': since such an exposition is contrary to other places in Scripture, wherein this kind of speaking perpetually signifieth an union in consent and agreement, or the like, but never an union in essence. This very apostle in his gospel, chapter 17 verses 11, 21, 22, 23, useth this same expression six times, intimating no other but an union agreement; yea, in verse 8 of this very chapter in his epistle, he useth it in the same sense.''

A pamphlet entitled *Twelve Arguments against the Deity of the Holy Spirit* was produced for circulating among a few friends in the West Country. But one of these "friends" betrayed Biddle to the Gloucester magistrates, and, though ill with fever, the thirty-year old headmaster was committed to the common gaol. About this time the celebrated Irish bishop Ussher (of Bible chronology fame) passed through Gloucester and was constrained to pit his erudite wits against the heterodox head. The upshot was that a rather impatient bishop eventually withdrew from the dialogue with a few wry comments on the utter stubbornness of John Biddle. The famous prelate was unaccustomed to having his vast patristic learning questioned so radically.

Biddle considered the bishop was enslaved to church councils instead of to the word of God:

> "The fathers of the first two centuries, or thereabouts, when the judgements of Christians were yet free, and not enslaved with the determinations of Councils, asserted the Father only to be that One God...".

Trial by Parliament

In 1646 Biddle was summoned to London and his case was considered by Parliament itself. He himself was confined in the Gatehouse at Westminster while the proceedings dragged on. In a correspondence with Sir Henry Vane, an acquaintance from whom he hoped to obtain a little aid in his unfortunate situation, Biddle wrote of his searchings and his spirit:

> "After a long, impartial enquiry of the truth, and after much and earnest calling upon God, to give unto me the spirit and revelation in the knowledge of Him, I find myself obliged, both by the principles of reason and Scripture, to embrace the

opinion I now hold forth. What shall befall me in the pursuance of this work, I refer to the disposal of Almighty God, whose glory is dearer to me, not only than my liberty, but than my life.''

He meant the last sentence, every word of it, for he remained in prison for five years. Indeed most of the rest of his life was spent there. The opinions he felt obliged to embrace ranged over a wide field of Christian doctrine, as will be seen, but it was principally his questioning of trinitarian views and formulas which earned him the bitter hostility of the Westminster divines. The case dragged on so long that Biddle in his confinement sought to hasten a verdict by producing detailed and penetrating studies of this particular doctrine. These are the only words of Biddle which can be considered in any way inflammatory. In them he showed the absence of trinitarianism in the earliest fathers, and the influence of Plato on third and fourth century theologians, who "did in outward profession so put on Christ, as that in heart they did not put off Plato". Dealing with the proposition that Jesus Christ was the creator of the universe and man in the beginning, he makes the reasonable deduction that when in Matthew 19 : 14 Jesus says: "He that made them in the beginning", he must have been ascribing that creation to a Being other than himself. The creation attributed to Christ is the new creation, the "reduction of things into a new state or order". The Scriptures indicate that Christ was foreordained, not personally pre-existent.

During Biddle's first long imprisonment his friends deserted him. He commented that almost his only comfort was a draught of milk from the cow morning and evening. He worked on an English edition of the Septuagint Old Testament for its London publisher, a necessary employment since he had to pay for his keep as a prisoner! The honourable House eventually passed this law, surely one of the most fantastic pieces of bigotry ever to be enacted by a national legislature:

> "Any who shall by preaching, printing or writing, controvert the deity of the Son or the equality of Christ with the Father, shall suffer the pains of death, as in the case of felony, without benefit of clergy. Any who shall maintain that man hath by nature free will to turn to God; that the soul dieth after the body is dead; that man is bound to believe no more

than by his reason he can comprehend; that baptizing of infants is void and that such persons ought to be baptized again; that the use of arms is unlawful; that the churches of England are no more churches nor their ministers and ordinances true ministers and ordinances (shall be imprisoned).''

This extraordinary law gives us an insight into the wide range of opinions and convictions on which Biddle had parted company with contemporary orthodoxy. Whether through independent searching or otherwise, he had taken up the identical position of the Polish Brethren, and they now undoubtedly began to consider him the principal English upholder of their cause.

On February 10, 1652, Biddle was released; he remained in London and there met in fellowship with some kindred spirits. A group met every Sunday "for the purpose of expounding the Scriptures and discoursing thereon" and for divine worship. He was not a pastor; indeed he seems to have had no particular office in the church since it was a group based on simple membership. He did, however, engage in active writing for the group, and frequently spoke to the assembly on Sundays. One such Sunday a party of visitors appeared at the meeting-house, led by one Dr. Gunning, later Regius Professor of Divinity at Cambridge. He came not to hearken or to worship, but self-confessedly to "confound and confute" Biddle. No sooner had he arrived than he challenged Biddle to a disputation there and then on the topic of the supreme deity of Christ. Though the defendant was unprepared, Gunning met his match as more than one member of the learned don's party afterwards publicly acknowledged. Biddle "acquitted himself with so much knowledge in the sense of the Holy Scripture that he gained much credit both to himself and his cause". The professor made surprise visits on two other occasions, the third debate being on the subject of the Atonement. Gunning found that he was not impressing either congregation or his own henchmen and he gave up the attempt.

Biddle's "Catechism"

The year 1654 saw the publication of Biddle's *Twofold Catechism,* probably prepared in the first instance for the use of his own London brethren in the instruction of candidates, though in the upshot it attained a far wider notoriety. It was a skilfully prepared pamphlet.

All other 17th-century catechisms were wordy, rambling dissertations upon the opinions of the sects promulgating them; apart from the preface Biddle's consisted almost entirely of Scripture verses, accompanied by a few brief comments. In rather more colourful language Biddle commented on this fact in the preface:

> "... all catechisms generally being so stuffed with the supposals and traditions of men that the least part of them is derived from the word of God, not one quotation amongst many being a whit to the purpose."

He pointed out that his work would be unique as a Scripture catechism:

> "Take heed therefore, whosoever thou art, that lightest on this book, and there readest things quite contrary to the doctrines that pass current amongst the generality of Christians (for I confess most of the things here displayed have such a tendency) that thou fall not foul upon them, for thou canst not do so without falling foul upon the Holy Scripture itself, inasmuch as all the answers throughout the whole catechism are faithfully transcribed out of it."

From this catechism would be banned all expressions and doctrines which the Scriptures do not own, such as Eternal Procession, Eternal Generation, God dying, God made Man, Mother of God, Transubstantiation, Original Sin, Satisfaction for Sins—the list exceeds a page of the preface. Instead there would be Bible answers to straight-forward questions. The reader was challenged to assess whether such a method was fair.

The catechism proceeded through 24 chapters, assembling first of all relevant Bible passages on the authority of the Scripture, God, and the Holy Spirit. Then follows a comprehensive series of chapters on the person and work of Christ as Saviour, Prophet, Mediator and King; on his death and resurrection and his coming again; on his example and commandments, especially in regard to taking the sword. It marshals Scripture evidence to indicate hell as the grave, the hope of the Christian as being resurrection, and the end of the ungodly as being to be "destroyed, corrupted, burnt up, devoured, slain, pass away and perish" and not eternal torture. There is a chapter on believers' baptism, and an important one on the universality of God's love ("God is not willing that any should perish, but that all should come to repentance"). This particular section, in which Biddle showed that the Gospel of the New Testament is offered to all men for the obedience of faith, grossly offended the Calvinist divines who were numerous in the honourable House at Westminster at that time. Indeed there was not a single chapter which did not run counter to contemporary theology in high places. As a modern Oxford scholar has expressed it:

> "Biddle's *Twofold Catechism* was the most sweeping indictment of orthodox Christianity that had yet appeared in England, and constructed in such a way that it was very difficult to refute. It embraced the whole field of Christian doctrine and attacked one by one (by the method of question and answer) all the accepted positions of orthodox theology, showing how they contradicted the words of Scripture."

Not only did the form of this work make it difficult to refute, but by framing the essential challenge to orthodoxy in the form of questions, leaving the Scriptures to answer, Biddle avoided using expressions of his own faith which could be taken up by his enemies. The pages reproduced show examples which are typical of the catechism as a whole (Plate V).

Repeated Imprisonment

As soon as the catechism came to the attention of Parliament, complaint was lodged and it received "ignominious censure"; all copies were ordered to be burnt by the common hangman. Biddle himself was ordered to appear in the Chamber in person, and on doing so he was questioned by various members. It was characteristic of Biddle that he was not overawed by the august assembly, but asked with his usual aplomb whether it was reasonable that one brought before a judgement seat as a criminal should accuse himself. With the example of Jesus' own trial no doubt vividly recollected, he told the Chamber that he had made his opinion clear in his books; there was no particular secret about his attitude to religious matters and those books were in no way seditious. He was convicted and sentenced to remain indefinitely in the Gatehouse at Westminster without writing materials or visits, and Richard Moore who had printed some of Biddle's books was also imprisoned. One party urged the death penalty, but their proceedings were cut short by political changes in Parliament.

One can imagine something of the feelings of some members of Parliament when two days after Moore's and Biddle's conviction a man appeared at the door of the Commons distributing copies of a booklet originating from the Polish Brethren, translated by Biddle and printed by Moore! This apparent effrontery was, be it said, due to an unfortunate misunderstanding; not even John Biddle was as brazen as that!

Oliver Cromwell was more liberal than his bigoted Parliament and Biddle was released in the following May through the Protector's influence. One result of the whole affair of the *Twofold Catechism* was that the large national churches, both Episcopal and Presbyterian, recognised a potential danger and began a policy of more thorough catechising of their own members, a movement which came to have profound effects upon 17th and 18th-century English church history.

Biddle returned to quiet but active work among a small circle of like-minded friends. He disliked controversy and trouble, but he was too honest to remain silent when his faith was challenged. A typical incident concerned a trinitarian Baptist named Griffin, who lost some of his members to Biddle's congregation. He challenged Biddle to debate, but, foreseeing further trouble, Biddle declined to accept the challenge until the pressure was such that he felt compelled by conscience to do so. In a meeting-house in the shadow of St. Paul's the disputation was held, some of the audience consisting of a band of fanatical rabble-rousers known as the "beacon-firers". Griffin opened proceedings in a pontifical manner by rising and calling out, "Does any man here deny that Christ was God most High?" Biddle with, it is said, "sincerity and firmness", rose and announced that on Scriptural ground he did deny it. From all accounts Biddle's formidable powers in debate were again in evidence and his adversary, "unable to support his cause", found it easier to use alternative methods of silencing arguments which he was unable to refute.

The trouble Biddle anticipated was not long in coming. Less than two months after his release from Westminster Gatehouse he was in gaol again, but this time it was the notorious Newgate prison. On an obsolete law he was remanded on a capital charge of blasphemy and heresy.

THE PROTESTERS

The trial was long and protracted, Biddle's lawyer pleading illegality. He escaped a capital sentence, but was banished to St. Mary's Castle, in the Scilly Isles, where he remained in confinement for three years.

A petition was drawn up to protest against this sentence by some influential persons; it has the following passage, asking

> "whether Biddle does not, in fact, profess faith in God by Jesus Christ. Is he not like Apollos, mighty in the Scriptures? Is his crime that he believes the Scriptures according to their most obvious nearest signification, and not according to the mystical and remote interpretations?"

His own writings support the petitioners' claim. There is a reasonableness and lack of mystification pervading them, though the quaint Elizabethan style deriving from constant acquaintance with the King James version creates a rather archaic effect:

> "He that saith Christ died, saith that Christ was not God, for God could not die. But every Christian saith that Christ died, therefore every Christian saith that Christ was not God."

Biddle was not idle while in St. Mary's Castle. He was not denied books or paper and one notable production of his pen resulted.

His *Essay explaining the Revelation* was the result of much study, not only of that book of the New Testament, but of the Bible as a whole and much else in the way of background reading. He wrote to say that he was still learning, and that the writing of this book had led him in many particulars to a clearer understanding of the divine oracles. The book concentrated attention on "the personal reign of Jesus Christ on the earth".

In 1658 he was released once more, and returned to London. This period of freedom lasted four years, and, though ill for a considerable part of the time, he was active among his friends and cemented associations with the Brethren in Poland. It was in this same year that the Polish Diet decreed their expulsion from that country and much correspondence passed between those associated with Biddle and the exiled Poles.

A Balanced Character

We can picture John Biddle at this period, a man of whom a contemporary wrote, "There is little or nothing blameworthy in him, except his opinions". Despite strong convictions, he avoided eccentricity. He was no narrow religious fanatic, being a man of wide literary and scientific interests. It is said that he carried his "reserve in his behaviour to the female sex to an unusual degree of delicacy and caution". He had a sense of humour which carried him through many a trying and difficult situation and a fantastically quick wit in repartee. But, unlike so many contemporaries, his speech was free from barbs and he always had a sense of the occasion. Biddle has been called the Father of English Unitarianism, but Biddle would have been horrified at the Unitarianism of the modern Manchester College variety. Although he was no believer in trinitarian mystifications, he always spoke of Christ with "deep reverence", believing him to be Son of God and Saviour. He could not, it is said, bear to hear the holy Name—or any sentence of Holy Scripture—used lightly or vainly, much less with scurrility. He worshipped Christ, as did the apostles, and often would say his prayers prone upon the ground. Perhaps the most outstanding aspect of his character was the rare combination of a brilliant intellect with a profound humility. "He quietly and unostentatiously endeavoured to practise what he preached."

Government agents followed Biddle frequently towards the end. Some of them were heard to "admire his strict, exemplary life, full of modesty, sobriety and forebearance, no ways contentious, altogether taken up with the great things of God revealed in the Scriptures".

On June 1, 1662, a sick man, he was holding a Bible Class in his own home. An armed party entered the room and carried him off to appear before a certain Judge Brown, a harsh and dominating incumbent of the King's Bench. Bail was offered on behalf of the ailing prisoner, but Brown petulantly refused. Five weeks later, worn out by the long trials and imprisonments and on fire with jail fever, John Biddle spoke with friends of his confidence through Christ of the resurrection of the dead and then "fell asleep".

14

STRUGGLES IN THE SEVENTEENTH CENTURY

SHORTLY after the accession of James I to the throne of England, a London businessman named Bartholomew Legate made a visit to the Netherlands and came into contact with a branch of the Brethren known as the "Seekers". Disavowing dogmatic creeds and fanaticism, they based their faith upon the conviction that a fair-minded, reasoned searching of the Scriptures would lead to a genuine Christianity. Legate was impressed and ultimately became a preacher for that community in London. His bold and fluent expositions of Scripture led him into trouble, especially his unacceptable view of the nature of Christ. He was imprisoned, and as he was a well-known person in London, King James himself desired or was persuaded to visit and interview the obstinate heretic. The royal visitor was pleasant until the prisoner ventured his view that although Jesus was called "God" on occasion in the New Testament, it was "not from his essence but from his office" as the revealer of God. A look of horror crossed the royal visage, and the king, spurning Legate with his foot, hissed "Away, base fellow!" and swung out of the room. The prisoner was taken to Smithfield and burnt in 1612.

Indictment by James I

Legate was known as a pleasant, moral and pious businessman and there was considerable public sympathy. Although the bishops still favoured the method—in the same year a colleague of Legate's was warned that if he persisted in his views "the law would take hold of him to fry him at a stake"—the view was gaining ground that the public burning of sincere Christians was a relic of the Roman Catholic Inquisition, and it became gradually less frequent. None the less, the indictment and sentence upon Edward Wightman, a

John Locke's notes on Volkel's De Vera Religione.
This book and many others from the Polish Brethren formed part of Locke's extensive personal library.

grocer of Burton-on-Trent, in the English Midlands, who was burnt "before the Guildhall at Lichfield" in 1611, are couched in essentially the same legal pomposity as in Michael Sattler's Rottenburg a century before:

"James, by the grace of God, King of England, Scotland, France and Ireland, Defender of the Faith, etc.

Whereas the reverend Father in God, Richard Bishop of Coventry and Lichfield, having judicially proceeded in the examination, hearing and determining of a cause of heresy against Edward Wightman of the parish of Burton-on-Trent in the diocese of Coventry and Lichfield concerning execrable and unheard of opinions by the instinct of Satan by him excogitated and holden, to wit —

— That there is not the Trinity of Persons, the Father, the Son and the Holy Spirit in the unity of the Deity;

— That Jesus Christ is not perfect God and of the same substance, eternity and majesty with the Father in respect of the Godhead;

— That the person of the Holy Ghost is not God co-equal, co-eternal and co-essential with the Father and the Son;

— That the (Nicene and Athanasian) creeds are the heresies of the Nicolaitanes;

— That the soul doth sleep in the sleep of the first death as well as the body and is mortal, and that the soul of the Lord Jesus Christ did sleep in that sleep of death as well as his body;

— That the souls of the elect saints departed are not members of the triumphant church in heaven;

— That the baptizing of infants is an abominable custom;

— That the use of baptism is to be administered in water and only to converts of sufficient age of understanding;

— That Christianity is not wholly professed and preached in the Church of England; etc., etc.

By divine sentence declared by the said reverend father, with the advice and consent of learned divines and others learned in the laws, he is justly adjudged, pronounced and declared to be an obstinate and incorrigible heretick; therefore as a diseased sheep out of the flock of the Lord, he hath decreed to be cast out and cut off, and the same Edward Wightman shall be in the same fire really burned in some public place in the city of Lichfield."

In general, however, as McLachlan has expressed it, James "politicly preferred that heretics hereafter should silently and privately waste away in prison rather than grace them and amuse others with the solemnity of a public execution."

The Early Baptists

The early 17th-century Baptists in Britain were a direct offshoot from the Brethren on the continent of Europe. They, like all the Brethren, rejected the nickname "anabaptists"—rebaptizers—and chose the denominational name of "Baptists" about the year 1613. Their earliest congregations had links with the Netherlands, and their earliest confessions differed little from other confessions of the Brethren elsewhere. The mortalist, antitrinitarian and millenarian elements of these early Baptist groups have proved an embarrassment to later Baptist historians writing from the standpoint of a Baptist church committed to a more orthodox theology. In later editions of Crosby's *History of Baptism* for example, reference to these beliefs was omitted. From one such omission is the following:[1]

> "We believe that there will be an order in the resurrection; Christ is the firstfruits; and the next, or after, they that are Christ's at his coming; then, or afterwards, cometh the end. Concerning the kingdom and reign of our Lord Jesus Christ, as we do believe that he is now in heaven, at his Father's right hand, so do we believe that, at the time appointed by the Father, he shall come again in power and great glory; and that at, or after his coming the second time, he will not only raise the dead and judge and restore the world, but will also take to himself his kingdom, and will, according to the Scriptures, reign on the throne of his father David, on Mount Zion, Jerusalem, for ever.

> "We believe that the kingdom of our Lord will be a universal kingdom, and in this kingdom the Lord Jesus Christ himself will be alone, visible, supreme king of the whole world.

---

[1] The author has been sent evidence which would indicate that it was John Thomas's citations from and reproduction of this passage which led to its suppression in later editions.

"We believe as this kingdom will be universal, so it will be also an everlasting kingdom, that shall have no end, nor cannot be shaken; in which kingdom the saints and faithful in Jesus Christ shall receive the end of their faith, even the salvation of their souls; where the Lord is they shall be also.

"We believe that the New Jerusalem that shall come down from God out of heaven, when the tabernacle of God shall be with men, and He shall dwell among them, will be the metropolitan city of this kingdom, and will be the glorious place of residence of both Christ and his saints for ever."

Concerning the rite of baptism itself, the following is typical (1644):

"The way and manner of the dispensing of this ordinance the Scripture holds out to be dipping or plunging the whole body under water, it being a sign of the interest the saints have in the death, burial and resurrection of Christ, that as certainly as the body is buried under water, so certainly shall the bodies of the saints be raised by the power of Christ, in the day of, and to reign with, Christ."

The rise of those churches in Britain calling themselves Baptist was marked by schism, and confusion in doctrine and practice; indeed in some instances almost the only common feature was a belief in believers' baptism. Some groups were ultra-calvinist in dogma; others played a prominent role in the Parliamentary Army under Cromwell and had no compunction about using force and often brutality. They thus became indistinguishable from the other Independents, "Fifth-Monarchy Men" (so called because they believed they were called to establish the fifth universal dominion of Daniel, God's kingdom) and sectaries who sought to build a moral paradise on British soil by means of the Ironside army. But there were others who were loyal to the faith and inspiration of the continental Brethren and resolutely refused to become involved in the internecine strife of the period. They protested at the unseemliness of Christians engaging in warfare, worldly politics or similar partisan entanglements. "The saints expect it as their portion patiently to suffer from the world, as the Scriptures direct them, than anywise to attain the rule and government thereof." One London group issued *The Humble Apology of Some Commonly (Though Unjustly) Called Anabaptists,* a document now in the Guildhall

Library. Signed by thirty men, it disclaims any seditious intentions on the part of their community, supports their position by quotation from an article, culled from a confession of faith, explains that they in no way involved themselves in insurrection, and requests legitimate freedom to worship God according to the pattern of His word, neither molesting nor being molested.

No Paid Ministry

As on the Continent, such groups aroused resentment by their egalitarian organisation, owning no special clergy or paid ministry.

> "There were preachers who were tailors, leather-sellers, soap-boilers, brewers, weavers and tinkers, but the important point is that these preachers carried conviction and wrought righteousness and constructed spiritual churches to the glory of God."

We can follow them one day in 1643 to the banks of the Bow River at Old Ford in London's East End ("that new Jordan", then a stream flowing through meadows, but today most unlikely to invite anyone to be immersed in its malodorous waters!) to baptize a new member. The candidate and the immerser walk out into the stream for the rite and as the baptism is completed the immerser grasps the hand of the new brother:

> "I am filled with much zealous joy to receive a new brother into our assembly who before had only the bare rags of Adam and was baptized by the ceremonies of Antichrist. We hold it utterly unlawful to baptize any until they come to full years of understanding, that they may answer for themselves and conform themselves to live according to that Name and baptism which they have received."

He goes on to urge the newcomer to the highest ideals of service and self-sacrifice, so that even the severest eye of justice will not be able to discern a wrinkle, much less a spot in his actions. The company disperses as inconspicuously as possible, for all too frequently an interested onlooker turns out to be a government informer.

A Battle of Books and Ideas

The middle years of the 17th century saw a great battle of books and ideas in Britain. Printing was comparatively cheap for the first time, though sometimes as much as thirty shillings, a princely sum then, would be paid for a book in high demand; literacy, often self-taught, was rising; and the chains of inquisition and superstition alike had been loosened. Many of the great libraries of Britain, public and private, were rapidly growing. Not only books, but broadsheets and pamphlets poured off presses, authorised and illicit, in an unprecedented stream, and it was no holds barred as far as language was concerned. Colourful and vigorous, the language of the title itself often had to convey the contents of the whole work, not only to arrest attention but also to convey a clear message, should it be confiscated or burnt.

> *"Of the Torments of Hell.* The Foundation and Pillars thereof discovered, searched, shaken and removed. With many infallible Proofs that there is not to be a punishment after this life for any to endure that shall never end."

If we can endure the grammar and read within, we find a Scripture treatise on the destruction of the rejected at the appearing of Christ. For an even more elaborate title there is Richard Overton's

> *"Man's Mortallitie,* or a treatise wherein 'tis proved, both theologically and phylosophically, that the whole man (as a rational creature) is a compound wholly mortal, contrary to that common distinction of soule and body: and that the present going of the soule into Heaven or Hell is a mere fiction; and that at the Resurrection is the beginning of our Immortality and then actuall condemnation and salvation, and not before."

The quaintness of style promised by the title is amply exhibited within; with delightful shafts of wit and pithy simile Overton wields his verbal sword against contemporary beliefs. Urging the illogicality of asserting that God condemns only the body by death, not the soul, he wryly comments:

> "... then the principal or efficient cause deepest in the transgression is less punished than the instrumental, the body being but the soul's instrument whereby it acts and moves—as if a magistrate should hang the hatchet and spare the man that beat a man's brains out with it."

STRUGGLES IN THE SEVENTEENTH CENTURY

The poet Milton had the post of censor of publications in the mid-17th century, but he was himself deeply influenced by the views of the Brethren and let many books and pamphlets through the net. In fact he himself on the whole favoured freedom and saw dangerous potentialities in muzzling the expression of opinion. Most of the time, however, the dangers attaching to the publishing, selling or reading of the literature of the Brethren or those favouring their views, were considerable. Heavy penalties were inflicted upon any who had the slightest connection or dealings with such literature. There was an especial furore when copies of a new edition of the *Catechism of the Ecclesias in the Kingdom of Poland*, the *Raków Catechism*,[2] began to appear in Britain. Several passages were read to the assembled Commons, who were scandalised and hurriedly passed an Act:

> "Resolved, that the book doth contain matters that are blasphemous, erroneous and scandalous.
>
> "Resolved, that all printed copies of the book be burnt.
>
> "Resolved, that the Sheriffs of London and Middlesex be authorised and required to seize all the printed copies of the book wheresoever they shall be found and cause the same to be burnt at the Old Exchange, London and in the New Palace, Westminster, on Tuesday and Thursday next."

A Pyre of Catechisms

Soon curious onlookers by the London Exchange watched a glowing bonfire and warmed themselves by the piles of flaming catechisms. A few years earlier, in 1644, Parliament had ordered that the "authors, printers and publishers of pamphlets against the immortality of the soul shall be diligently enquired for". One is left to guess at the purpose and result of the enquiry. The prevalence of publications questioning the Trinity was particularly worrying. It was even whispered that the chaplain at Eton—stronghold of orthodoxy—preached that the Holy Spirit was not one person of the Godhead emanating from another, but "God's activity in the world". Archbishop Laud rarely referred to the Brethren in a steady voice, but usually heaped on them epithets such as "those damnable and cursed heretics".

[2] See pages 118–123

THE PROTESTERS

A certain Daniel Featley, burgess of Southwark, annoyed by the worship in a small meeting-house of the Brethren near his home and unable to contain his displeasure at their disgusting rite of immersion, published a ferocious diatribe *The Dippers Dipt*. Nicholas Chewney, a provincial, supplied further information in his *Cage of Unclean Birds*. This work, extremely popular in its day—copies are still to be found on some old rectory bookshelves—is a travesty of scholarship, unreasonable in tone and full of outrageous and unproven allegations, yet it had a considerable influence in presenting to conforming Anglican clergy a brand image of the Brethren which persisted for a very long time.

Not all works published by the Brethren or their sympathisers were free from aggressiveness. There was, for example, Paul Best's tract:

> "*Mysteries Discovered;* pointing out the way from Babylon to the Holy City, for the good of all such as, during the night of general error and apostacy, have been misled with Rome's hobgoblins."

The somewhat fiery challenge of Best's tract is partly explained by the circumstances of its composition. Best was a Yorkshireman, scion of the squire of Emswell near Driffield. He had a distinguished career at Jesus College, Cambridge in mathematics and poetry. He then proceeded to travel widely in Europe, traversing Germany and Poland. In Transylvania he became a convert of the Brethren. On his return he confided his changed views to a Cambridge friend, who promptly betrayed him. His quarters were raided and he was arrested. On February 14, 1645, he was brought to Westminster for trial, and appeared several times before a committee of Parliament. He "persisted in his errors" and so was left to languish indefinitely in confinement. The House in fact seemed to have been considerably embarrassed both by Best's theological astuteness and by his dignity, and it postponed conviction again and again. It was to provoke some action that Best composed his inflammatory tract. One surviving copy of Best's tract, located by the present author, has Milton's own handwritten notes on it; most were burnt.

Contemporary with Best was John Biddle, whose case has already been considered. Reference here, however, can be made to the small groups of Brethren who continued Biddle's work after his death. Revered leader and guide of one such group which "went underground" after the Conventicle Act of 1664 was John Cooper. Born in Worcester and fellow of Balliol College, Oxford, Cooper became headmaster of the same school in Gloucester as Biddle himself. Originally an Anglican, he was ejected from a vicarage at Cheltenham with some violence. He was constitutionally delicate, "always composed and grave, but of a most sweet and obliging temper and conversation", but abuses from louts and ruffians broke his health and undoubtedly shortened his life. In a letter concerning the visit of a brother from Poland, Henry Hedworth, a member of the London congregation, makes a reference to Cooper, dying at 43, in somewhat flowery terms:

> "His great infirmities have now prevailed to deprive him of the light of the sun and us of the beams of his resplendent soul and countenance. His years and temperance promised us longer life; his sweetness of conversation, parts and virtues made him desirable and useful to all. My day in him seems to be obscured and my spring turned into autumn."

Hedworth had first met the Brethren in the Netherlands and through many difficult years guided an "ecclesia" in London until his death as an old man in the terrible winter of 1705. His will includes the following:

> "In the acknowledgement of the Most High God, the God and Father, the Only True God, and of Jesus Christ whom He hath sent to be the Saviour of the World, I commit myself to that my God through that Jesus Christ the Son of God, in the firm hope of the remission of sins, resurrection and eternal life."

The same will mentions Christopher and Samuel Krell, members of a family prominent at the Raków college, and Hopton Haynes, a close friend of Sir Isaac Newton.

Sir Isaac Newton

This leads to consideration of Sir Isaac himself, without question one of the most brilliant minds the human race has ever produced. His true greatness lay, however, not in his vast scientific erudition and perception, but in his deep and genuine humility. Though he could see a vast world of science opening up for man's ingenuity to utilise, yet as his own immense knowledge of the universe grew, it brought increasing conviction of the Divine and increasing reverence. It has even been suggested in biographies of Newton—those that show ignorance of his religious writings—that his religious interests coincided with periods of mental unbalance. Nothing could be further from the truth, as the painstaking work of scholars at Manchester College, Oxford has clearly shown.

To Sir Isaac religious faith was not only one of the facts of the universe to be studied along with all other phenomena but in a sense the greatest of them, since through it was distilled an ultimate and eternal relevance without which the music of the spheres was but so much sound and vanity. As one scholar has stated, the Christian faith aroused in Newton "the highest effort of his intellect and industry". He wrote in the region of a million words on religious topics, much of it on the highest level of scholarship. He sifted through early Christian and patristic sources, bringing to bear his acute critical qualities of intellect. He produced studies such as *Paradoxical Questions Concerning the Morals and Actions of Athanasius and his Followers,* in which he shatters any illusion that theological honesty was the keynote of the fourth-century church councils; *Twenty-Two Queries Regarding the Word 'Homoousios'*; and perhaps most noteworthy of all, his unpublished *Two Notable Corruptions of Scripture,* which dealt with corruptions of the text of the New Testament in the same period in the interests of trinitarianism.

Newton lived for a time in a house situated in a lane behind the National Gallery in London. Next door was a small meeting-house—it is still there and in use—which has an interesting history. Originally a Huguenot refuge, it seems to have been used in Newton's time by a congregation of Brethren and Newton himself appears to have had some connection with it. Sir Isaac disliked controversy, and the great majority of his religious writings were never published for fear of the furore which would certainly have ensued. To his contemporaries he appeared a rather vaguely nominal Anglican, but to a close-circle of friends, several of whom were either active Brethren or sympathisers, and in his writings, he emerges as a convinced student of the Scriptures after the manner of the Brethren, a powerful expositor and adherent of their principles and an assiduous reader of their literature. His own voluminous writings on prophetic and chronological matters bear as much the impress of Brenius and the Raków professors as they do the influence of Joseph Mede of Cambridge.

Repressive Government measures in Britain in the interests of established uniformity made any public witness on the part of the Brethren very difficult and naturally few records survive. For many years there was an active congregation in Coleman Street, London and others in the West Midlands. A very wealthy London merchant and philanthropist, Thomas Firmin, though never completely severing his connection with the state church, gave much aid to the Brethren, generously assisting exiles from Poland both in Britain and elsewhere. In days more tolerant he would no doubt have been a member, although he never hid his sympathy with the movement. He lived at Morden, Surrey, and his tombstone in the churchyard there lauds his benevolence but discreetly omits reference to his heterodox beliefs.

John Locke

John Locke, the famous philosopher and "apostle of toleration", friend of Newton and many Brethren, became convinced that their approach to the Christian religion was the only reasonable one. His library contained a great number of their works, indeed virtually all their major German and Polish authors. He made a *précis* of Volkel's *De Vera Religione* which is now in the Bodleian Library, Oxford. His little-known essay, *The Reasonableness of Christianity*, was his apology on their behalf and the following passages from it show how deeply he had imbued their spirit:

> "All men are mortal, and come to die. This is so clear that nobody can deny; only they differ about the signification of the word 'death'; for some will have it to be a state of guilt, wherein not only he but all his posterity was so involved, that everyone descended of him deserved endless torment in hell fire. But it seems a strange way of understanding a law, which requires the plainest and directest words, that by death should be meant eternal life in misery. Could any one be supposed, by a law that says 'For stealing thou shalt die', not that he should lose his life, but be kept alive in perpetual, exquisite torments? And would any one think himself fairly dealt with who was so used? I must confess that by death here I can understand nothing but a ceasing to be, the losing of all actions of life and sense.

> "By man came death, by man came also the resurrection from the dead. Whereby it appears that the life, which Jesus

Christ restores to men, is that life which they receive at the resurrection. Then they recover from death, which all mankind should have remained under, lost for ever, as appears by Paul's arguing in 1 Corinthians 15 concerning the resurrection. Christ will bring men to life again, and then shall they be put everyman upon his own trial, and receive judgement, as he is found to be righteous or not. And the righteous, as our Saviour says, Matthew 25 : 46, shall go into eternal life. The punishment of those who would not follow him is to lose their souls, i.e. their lives, Mark 8 : 35-38, as is plain.

"God nevertheless, out of His infinite mercy, willing to bestow eternal life on mortal man, sent Jesus Christ into the world; who, being conceived (by the immediate power of God) in the womb of a virgin that had not known man, was properly the Son of God. God, therefore, out of His mercy to mankind, and for the erecting of the kingdom of His Son, and furnishing it with subjects out of every kindred, and tongue, and people, and nation, proposed to the children of men, that as many of them as would believe Jesus His Son to be the Messiah, the promised deliverer, and would receive him as their king and ruler, should have all their past sins, disobedience and rebellion forgiven them. So believing, it was further required that those, who would have the privilege, advantage and deliverance of his kingdom, should by baptism be made citizens, and solemnly incorporated into that kingdom, live as subjects obedient to the laws of it. This is the law by which men shall be judged at the last day.

"He did not expect, 'tis true, a perfect obedience, void of slips and falls: he knew our make, and the weakness of our condition too well, and was sent with a supply for that defect. But that Christ requires obedience, sincere obedience, is evident from the laws he himself delivers (unless he can be supposed to give and inculcate laws, only to have them disobeyed) and from the sentence he will pass when he comes to judge. At which time, they shall all appear at his tribunal, to receive every one his doom from the mouth of this righteous Judge of all men. Matthew 16 : 27: 'For the Son of man shall come in the glory of His Father, with his angels: and then shall he reward every man according to his works'.

"This faith in the promises of God, this relying and acquiescing in His word and faithfulness, the Almighty takes well at our hands, as a great mark of homage paid by us poor frail creatures to His goodness and truth. The works of nature show His wisdom and power, but 'tis His peculiar care of mankind, most eminently discovered in His promises to them, that shows His bounty and goodness; and constantly engages their hearts in love and affection to Him. We have an example in Abraham whose 'faith was counted for righteousness', that he was called the 'friend of God'; the highest and most glorious title that can be bestowed on a creature."

Locke expressed his own outlook thus:

"I take the rule of my faith and life from Jesus' will, declared and left on record in the inspired writings of the apostles and evangelists in the New Testament, which I endeavour, to the utmost of my power, as is my duty, to understand in their true sense and meaning."

A Print-shop of the Brethren in Christ

15

"UNTIL THE DAY DAWN" — LONE LIGHTS OF THE EIGHTEENTH CENTURY

JOHN LOCKE died in 1704. By this time, the early years of the 18th century, the religious establishment in Europe felt satisfied that its version of Christianity was once again safe from Bible-based "heresy". The Inquisition had put aside (in most areas) rack, pincers and stake, but used subtler methods to ensure conformity. In most areas which the Catholics controlled, it was impossible to buy or sell, travel, trade, marry or find employment without having the "mark of the beast". The Protestant reformed churches had mellowed somewhat but had no intention of tolerating teaching such as the Brethren promulgated or of allowing free assembly by those who believed it (if they could find them). Nevertheless, the darkness had not totally overcome the many little lampstands of Bible believers scattered around Europe and the New World across the Atlantic. Although, surprisingly perhaps, documentary material is much harder to find for the 18th century than for the 16th or 17th, and detective work more difficult, yet from the limited available sources have come some exquisite gems.

A Typical "Ecclesia"

Through the eyes of the 18th-century French Romanist Bernard Picart[1] we can glimpse a typical "ecclesia" of Brethren at that period. Commenting that even thieves and robbers must have rules, he describes their church order, referring particularly to the fact that the qualifications for deacons are "good sense, a good conscience and tried fidelity" rather than learning. He considers

---

[1] This document, brittle and yellow with age, was found by the author in a London basement bookstore and purchased for one shilling. It failed to survive his brief handling.

their rite of baptism almost scandalous:

> "They think that no one can receive it unless he is able to know the difference betwixt truth and falsehood, to know God, and embrace the Christian doctrine by choice; besides which, they require piety and devotion, a humble sentiment of their unworthiness. Baptism itself is conferred, by immersion, in a clear running water. He puts one hand on the head, the other on the chin of the baptised, and thus dips them. A canticle is sung and the whole concludes with a prayer. By this baptism all these faithful become and are owned as members of the Christian antitrinitarian church. The day after they receive the Communion with suitable exhortations and acts of devotion.

> "The only place of communion is the church, the most proper time Sunday morning, it being a day set apart for piety and prayer, in brotherly union; the rest of the day may be employed in meditations on, and thanksgiving for, the benefits which God is pleased to bestow upon us. Their discipline allows that in a long distemper, when the infirm person earnestly desires to pay homage to Christ by this ceremony, an assembly may be held at his house."

We are introduced to a typical Sunday morning breaking of bread. A long table covered with a clean cloth provides the focal point of the room. Bread and an empty chalice rest on it. The Brethren enter and take their places around the table. The service is one of great simplicity. After hymns and readings and exhortation, an appointed one of the number stands and taking the bread gives thanks and passes it to the rest. He pours wine into the chalice or cup and passes it around, taking it last himself, seating himself to do so in order to emphasise that he is neither greater nor less than they. A "canticle" is then sung in imitation of the twelve at the Last Supper. (Plate VIII).

Picart provides an interesting insight into the marriage ceremony as conducted by the Brethren. They "disallow" marriages with those not in their faith, and have no place for "immodesty, excess and vanity" at either engagements or weddings. On the wedding day the couple appear quietly among their brethren and sisters. The presiding elder asks them to stand, and he then reads a portion of Scripture. This he follows by an explanatory discourse. The couple then solemnly "make to each other the usual promises",

Mountains, & be exalted above the Hills: And left any should think this hath been already fulfilled, the 4th Verse will tell us *no*; for it will be when *Swords must be beaten into Plowshares, and Spears into Pruning-Hooks*, and when *they should learn War no more*: And *Paul* tells us, that *in the last Days shall come perilous Times*; that is *the latter Part* of *the last Days*, 2 *Tim.* 3. 1: This is called also *the latter Times*, 1 *Tim.* 4. 1, when *some shall depart from the Faith. Job* tells us, that Christ *shall stand at the latter Day upon the Earth, Chap.* 19. 25. *Balaam* also prophesied what great Things God would do for *Israel* in *the latter Days*. I will advertise thee *what this People shall do to thy People in the latter Days, Numb.* 24. 14. *Hosea* also speaking of the *Calling* of the *Jews*, faith it will be *in the latter Days; Chap.* 3. 5. *they shall fear the Lord and his Goodness in the latter Days*. So that we see there is *the last Days*, and *the latter Part* of *the last Days*; and yet all this *long before* the *ultimate Day*.

There is yet *another remarkable Period of Time* which is yet *future*; and that will be at the *second* or *next Coming of* Christ. His *first Coming* was to put away Sin by the Sacrifice of himself; his *second Coming* will be without Sin to our Salvation, of which we have written before: his *first Coming* was mean in outward Appearance; his *second Coming* will be unspeakably glorious, *with Power and great Glory*, Matt. 24. *When he comes to build up* Sion, *he will appear in his Glory*, Psa. 102. 16: Then *he will come with Ten Thousand of his Saints*, and take unto himself his great *Power and reign*, and *all the Kingdoms of this World become his*, Rev. 11. 15; deal wonderfully with and for his People, *Joel* 2. 26.

I do not know any one Thing in Scripture more insisted on, than *the Glory of the latter Part* of *the last Days*, including the *Thousand Years* of the Kingdom of Christ, until the last Judgment. A short Account of several Things which will then be done, have already been given in this Discourse:

A Page from *A Brief Discourse concerning Futurities or Things to Come*, published in Boston in 1757.

the elder joining their right hands and placing his hand on theirs. Then they exchange rings which—seemingly to Picart's surprise, since he italicises this passage—are "made of purest gold, no joints or separations appear in them and their round figure admits no beginning or ending. Excellent types of the union and constancy of the married couple! Dancing, singing and fiddles are strictly prohibited at weddings as being only incentives to uncleanness."

On the whole our reverend French informant is not unfair in regard to the practice of the Brethren, though their objection to war would make them "useless to governments": "We cannot help commending", he says, "at least their moderation and seemingly charitable condescension." There is one comment of his which is particularly interesting: his reference to the origin of the community of the Brethren in "the sixteenth age (century), and *the astonishing progress it has made through Europe*". This coming from a priest in the 1730s, when persecution had extinguished many of their assemblies and reduced them to a thinly-spread, fugitive and poorly-organised remnant, is quite astonishing. Their underground influence, moreover, he sees as even more sinister and pervasive.

Adventist Movement

It is certain that there were, as Picart feared, many "hidden heretics", for what could not be done by overt ways in the sight of the sun by regular assemblies, could be done surreptitiously by those whose consciences were not those of martyrs. In fact the faith of the Brethren was, during the 18th century, far greater as a distinct and subtle influence upon other denominations than as an organised sect itself. It profoundly influenced the Unitarians, who went much further in rationalising Christianity; it undergirded the millenarianism of Bengel in Germany and John Robertson in England and provided the initial impetus for the whole Adventist movement which gained prominence in the early 19th century. Some communities of Brethren did actually survive almost unmodified throughout the 18th century, both in Europe and the New World. An Edinburgh tract of 1791 refers to "certain independent congregations", presumably in Scotland, and identifies the following as being some of their characteristic beliefs:

1. Man is mortal and has no immortal soul.

2. The dead sleep with their fathers until the morning of the

resurrection, when Jesus will judge the living and dead.

3. The Word, an attribute of Deity, was so united to Christ, as to be the principle of all his wisdom and wonderful works.

4. The wicked will be punished with everlasting destruction and annihilation.

5. It is absurd to believe that Jesus "sustained the wrath of God". He rather died as a supreme example of obedience. It is that obedience, not his literal blood, which saves us. He was sinless morally, but this perfection was the result of deep struggle, not of immaculate nature.

6. The corruptions of the heart are the only devils.

The existence of such congregations of Brethren in lowland Scotland at the threshold of the 19th century is most significant, since this area was one in which the same faith put down new roots in the 19th century.

The Kingdom of God on Earth

In private libraries in both Europe and America it is possible to find fine examples of very detailed expositions of Bible teaching on the Promises to the Fathers, the Hope of Israel, Christ's return and the millennial reign of Christ on earth. Though couched in quaint language (to us), the message is always clear, the Bible references exhaustive. One gem from 1771 is a treatise entitled *Observations upon the Prophecies relating to the Restoration of the Jews*. Published by Cadell of the Strand, London, it is from the pen of Joseph Eyre—but the present author has no knowledge as yet of an ancestral link!

In a prefatory note, Eyre briefly puts forward the Brethren's usual explanation of why Bible truth had been neglected for so many centuries:

"When the church, by an accession of wealth and power, was so corrupted as to mind little else but enriching itself, to the neglect of scriptural studies in general, it is not strange that the study of the Prophecies should be discouraged, and almost wholly neglected. During the Papal tyranny, we have so very few, and those erroneous, explications of Scripture prophecies in general. But when the Reformation began to take place, and the sacred Scripture, which had long been shut up from the people, was again laid open for the perusal of all Christians, the study of the prophetical parts began to revive."

A few paragraphs from the body of the work will reveal its straightforward, solidly scriptural substance:

"By the kingdom of *God* or of *Christ,* in its full and compleat meaning, or, as it is always represented as a state of *purity, peace,* and *happiness,* can be meant nothing less than that *thousand* years reign of Christ which is foretold in the *Revelations,* and to which a very great part of the Prophecies of the Old Testament do most evidently relate. This *millennium* has indeed been a very unfashionable doctrine for these last fourteen centuries, but it were very easy to show, that it was generally believed in the more early ages of the church, especially in those nearest to the apostolic age ...

"Almost all the writers on this subject, that I have met with, seem to me to have run, more or less, into the following error: They have generally applied the Prophecies relating to the restoration of the *Jews* to the church of Christ, as it has hitherto subsisted in the world; applying the words *Israel* the *seed of Abraham* and *Jerusalem,* in an allegorical sense to *Christians,* or the *Christian church;* whereas the great happiness, which is the principal subject of all the Old Testament Prophets, appears to me to be no way applicable to any state of Christianity that has ever yet existed, but to relate to the conversion and restoration of the *literal Israel,* the *Jews* and ten tribes, in the later times, and to the reign of Christ."

Joseph Eyre, like many sincere Bible believers during the 18th century, handles the question of the "times and seasons" with reasonable caution, knowing that much remained to be fulfilled before the Lord's appearing:

"It may be expected by some that I should say somewhat concerning the time when this restoration is to take place; to whom I answer, in the words of our Lord, that *it is not for us to know the times and the seasons, which the Father hath put in his own power.* All that we can be certain of in relation hereto, is, that *Jerusalem shall be trodden down of the Gentiles, until the times of the Gentiles be fulfilled,* as our Saviour tells us, *Luke* xxi. 24.

> What is meant by the times of the Gentiles being fulfilled, is, according to the most judicious expositors, when the times appointed for the duration of the dominion of the four monarchies shall be compleated.
>
> "We now live under the last state of the fourth monarchy, after the division of it into ten kingdoms, represented to *Nebuchadnezzar* by the feet and toes of the image which he saw in his dream; but the precise time when the stone cut out without hands shall smite the image *upon his feet* that were of iron and clay, or partly strong and partly brittle, as the angel interprets it, is not perhaps now discoverable by us.
>
> "That the time of this restoration is one of these secrets of Divine Providence, appears from the 12th chapter of *Daniel,* where, after the Prophet had been informed that *Michael shall stand up the great Prince which standeth for the children of his (Daniel's) people,* it is added, ver. 4. *But thou, O Daniel, shut up the words, and seal the book to the time of the end.* And again. *When he shall have accomplished to scatter the power of the holy people, all these things shall be finished.*"

This interesting work concludes by reminding readers that prophecy is a light shining in a dark place, until the day star arise; and it is also a powerful evidence of God's truth and His purpose throughout history:

> "The natural consequence of comparing the several prophecies relating to the *Jewish* nation with the events would be a thorough conviction in our minds of the truth of that revelation by which they were delivered to us. That they were to be *dispersed* and scattered among all nations of the earth is repeatedly foretold by the Prophets, and that they shall finally be *restored,* never to be again dispersed, is likewise as often predicted by the same Prophets. The first of these we see most literally fulfilled, and the latter therefore it is most highly reasonable to expect. In the mean time we see this people alone, by a singular miracle of Providence, preserved alive to this day, under persecutions and oppressions more than enough to have extinguished their race, preserved entire, and unmixed with the nations of the world, among whom they are scattered."

Gog, Magog and Armageddon

On the American side of the Atlantic, where, it should be remembered, both men and women in the 18th century were sometimes publicly whipped to death for opposing Calvinist orthodoxy, similar expositions appeared. Many of the writers, possessing treasured copies of the publications of the Brethren in Christ which had been carried from Europe, and warmed at the fire of the prophetic Word, endeavoured to inform their contemporaries just where they stood in time in the grand plan and purpose of God with His earth. We do not hesitate to cite another gem from mid-18th century at some length, as he explains about Gog, Magog and Armageddon:

> "*Gog* and *Magog* spoken of by *Ezekiel* are to be Contemporaries with the *Jews* either at the Time or not long after their Return to their own Land; as appears by the whole Story, Chap. 38 & 39, to which the Reader is referred. The Persons *against whom* they are to engage in this War are principally the Nation of the *Jews,* tho' it may be not only with them. The *Occasion* or moving Cause seems to be, either the Weakness of that Nation at this Time, as not being yet settled in their own Land, or their Security, or both, as ver. 11; but it was chiefly to spoil them, or to make a Prey of them, as ver. 12 . . .
>
> "As to the *Time* of this War: it is at or not long after the Return of the *Jews* to their own Land. *Preparation* thereunto will be under the pouring out of the *6th Vial:* When this Battle is over, there will be *a peaceable and prosperous State*. . .
>
> "So that if we view these Scriptures (Joel, Ezekiel, and the Revelation) we shall see that they all speak of the same Enemies, gathered together by the same Hand, engaged against the same People, at the same Time, upon the same Occasion, to be destroyed in the same Place; and the same Effects to follow, viz. terrible to the one, and comfortable to the other. So that you see this War is not a War, in which, the Enemies of God shall fight one against another, as they often do upon divers Occasions; but it will be a Combination of them all against CHRIST and *his People,* and *Specially his antient People.* And *these* are as I understand the *Gog* and *Magog* intended by *Ezekiel.*"

In their day, those 18th-century Bible believers could not foresee how it would be accomplished, but that scattered Israel would return to its ancient homeland, they were certain. The Day of Christ could not come until it was a reality. So God Almighty would make a way. A full century before John Thomas' *Elpis Israel*, yet in virtually the same familiar turns of phrase, the challenging message is sounded forth in a passage which hardly allows us to draw a breath:

> "I rather incline to think, that God will some Way or other, first bring them into their own Land, and give them Advantage to return by *drying up the River* EUPHRATES, that is as I conceive by diminishing and abating the great Power of the *Turk* in and about that Part of the World; and that either by intestine Commotions, or Wars with other Nations, or both; that so a Way may be prepared for *these Kings of the East* to return: and this is to be done under the *pouring out* of the *6th Vial:* and that is the Time when *these dry Bones will come together and stand upon their Feet, and become an exceeding great Army, and have Breath breathed into them,* and have a *civil Life* put into them, but *no Spiritual Life* till they be in their own Land, and at the *Sound of the 7th Trumpet* and the *pouring out of the 7th Vial:* and *after this great Battle,* when God will destroy all Nations that come against *Jerusalem, then he will pour upon them the Spirit of Grace and Supplication;* and then, will CHRIST *personally and visibly appear, and they shall look on him whom they have pierced and mourn,* with a penetential Mourning; and when *his Feet shall stand on the Mount of Olives,* from whence he ascended, *then he will come and all his Saints with him,* Zech. 14.3-5. *And this is the great Day of* JEZREEL, *when the Children of Judah and the Children of Israel shall be gathered together and appoint them one Head.* Hos. 1; *when the Lord shall be King over all the Earth,* Zech. 14.9; and *all the Kingdoms of this World become his,* Rev. 11.15."

The Hope of Israel

The characteristic Christadelphian view of the Gospel as being the "Hope of Israel", and a development of the covenant God made with Abraham, is evident in the writings of Joshua Spalding who was acquainted with George Washington. Copies of his published works are now exceedingly rare and viewed as collector's pieces by the American Antiquarians' Society. Although not considered famous enough to merit a place in the *Dictionary of American Biography,* at the time Spalding seems to have had considerable influence. He frequently offended people by reminding them that they were like the beasts that perish, and that human nature is now basically depraved. In the 1790s he held a campaign in Salem, Mass., then one of the major towns of the United States. It consisted of a series of addresses on "The Coming Kingdom of Christ" and he personally describes the synopsis of this series thus:

> "What will be the constitution of this world to come, which is the grand theme of all the prophets, what the nature of its kingdom, its heavenly power and transcendent glory."

The lectures were published and created a typical furore of opposition among the dominant Calvinists. Some years later Spalding wrote rather sardonically, but truthfully:

> "My opponents may affect to treat that book with indifference, but they have it not in their power *fairly* to answer the arguments therein adduced. No one has come forward publicly, to examine the sentiments supported in those lectures, and refute the copious proofs therein offered from the plain sense of the Scriptures."

His style was often rather tortuous and complex and has not the warm sparkle of Hübmaier or the cool logic of Stegman. But the following is clear enough:

> "The world to come, of which all the prophets have spoken, and which is the express object of all the promises and the grand article of the faith of the just, will be in all respects a new world. It will be as really the world of man as was that before the flood or as the world that now is. It will be composed of a heaven and an earth, of cities and countries and rulers and subjects, and of everything necessary to constitute a proper world and kingdom.

> "Some have supposed because this country is called an heavenly, and its city is the heavenly Jerusalem, that it must be the world of spirits above. But when the Scriptures are carefully compared, it will appear beyond controversy that this 'world to come' is called an 'heavenly' because it is put in subjection to the Lord from heaven, subject to the high authority of the Lord Jesus Christ.

"It is acknowledged by all that the land of Canaan was shown to Abraham as the premises named to him in the promise, bounded by the Euphrates and the River of Egypt.

"Psalm 37 : 9; Matthew 5 : 5: the meek shall inherit the earth. This cannot be understood of the present world, for it is not worth inheriting. And it cannot be better explained by supposing that this world is pointed to as a figure of heaven; for what propriety could there be in using this dunghill world as a figure of celestial mansions above? But there is no obscurity as to this subject in the Scriptures. See Isaiah 45 : 17; 46 : 22; 2 Peter 3 : 13; Rev. 21 : 1; Heb. 11. The world to come, its realms and its Lord, has ever been the grand object of faith.

"The resurrection of both the just and unjust will take place. The dust of believers, being united to Christ, will be quickened and raised up by the glorious appearing of the Sun of Righteousness, as a *seed* possessing the principle of life is excited and springs up under the genial influence of moisture and heat. Thus the prophet describes the hope of the resurrection in Isaiah 26 : 19.

"Watch ye therefore and pray always ..."

The exceedingly rare work from which the above is taken—*The Divine Theory*—is chronological rather than thematic in its treatment of the Gospel, dealing first with the Creation, the fall, through the promises made to Abraham and David, to the Kingdom of God in the future. This departure from the general convention of the Brethren, whose thematic approach often followed the doctrinal order of the Apostles' Creed, was continued later by John Thomas in *Elpis Israel* and by other Christadelphian writers. Spalding is of considerable interest in that he revived the consistent use of the term "Hope of Israel" to describe the New Testament anticipation of the reign of Christ on earth, and stressed for the first time in an elaborated form the importance of the promises and covenants made to Abraham and David as foundation blocks for understanding the doctrines of the resurrection and Kingdom of God. Though referred to many times in earlier writings by the Polish Brethren particularly, the consequence of the fundamental covenants in the Old Testament had been assumed rather than been the starting point for sustained exposition.

"UNTIL THE DAY DAWN"

One episode in the 18th century is of considerable interest, though its documentation is scanty. An abundantly whiskered Swiss by the name of Abraham Stemler, connected in some way with the Swiss Brethren, published a delightfully written millenarian work, *The Hope of a Better Time,* about 1712. Carefully and moderately reasoned, it drew a swift rejoinder from the Swiss Reformed establishment. Dr. Christoph Sonntag (clearly a pseudonym for a fanatical advocate of Sunday sabbatarianism!) wrote a "refutation" in flowery but uncompromising Latin. This document, now a fragile, yellowed tissue, is for some strange reason in the U.S. Library of Congress. Another publication, this time in England (copies also reached the U.S.) was that of Thomas Hartley in 1764 entitled *Of Christ's Glorious Reign on Earth—A Testimony to the Doctrine of the Blessed Millennium, with some Considerations on its Approaching Advent from the Signs of the Times,* later republished as *Paradise Restored.* These are only two examples of many during the 18th century, but they are indicative of the fact that although the century has historically been considered "irreligious and thoroughly secularised", the salt had by no means entirely lost its savour.

16

WITNESS TO TRUTH IN 1807

THE search for Bible truth by a New Englander, Elias Smith, illustrates the way in which the seeds of the gospel constantly generate new plants in unexpected and sometimes most unlikely places.

Elias Smith was born in 1769 at Lynn, a town about ten miles from Boston, Mass. His education was in the strict puritan tradition of the area and included weighty indoctrination in the Calvinistic Catechism and committing to memory "the greater part of the New Testament". He was 20 years of age when he finally decided to affiliate with the Calvinist Baptist church to which his father belonged. He had earlier been "sprinkled" by the Congregational church which his mother attended, an occasion he always referred to afterwards in a tone of undisguised disgust.

Being of bright intellect, he was encouraged to train for the ministry, and he was "ordained" at Lee, New Hampshire. Shortly after his marriage at the age of 29 he was appointed pastor of a congregation numbering several hundred at Woburn, Mass.

It was about this time that he began to be very unhappy both with his message and its fruits. He noticed that the Calvinist doctrines of predestination and election confirmed people in their pride rather than induced them to humility. On the other hand, those who had no confident assurance of being divinely chosen were hardened the more into sin. The preaching of Dr. Hopkins' "system of divinity", in which he had been rigorously schooled, only served, he wryly commented later, "to stultify my audience".

Despite his admitted fears of the bishop's wrath, he decided on a total re-appraisal of his message, and set about it in a typically thorough manner. "I threw divinity books out of my bookcase, and began to think of the extent of the love and grace of God to man." He examined afresh the catechism which he had accepted for many years and "found it contained contradictions and impossibilities and was contrary to the plain declarations of the Scriptures".

His bishop was furious and Smith was unceremoniously ejected from his pastorate. But he was undeterred. In revulsion from the Pharisaism of Calvinist doctrine he turned towards Universalism, then being propagated from the colleges of New England. He shrewdly noted that although apparently different, Universalism was really based on Calvinism, the only difference being the number to be saved! In neither case was faith a real power. He decided to "drop both and study the Scriptures". His next step was to repudiate the dogma of the Trinity as unscriptural scholasticism.

Single-minded Zeal for Truth

Intrigued and spurred on by a zeal for Truth, Elias Smith then got down to serious Bible study. "I endeavoured", he wrote some years after, "to attend closely to the plain declarations of the Scriptures of Truth, without any regard to the opinion of man. My Bible and Concordance are almost the whole of my books. In my search after Truth in the Scriptures, I have been led to reject many things which others hold, and to embrace many things which some reject, because they do not search after what God has said in his word."

There is no doubt, as in other well-known cases, both before and after Smith, that he was sincere and honest in his claim to be objective and unaided in his search for Truth. There is no need to doubt that he allowed the Word to imprint its message upon his mind. Yet he mentioned himself that he was familiar with the writings of the Joshua Spalding, referred to earlier, Newton and others who had taught about the Hope of Israel, the Personal Return of Christ, the Promises, the Resurrection and the Millennium. No man is an island.

By the end of the 18th century Smith had enough confidence in his new found Scriptural convictions to commence a career of preaching, magazine editing and writing that became typical of many other self-taught religious men of the 19th century. Called

THE PROTESTERS

"quaint and eccentric" by others of lesser courage, he ranged around the New England townships giving lectures which both stirred and infuriated. Several times he narrowly escaped mob violence. An ancient copy still survives of a discourse on Nebuchadnezzar's image given in the Jefferson Hall (town unspecified) in 1802. He gathered a congregation of like minds at the town of Portsmouth, New Hampshire. They repudiated "all names and denominations of Christendom", acknowledged no creed but the Bible and called themselves simply Christians.

Smith then commenced to publish a weekly newspaper, *The Herald of Gospel Liberty,* later *The Herald of Life and Immortality.* This is usually considered to be America's first religious weekly periodical. The trend of his thought is illustrated by other titles such as *The Day of Judgement* (1805); *The Doctrine of the Prince of Peace and his Servants* (1805); and *The Lovingkindness of God Displayed* (1809).

In 1807 a remarkable series of addresses was given at Exeter, New Hampshire, a town about 12 miles from Portsmouth. They deserve our interest for they clearly and closely foreshadow, not only in content but in very format and style, Christadelphian Bible campaigns of today.

Let us in imagination flash back in time, slip into a packed clapboard meeting house among the maple trees of the New England countryside, and listen to the persuasive preaching of the 38-year old Elias Smith in the prime of his powers. After a preliminary discussion on believing the Bible, he takes the first key to understanding the Bible:

> "The foundation of all the glorious things which are to take place concerning the kingdom of Christ, the seed of Abraham, appears to be laid in the promises made to Abraham, Isaac and Jacob."

A detailed Scriptural exposition follows—explaining the Promises of the Seed, the Land, the Resurrection and the Kingdom. Then he asks:

> "Can any person of common sense suppose that God fulfilled all promised to him (Abraham) while he lived a stranger in that land, having no possession at all, living a stranger and a pilgrim? There is something greater than this for him; which

will be given him when he shall rise again with the other saints and reign there (Canaan) with Christ a thousand years."

The Return of the Jews

Subsequent lectures take us on to the Davidic promise, the Hope of Israel and the return of Christ. The return of the Jews to their land (remember this is 1807!) is dealt with as confidently and plainly as if he was living a century and a half later. He examines systematically dozens of passages from the prophets, showing the various steps required before the coming of the Lord. After dealing with Isaiah 62 he comments: "It is not possible for language to express anything plainer than that the return of the Jews is here described." Then again after a consideration of Isaiah 60 he adds:

"How can any person read Isaiah 60 and doubt the return of the Jews to the land of Canaan? It is certain that there has never any such thing taken place among the Jews, or any other nation, as is mentioned in this chapter; therefore it is yet to come to pass. The Lord hasten it in His time. Amen."

This is faith to match Jeremiah, Habakkuk and Daniel as they faced apparent delays in the accomplishment of the purpose of God revealed. His voice rising in eloquence, Elias Smith spans two centuries of turbulent history in confident anticipation:

"What a remarkable day it will be (a day near at hand) when the inhabitants of Europe, Asia, Africa and America shall hear that the Turks who have long trodden down Jerusalem and laid waste the land have agreed to resign the whole land to the Jews and to leave the country... when a proclamation shall go forth into every place where a Jew is found calling him to join the great company who are returning to the land of their fathers! When the ships of Tarshish first and others after shall bring the sons of Abraham from distant lands... this will be one of the last signs of the coming of the Son of Man to reign on the earth a thousand years, when wars shall cease to the ends of the earth and all nations shall call him blessed.

"While I look over these prophecies, see their agreement, and know from the present state of the Jews that they will ere long return to their own land, and there be a great blessing to the world, my soul leaps for joy, I am filled with wonder, joy and love."

In the tradition of the earlier Brethren in Christ, Smith identifies the Man of Sin with Rome, and a Christendom astray from Truth is seen as the "falling away" foretold by the Apostle Paul. Reviewing a mass of Scriptural testimony, he modestly sums up this topic:

> "From all these scriptural testimonies I feel certain that Jesus, who once suffered on earth, will hereafter be honoured on earth, beyond what my tongue or pen can describe."

In a subsequent lecture we hear the clearest evidence that eternal hell fire torture for the damned is a horrifying distortion of truth. We are shown that the words used to indicate the fate of the wicked are *destroy, perish, devour, consume, burn up, perdition* and *end*. In typically persuasive fashion Smith points out:

> "In the Scriptures the end of the wicked is said to be *destruction* and to be burned as briers and thorns. There cannot be plainer words to describe the complete overthrow of the wicked. The END of the righteous is life, the END of the wicked is death, which cannot mean existence in any sense whatever."

A Moving Appeal

The final address in the series is a moving appeal to heed God's Word of grace and Christ's call to discipleship rather than the vain traditions of men. Its style is eloquent, moving yet simple, an example for us as preachers of God's Word today. Here is no love of controversy for its own sake, no desire either to tickle the ear or needlessly antagonise. This is an earnest call to sincere men and women to love and believe God's offer of life eternal. We do well to pause and listen awhile:

> "People have a kind of general system of what is to be hereafter, and thinking this system is right, they suppose the Scriptures must mean their systems, let it say what it will. This is a very great disadvantage to people. We are in general taught...that there is a wonderful place called Heaven and a place called Hell where the wicked will be tormented without end and be eternally raging and blaspheming God. The small knowledge which people in general have of the Scriptures is used to support what they are taught to call divinity.

> "So long as people believe that the plain declarations of Scripture do not mean as they say, so long will they remain

ignorant of the real beauty and excellency of the sure word of Prophecy . . . whatever things this light discovers we ought to believe and consider true.

"How must every believing heart grow warm while he views the promises made to Abraham, Isaac and Jacob, and when he considers that God will ere long perform all He promised these men, as it respects themselves, their land and their children!

"How glorious do the prophecies appear which speak of the new covenant with the Jews, which shall hereafter be made with that long neglected people, when they shall come from different parts of the earth where they are now scattered, and be settled in the land of their Fathers. While we read that Jesus shall return to the Mount of Olives to overcome his foes, deliver the Jews, reign over Jerusalem, and be the King over all the earth, causing wars to cease to the ends of the earth—how glorious is the prospect before every believer! Especially when he reads in this prophecy of the glorious event that all the dead saints shall rise to reign with him . . . in the new Jerusalem where changes, troubles, sorrow and death are no more. These things I believe in, rejoice in, look and long for.

"To attend to the prophecies as recorded is doing well because it gives us an exalted idea of what Christ, under God, will do before he gives up the kingdom and what he will have when he reigns in the new Jerusalem with all his saints forever.

"To take heed to the prophecies is doing well for ourselves in this way, we have a light all the journey through life in whatsoever situation we are in, if poverty, affliction, pain or loss attend us, the prophecy of future glory will lead us to glory in tribulation, knowing that through much tribulation we must enter into the kingdom, where the righteous shall shine as the sun forever, in that day which will dawn at the resurrection of the just, a day without night, sorrow, death or crying."

Bible Campaigns
We do not know the lasting effects of this and other Bible campaigns Elias Smith conducted in the ten years between 1807 and 1817. Some of the lecture titles are suggestive: "New Testament Baptism, with a History of Infant Baptism"; "The Whole World governed by a Jew, or The Government of Christ as King and Priest"; "The Light not

Clear nor Dark; or a Mixture of Human Inventions called Christianity." He and a friend Abner Jones produced hymnbooks, large and small, including many hymns written by themselves. However, neither, it should honestly be said, were particularly gifted poets!

Determination to avoid a sectarian label undoubtedly limited the effectiveness of Elias Smith's work. Also he rather disgusted his friends and converts by a five year flirtation with the Universalists (through having too close a friendship with one of their number).

Although he abjured his regrettable lapse, the last 23 years of his long life were mainly spent as what today would be called a quack doctor, building up a sizeable practice with a partner of like interests.

Many who had become "Christians" through Smith's teaching drifted into the Campbellite "Reformation" in the 1830s. Their Scriptural views were apparently something of an embarrassment as this was developed into a broad, popular "orthodox" movement. In this way at least Elias Smith paved the way for John Thomas. Campbell himself recognised the connection, mentioning in his *Millennial Harbinger* of 1837 that Dr. Thomas quoted Smith without necessarily having borrowed his ideas wholesale. Similar phrases and clichés are used by both of them in their writings, some indeed having passed down from still earlier writers.

Elias Smith travelled little. He refused to found a sect. But the leaven of his witness at the very beginning of the 19th century in one small corner of the United States did an unseen work. In commending one publication in 1808 to the 200 New Englanders whose subscriptions had defrayed the costs of printing, he penned words which can live today:

> "To the blessing of God I commend this feeble attempt to increase the knowledge of the sure word of prophecy ... conscious that I have written according to the understanding God has given me by His Word and spirit, which taught me to know and love the Truth as it is in Jesus.
>
> "It is possible that many who read this work may never see my face in time, and it is likely that some at least will read it when I am laid away in dust.

"I have one request to make, that is, not to believe or disbelieve what is stated in this book on my testimony barely, but to search the Scriptures whether these things are so. If you are an unbeliever, repent, and believe the gospel. If you are believers, pray for me, for yourselves, live as pilgrims, and long for glory. Such, through grace, I hope to meet in the New Jerusalem, where Jesus shall be our light, our glory and our joy forever. To him be glory in the church, throughout all ages, world without end. Amen and Amen."

17

OLD WINE IN NEW BOTTLES

The Second Coming of Christ

THE last decade of the 18th century and the first three of the 19th saw development of a distinctive movement to revive conviction in the second advent of Jesus Christ. The seeds of this were sown by Sir Isaac Newton and Joachim Stegman and other Polish Brethren, the influence of whose writings continued long after their death. With somewhat increasing tolerance, libraries and private collections preserved copies of their work and active revival of the position they represented was not infrequent. Some of the writers were "orthodox" theologians within the established church who adopted certain advent and prophetic views and little else. Others were more radical. It is intriguing to trace this stirring of interest in the return of Christ and the establishment of the Kingdom of God on earth, since the seeds sown germinated in many places after the end of the Napoleonic wars. Three early 19th- century centres of germination can be recognised. One was in Germany, another in central and western Scotland, and the third on the American frontier.

Over a number of years through use of public platforms and publications various individuals were linked into like-minded groups, but for the first thirty years of the 19th century at least the movement had little formal organisation. But of the strength of conviction of individuals there can be no doubt. One group, however, is of considerable interest, since it bears directly on the subsequent line of development traced in this book. It has been associated by some ecclesiastical historians with the name of Edward Irving; in fact, though prominent in an early phase, his part in the movement was a temporary one. Another member for a time was Wm. Drummond. He and Irving later had much to do with the organisation of the ill-fated Catholic Apostolic Faith.

Strangely, it was not writers who provided a direction for the movement, but a group of liberal-minded Irish and British publishers who for many years financed and supported publications of a millenarian-mortalist flavour, largely by developing the subscription method of sales. Prominent among these was James Nisbet of London, whose descendants after 150 years are still in the publishing business (though not with the same flavour!) and R. T. Tims of Dublin. A typical work is reproduced overleaf. The author, James Begg, was a fervent Scots Calvinist until one day in May 1828 he travelled from his home in Paisley all the way to Edinburgh to hear a lecture on the return of the Jews to Palestine. (At this date John Thomas, of whom more later, was writing lectures on obstetrics.) Begg returned to Paisley and immediately began an intensive study of the Scriptures; the first edition of the work illustrated appeared less than a year later. It is well reasoned, packed with references and close, cogent argument. Except perhaps at the end, where he launches into a diatribe against the "mother of harlots", it is free from polemic, and its style is fresh and amazingly similar to later Christadelphian works. Although there is no direct evidence that Christadelphian writers drew directly on works published by Nisbet such as *A Connected View*, the present writer finds it hard to believe that there was no connection at all, so close and even identical are the language and the concepts and even the clichés used.

No Premature Anticipations

Typical chapters in *A Connected View* indicate the purpose and message it offered: "Restoration of Israel to Palestine"; "The Whole Earth Blessed in Israel's Restoration"; "Review of the Promise of the Presence of the Lord"; "First Resurrection and Reign of the Saints"; "The Submission due to Revealed Truth". In refutation of detractors' jibes that believers have always expected the imminent return of their Lord to be "just around the corner", Begg had too sound a knowledge of the revealed purpose of God to be misled by premature anticipations:

> "The 'consummation' has not yet arrived. God's controversy, or 'war', with His ancient people has not yet ceased;

A
Connected View
OF SOME OF
THE SCRIPTURAL EVIDENCE
OF THE
Redeemer's Speedy Personal Return,
AND
REIGN ON EARTH WITH HIS GLORIFIED SAINTS,
DURING THE MILLENNIUM;
ISRAEL'S RESTORATION TO PALESTINE;
AND
THE DESTRUCTION OF ANTICHRISTIAN NATIONS:
WITH
Remarks on Various Authors who Oppose these Doctrines.

" *Thus saith the Lord, I am Returned unto Zion, and will dwell in the midst of Jerusalem. . . . If it be marvellous in the eyes of the remnant of this people in these days, should it also be marvellous in mine eyes, saith the Lord of Hosts ?*"—ZECH. viii. 3, 6.

BY JAMES A. BEGG,

THIRD EDITION, ENLARGED.

THE PROFITS OF THIS EDITION TO AID THE FUNDS OF THE LONDON
PHILO-JUDEAN SOCIETY.

PAISLEY:
PUBLISHED BY ALEX. GARDNER:
M. OGLE, W. COLLINS, J. REID, AND O. GALLIE, GLASGOW;
W. OLIPHANT, WAUGH & INNES, W. WHYTE & CO., J. BOYD, AND
J. LINDSAY & CO. EDINBURGH; J. ANDERSON, DUMFRIES; BROWN & CO.
ABERDEEN; W. M'COMB, BELFAST; R. M. TIMS, DUBLIN;
AND JAMES NISBET, LONDON.

1831.

Title-page of James Begg's *A Connected View*

nor has 'that determined' been wholly poured upon its objects. But, as we have already seen, 'the end' or 'consummation' will come when the gospel has been 'preached in all the world for a witness unto all nations' and when the city and sanctuary cease to be 'made desolate'. God's controversy with His ancient people must cease before the Millennium. The prophet also foretells the awful tribulation by which it is preceded: 'Behold, The Lord maketh the earth empty...therefore the inhabitants of the earth are *burned and few men left'* (Isaiah 24 : 1-6, 23). The tribulation of which our Lord speaks must *still be future*...''

Israel's Inheritance

Begg, like editors of *The Christadelphian* magazine in later years, sought for the smallest confirmatory evidence that the shaking of the dry bones of Israel was commencing—a healthy indication of his attitude towards the Bible. He refers to a note in the *Jewish Expositor* of January 1830 that one hundred Jews, from Constantinople, had arrived at Jaffa. With the wisdom born of diligent searching of the Word, he commented on its significance, predicting that it was the tiny, unnoticed precursor of a mighty mass migration. Then, he continues:

> "In the plenitude of their uncontrolled power, earthly potentates may indeed combine, and with a view to perpetuate their systems of iniquity, may create kingdoms at will, allot them the territories they shall possess, and appoint the kings by whom they shall be governed, without asking counsel of the Lord. In all their calculations Israel may not be reckoned; in their disposal of territory, no portion may be assigned for their inheritance. But the God of Jacob has purposed, and who shall disannul it? Ezekiel 36 : 8."

As a prophecy of the sordid political intrigues of 1918 and the subsequent events of 1948, no reader of this book needs reminding of its perspicacity. Like the 18th-century writers quoted in an earlier chapter, Begg was confident that, as on so many occasions in history, God's revealed purpose would triumph, whatever the human obstacles that might have to be removed to accomplish it. It is reminiscent also of another famous passage in John Thomas' *Elpis Israel,* published in 1848.

Begg, also like John Thomas, did not share the optimistic

expectation current among evangelicals of that time (and since) that the world will be brought to bow the knee to Christ by the preaching of missionaries in "heathen" lands:

> "We are bound to thank God for what success He has been pleased to bestow on missionary operations—the present extent and anticipated increase of which must afford the purest delight to all rightly exercised Christians. The Millennium, it is supposed by many, will be the gracious result of the mere preaching of the Gospel. But the Scriptures do not represent the nations as having generally received the gospel at the period of Christ's return, nor is it the expectation of those who are now looking for that blessed hope and the glorious appearing of the great God and our Saviour Jesus Christ (Titus 2 : 13). He ordained that the gospel should first be preached in all the world for a *witness* unto all nations. When the Jews had filled up the measure of their iniquity, He let out His spiritual vineyard unto other husbandmen. The gospel was then entrusted to certain nations of the Gentiles, with the assurance that if they continued not in the goodness of God, they also should be cut off (Rom. 11 : 22). Instead, however, of profiting by the warning of God and the fate of Israel, these nations have perverted the gospel. While other nations are being put in possession of the gospel as a witness, those which have long been entrusted with God's Word and ordinances are ripening for judgement."

Another associate of the Irving-Drummond group, Harriet Livermore, of Philadelphia, spasmodically edited the *Millennial Tidings* in the early 1830s. She was in close contact by correspondence with Begg and others, and insisted also on the necessity of a Jewish return before the consummation. However, one element in her periodical which has interest here is her exposition of the Letters to the Seven Churches in the Apocalypse, in which her identification of seven stages of apostasy is a clear anticipation of the fuller treatment of this in John Thomas's *Eureka*.

It is clear that the religious faith and ethical ideals of the Brethren in Christ, despite persecution, dispersal and schism, still had power, continuing to generate groups, communities and isolated spirits in many places. In the early 19th century denominational labels were held in abhorrence by many of the more Biblically minded, and the existence of dozens of different names of independent local communities masks broad unity of outlook while accentuating minor differences. The pioneer spirit of the age, especially on the North American frontier, a certain independence of mind, the vast distances and the difficulty of travel, all meant that contact between groups was limited. Emigrants from Europe carried the views, ideals and hopes of the Brethren across the ocean and spread them thinly over a vast continent. Tracts, books and periodicals were cherished and passed around.

"In journeyings often"

There were men of resolute stamp for whom the New World held challenge rather than difficulty. Using mainly the saddle they travelled widely over the fringe lands of the United States and Canada in the first decades of the 19th century, providing the only links, other than tenuous correspondence, between small widely scattered congregations.

> "The proclaiming of the gospel of the kingdom of God to be established on the earth was by means mainly of itinerant preaching. It was a gruelling and hard life. Method of travel was varied. Not infrequently it was by horseback, stage coach, canal boat, river steamer or plain walking. These men frequently would meet with brethren in conferences at various places. Outside of normal hardship and suffering from travel and exposure, the preacher would often be down with swamp fever, typhoid fever, lung fever and other sicknesses caused by the exposures and bad water. Despite these, he carried on and attempted to maintain his appointments. He was poor, oftentimes extremely so, as far as material goods were concerned, but rich in his faith in the return of Jesus Christ to set up his kingdom upon the earth, raise the saintly dead and change the living to a life of immortality" (Hatch).

The rigours of log-cabin life on the American frontier, especially in winter, appal us in these gentler days. Often a preacher would be invited to sleep on straw in a hut with glassless windows and arctic blasts filtering through every chink between the logs. Religion was a powerful inspiration, since many of these immigrants or their forefathers had a religious motive for their coming to the land of freedom. And the freedom was exercised to the full, with controversy playing a major role in religious life. Minor theological points were hotly debated and congregations divided and re-formed with bewildering abandon.

New Periodicals

The pen was also mighty in the fray. If the 17th century was the age of tracts, the 19th century was the age of the religious periodical. Periodicals were born, flourished for a while and then changed their name and place of publication, or disappeared. The *Expositor and Advocate,* published by Joseph Marsh in Rochester, New York, was a rallying-point in the third decade of the century, and *The Voice of Truth and Glad Tidings of the Kingdom,* emanating from the same city, a few years later. There were several magazines called *Messenger,* and several called *Investigator;* these and others delved into Biblical prophecies in great detail, causing a ferment of adventist speculation and anticipation. These magazines and broadsheets circulated among a loose network of fiercely independent congregations in the north-east and mid-west of the United States; the origin of most of them is now obscure, but undoubtedly they had tenuous links through migration with communities of Brethren in Europe. Many of these steadfastly resisted the imposition of a formal creed, preferring like the "Seekers" of the 17th century to have an open-minded and undogmatic approach to the Bible, though in practice doctrinal differences were not great. They would readily welcome any speaker into their midst and hear him if they believed he had any views or expositions worth contributing. They gathered in simple meeting-houses such as that in Illinois illustrated in Plate VII, and it was in this atmosphere of religious freedom, fierce controversy, a stern piety, eager and in many cases open-minded audiences, that men such as Joseph Marsh and D. I. Robinson in the twenties and thirties, B. B. Brown and particularly John Thomas in the forties of the century travelled, preached and published.

John Epps

Before considering the work of John Thomas, reference should be made to a fellow-Londoner who was a contemporary of his, John Epps. Like John Thomas, Epps was a medical practitioner, but despite almost identical views on the interpretation of Scripture, and the fact that both were keen in propagating their views, evidence is lacking of any certain contact between the two men. Epps, however, while a vigorous exponent of the views shared by both, never endeavoured to develop a community which would survive him.

Epps was born into high Calvinist circles, in comfortable circumstances in a south-east suburb of London, in 1805. Disgusted with the religious atmosphere in which he found himself, he went to Edinburgh to study medicine. There was a broad crusading spirit in Epps' character, for he disseminated his not inconsiderable energies over a wide range of causes. He campaigned for the new ideas of homoeopathy, for phrenology, for social justice, for educational reforms and above all for his views on Christianity. In fact his encyclopaedic mind and extensive interests were such that he made little permanent impact in any single field, which was a pity since many of his ideas were far ahead of his time. He "incessantly lectured, wrote letters, spoke at public meetings in connection with religious and social reforms". The titles of these lectures cover a fantastic range of topics: "Influence of Parents on their Offspring"; "The Observations of Linnaeus"; "Degeneracy of Plants grown perpetually in the same Soil"; "The Devil"; "The Fall of Man". From 1835 to 1839 he published the periodical *The Christian Physician and Anthropological Magazine,* and two years later he gave a celebrated—or notorious, according to one's viewpoint— series of twelve lectures in the Working Man's Church in Bermondsey, London. These considered the fundamental doctrines of first-century Christianity: resurrection, the soul, hell, sin, communion, the devil. In 1842 he was prevailed upon to publish anonymously his most controversial work, which a reverend critic called "a laboured attempt to dispose of the existence of the devil, adding one more proof of the awful fact". His own title was *The Devil: A Biblical Exposition of the Truth concerning that Old Serpent, the Devil and Satan and a Refutation of the Beliefs obtaining in the World regarding Sin and its Source.* Clearly the 17th century did not have a monopoly of long sub-titles! Much opposition was aroused by the publication, and a lecture given shortly afterward to the Tooting Institution at the Mitre Inn in that London suburb caused serious offence and led to widespread ostracism and hostility.

In *The Devil*[1] and other publications Epps rejects the doctrine

[1] This booklet was republished by a group of Australian Christadelphians in 1944 without their knowing the identity of the author.

of the soul's immortality and expounds from the Scripture the hope of resurrection. Hell is the grave; the devil and satan are in the main to be understood as personifications of the lustful principle in man. He rejects the trinitarian view of Christ, showing that he prayed to "God", not just to the "Father"; Jesus is the Son of God, by nature man; the second coming of Christ is emphasised. All the cherished principles held by the Brethren in earlier days are there. So is their language concerning larger Protestant churches as being the "harlot daughters of Rome". He speaks out vigorously against the glorification of war-heroes—"the honour of the British flag is a specious phrase which blinds men's eyes to right and wrong". He had a broad vision of the international role of the Christian Gospel.

His own childlike humility and submission to the dictates of the Bible revelation were such that he remained puzzled to the last by the immense variety of creeds that claimed derivation from the same Bible, some so patently in contradiction with it. Epps was in many ways in his personality and interests, in his piety of spirit and widely questing mind, in his dynamic energy, an embodiment of the early 19th century. Yet he was in more important ways treading in the footsteps of Biddle, Wiszowaty and Hübmaier.

Short and stocky, reportedly with a beaming, self-confident expression, the energetic doctor was never lost for words. They flowed like a Niagara from the moment he grasped the rostrum, sonorous and animated. The sheer nervous effort of giving countless lectures—many of them hours long—and writing the voluminous articles on dozens of different topics must have hastened to a somewhat agitated close a fantastically busy life. His closing days were occupied with investigation into animal magnetism.

18

JOHN THOMAS

JOHN THOMAS was born in 1805, the same year as Epps. The son of a rather restless minister of religion, the young Thomas did not take a very serious interest in religion early in life. He spent part of his childhood at boarding-school, and was apprenticed to a surgeon at fourteen. A frightful Atlantic crossing on the "Marquis of Wellesley" while emigrating to the United States caused him to vow to seek and follow Christian truth. The early contacts in the United States were with the so-called "Reformation", or Campbellites, now the Disciples of Christ. But Alexander Campbell, organiser of this "Reformation", was chiefly interested in a broad non-denominational Christian union without creeds, membership of which was not dependent upon assent to doctrine. John Thomas was of a very different turn of mind; his spirit was that of the early Brethren—a submission to a straightforward understanding of a divinely-inspired Bible unmodified by later creeds and ecclesiastical traditions.

He occasionally claimed, and others even more vigorously claimed for him, that his matured views on the Scriptures were solely the result of the study of them alone, and that he owed nothing to others. In this he can be compared with John Biddle, who also had made something of the same claim. There is much truth in the claim made by John Thomas; his study was no doubt as impartial as it was possible to be in the circumstances. He had an independent and sincere turn of mind and was not likely to follow consciously interpretations that bore the stamp of any particular theological school. However, as in Biddle's case, it is difficult to avoid the conclusion that there were subtle and unconscious influences at work outside the study of the Bible itself.

Despite incessant lecturing and controversial correspondence he was a reader of amazing breadth. How this was possible since he was continuously on the move is something of a mystery. But the writings of his formative period—when he also travelled widely—show close and accurate familiarity with Plato and other Greek writers; 3rd and 4th-century Christian writers; medieval history; the poetry of Burns; first-hand sources of the 16th-century Reformation; Milton, Newton, Hobbes, Locke and other 17th-century authors whom he quoted at great length *verbatim;* Gibbon's *History of the Roman Empire;* an extensive knowledge of most of the principal writers on Biblical prophecy during the previous 70 years, including some, such as Bicheno, who were extremely obscure; and digestion of the enormous contemporary output of books, tracts, broadsheets and periodicals dealing with prophetic, millenarian and general religious topics.

Apocalyptic Study

The mid 19th century was a period of feverish apocalyptic study among Biblical Christians. John Thomas entered this field with fervour, his work culminating in his three-volume *Eureka,* which was produced in instalments in the fities and sixties. Close affinities are apparent between *Eureka* and Elliott's *Horae Apocalypticae* published in 1844. Thomas was certainly thoroughly familiar with Elliott. But *Eureka* is not based on *Horae Apocalypticae,* since all its main interpretations appear in periodical form in the magazines published by John Thomas *before Elliott's work appeared.*

Rather, both Elliott and *Eureka* draw their thematic structure and broad lines of interpretation from a common stream, like distributaries in a delta. The source actually lies back through Newton and Biddle and Brenius to the early days of the Brethren. At that time, with Ferdinand's edict of destruction bringing suffering and martyrdom to so many pious Bible-lovers, the identification of the beast of Revelation 16 with Vienna was more natural than it was in the later 19th century. At that time also the Turk was the "bogeyman" of Europe and it was not difficult to see his role in the Revelation.

The identification by John Thomas of the slain witnesses of Revelation 11 as being a faithful remnant at the period of the 16th-century Reformation is also shared—with some variation due to availability of supporting historical material—by earlier writers among the Brethren. Probably because of the historical sources available, Thomas emphasised the role of the Huguenots. He was clearly in some difficulty here, since he was not in doctrinal agreement with the Huguenots and did not approve their use of force; consequently the interpretation at this point is strained. Had he known more of the views and witness of the Brethren, he would have given them more prominence in his interpretation of this period.

Quotations from Earlier Authors

He was, however, not ignorant of them, even though his sources were poor. He never considered himself the only one to have gone unbiased to the original Christian sources and come to the same considered view of "primitive Christianity". He refers to the 16th-century "anabaptists—as they were ignorantly styled"—and states his conviction that in their age they had "preserved the truth from dying out". In his quotations of Milton, Sir Isaac Newton, and other 17th-century writers, Dr. Thomas intimated that he was aligning himself with a tradition going back centuries. He considered that he was reviving not only original Christianity, but a faith of the 17th-century that had been lost or corrupted in the 18th, and quotes with approval the 17th-century Baptist confessions[1].

In addition to these recognised historical affinities, John Thomas had other links with the past and with kindred spirits. Mention has been made of certain periodicals published in Rochester, New York. Dr. Thomas subscribed to at least one of these and endeavoured—unsuccessfully, it should be said—to gain an opening for his views through it. He viewed it as representing a standpoint with which he was in general agreement. On at least three occasions he visited the Illinois River region of the Middle West and came into contact with some of the groups of independent Christians referred to earlier in this chapter who had similar views to himself.

These contacts were not productive of any close association, and there appear to have been clashes of personality and leadership jealousies. Some associated with John Thomas, while others later federated into what is at the present time the Church of God Conference (Abrahamic Faith) in the United States, with general

---

[1] See p. 145

offices at Oregon, Illinois. An official history of this community by Hatch claims that Thomas's work was an "interesting alignment" to their own. Because of the abhorrence of denominationalism prevalent among all these groups, their loosely organised federal structure and the prevalence of locally dominant leaders of strong personality, it is not likely that there was complete uniformity of doctrine and practice among them. John Thomas proceeded to encourage the formation of communities of people sympathetic to the views expressed in his periodical the *Herald of the Kingdom,* but these were at first very loose in organisation, and while some adopted the title "Baptised Believers in the Kingdom of God" and others "Bible Christians", there was no unanimity and a variety of designations appeared.

The American Civil War precipitated the need for some name. True to the principles for which they stood, John Thomas and his colleagues refused to take part in the hostilities. In Richmond, Virginia, he publicly called attention to the position:

"If the Southern and Northern Methodists, Baptists, Campbellites, Presbyterians, Episcopalians, and Papists think fit to blow one another's brains out, let them do it to their heart's content, but let not Christians mingle in the unhallowed strife."

Brethren in Christ

It was typical of John Thomas' general attitude of not assuming any personally dominant leadership that in presenting in his *Herald* this important element of faith, he used an article by Dr. Grattan Guinness, who was not associated in any way with him. In 1864 the name Brethren in Christ or Christadelphians was registered at the County Court House at Oregon, Illinois, and application made, asking that this name be accepted as the official title of a religious body. It was an interesting moment when John Thomas chose for his friends the same name as had come into being in Switzerland three hundred and forty years earlier, to designate those who refused to "engage in the armies or navies of any government".[2] In 1865 a petition was made to the United States Senate asking for exemption from military service for members of the community.

[2] The late F. W. Turner of *The Christadelphian* provided the author with evidence from correspondence that the choice was a deliberate reference to that of the 16th-century Swiss Brethren.

JOHN THOMAS

Six years after the Brethren in Christ or Christadelphians had thus officially come into being as a distinct body, John Thomas died in the vicinity of New York. He was a controversial figure, with a stabbing, pungent style of writing. He seemed to attract some to adulation and drive others to distraction; but he bored no one. He made no apology for engaging in verbal polemics. Disciples, he stated, obtain peace in this age in proportion as they are indifferent to principle. Because of the controversies he inevitably stirred up wherever he taught, it is difficult at the present distance to make an accurate assessment of his personality. During his lifetime opinions varied. "He was fatherly, kind, domestic, disinterested and truly humble." "He was quiet, gentle, courteous, well-mannered, modest, absolutely devoid of affectation or trace of self-importance." "He was the most uncompromising, stubborn, self-willed and dogmatical person ever known; having large self-esteem and firmness and deficient benevolence, though a good intellect, and all this hardened by a bilious temperament." Clearly he was a many-sided man!

He was invariably warm to close friends, but bitter experiences with false friends made him somewhat cold and distant with both opponents and strangers. Those who knew him best invariably came into the closest fellowship with him. Memories of him (and a hat of his) still survive and are cherished in the tobacco country of Virginia where so much of his work was done. The author had in 1968 the great privilege of talking with one of the last surviving persons to attend his lectures. He was known far and wide among the Virginia and Maryland planters for his hard riding, firm convictions, and his enjoyment of conversation. A great friend of his in Virginia, and one who in fact stoutly defended the worthy doctor on more than one occasion from outraged hearers, was Albert Anderson, known throughout southern Virginia as "the walking Bible"; great-grandchildren of Anderson are Christadelphians in the same area today.

In intellectual stamina and breadth Dr. John Thomas rivalled Epps, though he concentrated his energies in a far more organised way. On a typical lecturing tour it was not uncommon for him to deliver 130 two-hour addresses on a variety of topics in a matter of two or three months. And it was rare for any of these to contain inaccuracy in any of the Scriptural and historical references with which they were always liberally sprinkled. He ascended the speaker's dais in an unostentatious manner, and rarely worried about conventional introductions. "It is written in the prophets..." he would begin and follow with an expansive and analytical treatment of his theme.

The "Revealed Mystery"

Because prophecy figures large in his major written works *Elpis Israel* and *Eureka,* the breadth of his religious interests is often overlooked. The clearest and most balanced in content of his works are to be found chiefly in the periodicals he edited. One of the shorter works, *The Revealed Mystery,* may perhaps be chosen as representing most fundamentally his overall view of the Christian faith. Though differing in style and order of presentation, its view of that faith is basically the same as the *Twofold Catechism* of Biddle, the *De Vera Religione* of Volkel and the confessions of the early Brethren. Significantly the order is not modelled on that of the Apostles' Creed like so many of these last, but leads from a consideration of the faith of Abraham through the "new covenant" to the last judgement. The following excerpt is thoroughly typical of John Thomas in mid 19th century:

> "Immortality is deathlessness. God only has a nature in which the death principle never existed. Incorruptibility and life constitute immortality; so that immortality may be defined as life manifested through an incorruptible body. A diamond is incorruptible, but not living; therefore, it is not immortal. Paganism defines immortality to be a particle of divine effluence in all men, hereditarily transmitted, and having personality and consciousness after death! The Scriptures, however, reveal no such conceit. The immortality they bring to light is 'life and incorruptibility through the gospel'; or 'eternal life through the Christ Name'. Immortality is promised only to those who are justified by the name of Jesus; and, being justified, walk worthy of the same.
>
> "Immortality is an investment imposed by divine power upon certain who come forth from their graves; and who, on judicial inspection afterwards, are accounted worthy of glory and honour in the kingdom of the Deity then about to be set up. In this, the resurrection-epoch and era of Israel's regeneration, the earthy bodies from the grave, to wit, the bodies of Christ's accepted brethren, together with the living

of the same class who are contemporary with the crisis, are clothed with incorruption or spirit from heaven, which, in the twinkling of an eye, transforms them into spirit, and makes them consubstantial with the nature of the Father and the Son."

The *Discourse on Eternal Life* which was later printed along with *The Revealed Mystery* was quite different in approach, illustrating a considerable versatility of character in the author. It shows in fact remarkable similarities in style and method of presentation to the best work of the Raków authors such as Wiszowaty. Its theme is in fact stated in the "fourth proposition" listed in the essay: "Eternal life, though the free gift of God, through Jesus Christ to the world, is nevertheless conditional." In considering this fourth proposition he lists twenty-three passages of the New Testament as "proofs":

> "Now, I do not hesitate to say that these passages prove that eternal life is conditional. The expressions 'if', 'he who', 'unless', 'whoever', 'as many as', 'to take from among', 'to everyone who', 'them who', 'to them who', 'that you may' and so forth, are all terms of condition."

Missionary Work

John Thomas travelled widely in the United States, Canada and Britain. His biography, by Robert Roberts, revised and enlarged by later writers, is happily still in print[3]. For details of the "missionary" work of John Thomas after his baptism at Richmond, Virginia in 1847 readers are referred to that book. It is through deference to an excellent existing work and not a minimising of his contribution that only one or two significant highlights are mentioned in a very colourful career. In his travels during the civil war in America, a brutal conflict which, over 120 years later, is still undergoing almost sickening glorification, he passed alternately from one side to the other to encourage his brethren, sometimes making his way through devastated villages in Virginia before even the smoke of conflict had disappeared. In these difficult and discouraging days he showed a courage and devotion to match any of his 16th-century forerunners. He was utterly sickened in his sensitive soul by the bestiality of the war and it is not surprising that he looked longingly across the Atlantic to his native Britain

---

[3] Obtainable from *The Christadelphian* Office.

THE PROTESTERS

John Thomas

Robert Roberts

as offering more opportunity for the Word.

Another factor was the strange parochialism of outlook of the American people, for some of whom the rest of the world might not exist. He complained that "news" for the average American consisted of the domestic doings at the White House and the scandalous corruptions of local politicos. He found a segment of British working folk more amenable to his lengthy expositions of world affairs in the light of the Scriptures, and some of his most thrilling moments were undoubtedly experienced during his visits to Britain.

As a preacher his greatest opportunity came when he spoke on the regeneration of the world in the City Hall of Glasgow, Scotland; the huge auditorium holds six thousand people and night after night not only was the place crammed to bursting point but it is reported that "multitudes could not gain admission". Elated he must have been; conceited certainly he was not. It must be remembered that John Thomas did not appear before that vast concourse as a Christadelphian lecturer—at that time he disclaimed all names and denominations. But from this campaign *Elpis Israel* was begotten; the fact that Christadelphian ecclesias exist in Glasgow today as a memorial to this campaign is almost accidental, for he made no deliberate effort to found a sect and was pressured into the publication of this work only through a soirée held afterwards in Paisley, which at that time was the leading stronghold of millennialism in Britain. Another unusual experience was the opportunity John Thomas had to preach in the Virginia State Capitol, to a very heterogeneous audience of legislators and others. There are Christadelphians in Virginia today whose great-grandparents attended these meetings. Also in the 1850s, during a visit to Washington, D.C., he held a series of open-air meetings on the steps of the United States Capitol. William Champion, a Quaker, was a blacksmith employed in the building. According to a relative: "He went to every one of Dr. Thomas' lectures and came home to his wife saying, 'Eureka—I have found it'." So, with his wife and another person, the Washington ecclesia was born, with five generations of theirs giving their loyalty and service to its witness and fellowship to this present day.

It might be wondered why distinct communities have survived the work of John Thomas, while Begg and Epps have been forgotten. There were two main reasons. One was undoubtedly the long connection and association John Thomas maintained with the Campbellites, years indeed after he had departed from them in terms of doctrine and spirit. He used them as a valuable platform, as Paul used the synagogue, as long as they were willing. From them he drew many friends, as well as from older groups of independent Bible Christians in the mid-west of the United States, Scotland and elsewhere.

Robert Roberts

The other reason was the conversion of Robert Roberts. John Thomas was a rich expositor, but he did not appear to take a very deep interest in the actual organisation of the Christadelphian community. It was in fact his view that, if the "principles of the truth" had taken possession of the hearts of a number of men and women, love rather than organisation would build the spiritual edifice of each "ecclesia". He hated crotchets, as he used to call them, and despised little-minded men who were more concerned about technicalities of one sort or another, and usually had self-conceited opinions, rather than a broadly based outlook on the real and permanent interests of the Gospel. He would often remind more businesslike individuals that if this possession of, or rather by, the truth was absent, no amount of organisation could bring it to fruition. It was left to Robert Roberts, a dynamic Aberdonian, to lay more organised foundations for the community. It is a testimony to the permanence of the message and the principles which are the theme of these pages that although Robert Roberts, unlike his mentor John Thomas, knew little or nothing about most of the people, events and ideas which they recount, yet the ecclesial structure, mode of life, faith and practice remain essentially the same.

To conclude consideration of the work and personality of John Thomas, it might be said that from the very nature of his beliefs he was bound to generate hostility. Yet especially later in life, he disliked replying in kind, though that was the spirit of the times. That he was of the same spirit as those mentioned earlier in this book is shown by the following prayer—to the present writer the most revealing of all the multitude of words that passed his lips or flowed from his pen:

"O Lord God in heaven above, merciful and gracious

Father, what can we render to Thee for Thy goodness? Thou hast appointed a day in which Thou wilt judge the world in righteousness by Jesus Christ! Blessed be Thy holy name. We shall all be judged before his tribunal and not man's. Then the hidden things of men shall be brought to light, and their secret thoughts shall be unveiled, to their justification or reproof! Thou God seest us all, for all hearts are open before Thee! If Thou beholdest any thing in me displeasing in Thy sight, let me fall into Thy hands, and not into the hands of those who thirst for my destruction! Grant me patience to endure their unrighteousness, and by fidelity and perseverance to overcome the iniquity of their doings; and may the word of the truth concerning the hope of the glorious gospel of Jesus be established in these countries; and may those who now oppose it, in ignorance and unbelief, find mercy of Thee, repenting of their waywardness, and purifying their hearts by faith, that they may be accepted when the Lord comes! 'Forgive them, for they know not what they do'; and may we all at length find an abundant entrance into the kingdom of the future age, to the glory of the great Immanuel's name! Amen! Amen!''

Note Added in Proof: Detailed genealogical studies by Christadelphian Charles Blore have established that John Thomas was of Huguenot ancestry from the Kleve (Cleves) area of the Rhineland, Germany.

19

THE FAITH AT THE END OF THE AGE

IT is not the purpose of this chapter to present a detailed history of the Christadelphian body, nor to recount biographies of its past pioneers or present proponents. Its essential aim has already been accomplished in the preceding chapters; to trace loyalty to the teaching of the Lord through his long absence in the far country. For one thing, the present author, while possessing an antiquarian bent and consequently quite widely read in Christadelphian material ancient, if not always up to date on material modern, knows that there are many others far more competent to write such histories, if ever they should need to be written. In any case "books" will soon "be opened" which will unfold a far more accurate account than any mortal man could write. But for a second reason, a number of excellent publications already exist which document at least the last half of the 19th century and many Christadelphians older than the writer can tell much about the 20th. These publications only need acquiring or in many cases taking down, dusting and reading again. Among these are *My Days and My Ways,* Robert Roberts' autobiography (like all modest men he only wrote such a book reluctantly after repeated urging), Islip Collyer's sensitive study *Robert Roberts* and the centenary booklet *One Hundred Years of 'The Christadelphian'*.[1]

Yet diligent search among large amounts of periodical and documentary material on two continents has convinced the writer that the proverbial half of the story has not been told. It is not proposed to recount that missing half, but search has suggested that in one last chapter the torch carried through the centuries may

---

[1] The first two titles are available from *The Christadelphian* Office; the third is now out of print.

be seen taken and raised aloft by those nearer in time and bearing the same name as the author and many of the readers of this book. Therefore in an expanding witness only what seem to him to be highlights will be briefly reviewed. Choice is inevitable, and the choice is mainly of those elements which have been little emphasised in existing works or seem to represent key concepts, individuals or movements. In an age when much that is 30 years old is considered barely worth a sidelong glance and criticism is rifer than emulation, the young and new to the faith for whom this work is mainly written may do well to take inspiration from an earlier generation of Christadelphian faithful. The author accepts full responsibility for his purely personal and somewhat arbitrary selection of material.

God-Manifestation

In the light of the preceding chapters, the most outstanding contribution of Christadelphian writers in the author's view is their exposition of the principles of "God-manifestation". The beliefs of the Polish Brethren concerning the Godhead were Scriptural, soundly based and reverent. But it was the fires of controversy over Christology which brought forth the rich understanding on this subject evidenced in such works as *Phanerosis* (John Thomas), *The Blood of Christ* (Robert Roberts), *God-Manifestation* (John Carter), *Theophany* and *Witness for Christ* (C. C. Walker), and others. A simple outline of this approach is seen in the following from Robert Roberts' *Christendom Astray* (originally published in 1862 as *Twelve Lectures on the True Teaching of the Bible*):

> "Christ was a divine manifestation—an embodiment of Deity in flesh—Emmanuel, God with us. 'God gave not to him the spirit by measure', says the same apostle (John 3 : 34). The spirit descended upon him in bodily shape at his baptism in the Jordan, and took possession of him. This was the anointing which constituted him *Christ* (or the anointed), and which gave him the superhuman power of which he showed himself possessed. This is clear from the words of Peter, in his address to the Gentiles in the house of Cornelius: *"God anointed Jesus of Nazareth with the Holy Spirit and with power:* who went about doing good, healing all that were oppressed" (Acts 10 : 38).
>
> "When Jesus said, 'He that hath seen me hath seen the

Father' he did not contradict the statement that 'no man hath seen God at any time', but simply expressed the truth contained in the following words of Paul: Christ is *'the image of the invisible God'* (Col. 1 : 15); 'the brightness of his glory, and the express image of his person' (Heb. 1 : 3). Those who looked upon the anointed Jesus, beheld a representation of the Deity accessible to human vision.

"Jesus said, 'I and the Father are one' (John 10 : 30). He could not mean, in view of all the testimony, what Trinitarians understand him to mean, that he and the Father were identically the same person ('the same in substance, equal in power and glory'), but that they were one in spirit-connection and design of operation. This is apparent from his prayer for his disciples, 'That they may be one, *even as we are one'*. The unity is not as to person, but as to nature and state of mind. This is the unity that exists between the Father and the Son, and the unity that will be ultimately established between the Father and His whole family, of whom Christ is the elder brother."

This book with the provocative title, privately circulated in the 1860s following the lectures in Huddersfield, England, which formed the basis of the work, was probably more effective than any other human publication referred to in these pages. Only thirty years later it could be stated that "it has revolutionised the religious convictions of great numbers of people". For more than a century it has done so, the present writer himself owing an enormous debt to its influence. Probably its greatest effect was in the 1920s and 1930s when editions by more than one publisher were distributed by the thousands. For an admittedly sectarian book that has never appeared in a general publisher's list and which has often been offered to the public *gratis,* its record is remarkable.

A Man of Many Parts

So also was its author. A man of many parts, possessed in the long run of unquenchable optimism and buoyancy of spirit, he led the brotherhood through fair weather and foul in what was virtually a continuous crusade. His appeal was self-confessedly to "the devout but distressed, whom popular theology bewilders, atheism revolts and scientific agnosticism chills and blights". It was from the ranks of exactly the same type of serious minded, honest Godfearers that

THE FAITH AT THE END OF THE AGE

the Swiss Brethren and Polish Brethren had drawn their zealous converts. Robert Roberts found it so again. In cities where an intelligent, yet pious independence rather than conformity in religion prevailed, he drew enormous crowds—Birmingham, England, and Melbourne, Australia, being perhaps the most outstanding examples. In both of these cities hundreds failed to gain admission to the cities' largest halls on some occasions. In both these cities also he resided, and converts were numerous. The apex of Robert Roberts' career was in 1893 when the Birmingham City Hall lectures were given "before thousands of people" on four midwinter Sunday evenings. It is probable that more baptisms resulted from this campaign than any other in Christadelphian history. Even though the copies of the proceedings are now yellowed, brittle, and antique looking, it is not difficult to envisage the scene on the concluding night and hear again the sonorous polysyllables of his peroration pouring forth from a vessel filled to overflowing with the same sense of urgency and intense concern of which Blaurock, Hübmaier, Biddle and others of our earlier drama's cast were so possessed:

---

411 **Christ in the Earth Again.**

LECTURES in the TOWN HALL,

BY

ROBERT ROBERTS,

Sunday, Feb. 12, 19 & 26, also Mar. 12, 1893.

TO COMMENCE AT 6.30.

ADMIT TO PLATFORM (Entrance Door A, Congreve St.)

A Ticket for the Birmingham Town Hall Lecture Series

" 'Not every one that saith unto me, Lord, Lord, shall enter the kingdom, but he that doeth the will of my Father.

Now is the time for the doing of that will as revealed. Separate yourselves from the multitude that refuse to do it. Don't wait until the only permissible response to your frantic appeal, must be 'Too late; too late; too late'. Now is the accepted time; now, while God is dishonoured; now, while all is darkness; now, while the Bible is unheeded; now, while there is nothing but promise; now, while men blaspheme; now, while the voice of wisdom is a still small voice on the ear of reason, from which fools turn away. This is the time for that victory of faith, without which it is impossible to please God.

"Whether you choose or refuse, a pall overspreads the political sky. It has been a long time gathering, and it grows denser every year. A storm is visibly brewing before the eyes of all men. The nature of the storm is known only to those who know the Bible. Christ is in that storm, and therefore they will not fear when it bursts . . . Low at last will be laid the greatness of man, and all the inventions and institutions of his folly.

"When the storm is spent, the clouds disperse; light will break forth; the sun will pour his healing beams from a cloudless sky; all nature will smile through her tears. His kingdom alone will prevail, and all the children of wisdom in unutterable thanksgiving will rejoice in the arrival of the glorious, long-promised day when mankind, weary of their own folly, and their incompetent ways, will find peace and well-being under the shadow of the Messiah, in fulfilment of the promised blessing of all families of the earth in Abraham and his seed."

The late 19th century was the heyday of the week-long debate, and Robert Roberts, along with many other Christadelphian preachers, rarely missed the opportunity to throw down a glove—whether the adversary advocated socialism, British-Israelism, atheism, or (to his certain confusion) heaven-going. If the adversary sometimes seemed to show an advantage, it was frequently because the Christadelphian was too straightforward and honest a debater, and rarely stooped to the worst tricks of the debating technique. But the present writer knows more than one person who left such a verbal battleground a wiser and a convicted soul.

Robert Roberts travelled more widely than the bearded doctor whom he adored. He was in fact on a world tour when his death occurred in San Francisco in 1898. Despite several deep schisms, the period from the death of John Thomas to the end of the century was a period of keen missionary fervour carried out on a shoestring by a small community which at that time was very poor indeed. After the pattern of the 16th-century Brethren and of course the earliest Christians, the dictum of Jane, wife of Robert Roberts was: *"Every Christadelphian is a missionary."*

A "Missionary Phase"

In areas where unusually sizeable Christadelphian populations now exist—Birmingham, London, the U.S. eastern seaboard, Arkansas, Ontario, California, Texas, and the cities of Australia and New Zealand—deep roots were put down before the end of the 19th century, during this "missionary" phase. In the body's subsequent tendency to honour two or three "pioneers" whose influence lay in editorship of the community organs, the works of many other outstanding but much lesser known sowers of seed should not be forgotten. There was no financial backing for members who promoted their faith in lonely places. Tragedy often dogged the work, which could not be followed up effectively. Converts were isolated from one author, and frequently lost contact; in India, Africa and South America (in Guyana—then the "end of the world"—there were at one time in the 19th century hundreds of members) whole ecclesias were "lost". Some were located again after as long as 50 years; others were not. Some efforts of desperately impecunious preachers of the faith in the 19th and early 20th centuries make us boggle today, and we badly need to light a spark from their fires. And where zeal flowed forth, Providence opened channels of opportunity.

"By chance", two men whose homes were a thousand miles apart met on a mountain peak in the Great Smokies, talked until one was convinced and was baptized in a cold mountain spring below; and so Isaac Jones learnt the Way and first brought it to Florida. Later, in 1877, he became a "missionary" to Bermuda and founded an ecclesia, descendants of whose first members still adorn the Faith today. "By chance", two men met on a river boat in the Ganges River. One, the captain, had been given a copy of *Elpis Israel* by a friend. The other borrowed it, and subsequently baptized himself in the "holy" waters for an altogether holier purpose—and so began the ecclesia in Calcutta[2]. The captain, himself now baptized, heard of it and wrote of the joyous event:

> "It was a memorable day—the firstfruits of the sounding of the pure Gospel in the East, the land of gross idolatry and heathenism. May it please God, the Father of us all, that it may be but the first stone of the ecclesia in this renowned city of palaces."

In 1865 there were more baptisms reported in India than in Australia. A group in Hong Kong at the same period, known as the "Christadelphian Synagogue", distributed literature in "Japan, the Philippines, Cochin China, Malaya, Borneo, Singapore, and India."

The brothers Oatman, rugged individualists both, rode the range on the Texas frontier years before the cowboys and Indians had finished scuffling, "travelled the length and breadth of the state", held debates and camp meetings, and are reported to have baptized "a hundred men and women with their own hands"— including forbears and relatives of former President Lyndon B. Johnson.

The Pottowatomie tribe of Plains Indians had for a long time before the coming of the white man to the West revered as sacred an old volume the origin and language of which was unknown. Among the first white men to meet the chief of the tribe was a wandering Christadelphian preacher. To the latter's utter amazement he recognised the "book" as a portion of the Old Testament in Hebrew—an identification later confirmed by scholars in Chicago to whom it was sent. He told the chief he could explain the contents of the mysterious book—and the chief became a respected Christadelphian as a result.

While slavery still existed in the United States (and elsewhere), coloured and white, even in the South, met as one around the Lord's Table. The Washington D.C. ecclesia had a much beloved negro member while the Civil War still raged. Another, described as "a diligent student and a preacher of persuasiveness", sowed and watered effectively in the New York area. Yet another dynamic

---

[2] "Lost" for nearly a century, its last surviving aged member was "found" by a curious "coincidence" in the 1950s. Further major ecclesial development in India had to wait until the 1970s and 1980s.

preacher was John Blenman, a West Indian baptized in London in 1878, who carried the message to his native Barbados, and also to Guyana and Jamaica. In June 1890 Robert Roberts received the following, signed by two Jamaicans:

> "I am compelled to communicate with you on behalf of myself and others who require direction. Some time back a young man by the name of Blenman came to our island for a few months, and preached the Christadelphian doctrine, to the astonishment of myself and others. From Mr. Blenman we received a few small books, and after reading some I was compelled to seek him, but he was not at home, and in a few days I heard that he had left the island. I afterwards sent for *Christendom Astray* . . . to be short, our desire is to be baptized, but there is no ecclesia here to baptize us. What are we to do? We have only been christened in our infancy."

Robert Roberts gave advice, and the Kingston ecclesia came into being[3].

In 1879 James Hepburn, a Scot from Newburgh, set out abroad, and after many vicissitudes, arrived penniless at Barbados in the West Indies. To the friends he made in the first few weeks, he set out the first principles of the Word of God in a floorless shanty by the wayside. Three of them were baptized and one of these became for many years the anchor of the ecclesia. "It is most gratifying", he wrote, "to see the people's interestedness night after night, Bible in hand, hearing and asking questions". (This situation is by no means unparalleled in the same region today.) It must have required uncommon endurance and devotion to handle four-hour meetings nightly for months on end in this tropical climate.

One day a young man approached Hepburn in the street, explained he was convinced of the Truth generally, but had serious doubts on one or two issues. "I requested him to come to my lodgings", is the subsequent comment, "where we discussed the matter for twenty-two hours with satisfactory result." After two or three months a fair sized ecclesia was in being. It was desperately short of literature for its preaching, and the expedient was adopted

---

[3] In 1958, the present writer, by an unusual "coincidence", met the son and other relatives of one of the signatories, and learned much about faithfulness to the truth in total isolation.

of writing out tracts and leaflets in longhand, lending them and then calling back for them in order to lend them to someone else. The *Bible Companion* did excellent service, as it has for generations of Christadelphians; many people started to read their Bibles. "They searched the Scriptures, therefore many of them believed": boatmen, stevedores, painters, doctors, shopkeepers, and an orthodox missionary working with the American Baptists. The ecclesia so founded subsequently underwent many trials and troubles born of decades of complete isolation, but it has survived.

"Christendom Astray" Translated

In 1884 a Swiss named Malan who had been baptized while in Birmingham, returned to his native Geneva determined that his light should be under no bushel. Although completely alone in the city he hired a hall holding 400 people, advertised a series of lectures, had handbills printed, and distributed them himself. He was in no way an orator. It is doubtful, indeed, if he had ever spoken in public before. He decided that the best procedure would be to translate *Christendom Astray* into French, and deliver the various chapters as separate lectures. The first evening the hall was packed. The theological colleges, masters and scholars, turned out in force. The lone witness acted as president, doorkeeper, and lecturer. At that time a small lightstand was in fact established in French Switzerland and the financial records of the Birmingham ecclesia show that a sum of £6, then no small sum, was contributed to print a pamphlet in French to assist its work.

Few in this generation will have heard of either Victorine de Verbizier or Peter Doycheff, but both were remarkable Christadelphians. The first was a French Christadelphian of aristocratic lineage who witnessed to the Faith in the south Pacific island of Tahiti. She came to a knowledge of the Gospel in that remote place and was subsequently baptized. About the end of 19th century, in her extreme old age, she "chanced" to meet another French Christadelphian while in Paris and had the blessings of fellowship during her last days. The second, Peter Doycheff, was a vigorous Bulgarian Christadelphian who lived in Plovdiv. For a couple of years he gave addresses on the Bible to a congregation in the town of Yamboli which had been deserted by its regular pastor. He set about publishing pamphlets in Bulgarian, of which the first appeared in 1898 under the title *Are the Dead Conscious?* Two others followed later; then a war of independence broke out in Bulgaria, and Plovdiv became the scene of bitter fighting. Nothing more was ever heard of Peter Doycheff.

In the Southern Hemisphere

Mention may be made of D. M. Maartens, Adam Shrosbree, and James Markham, who in the 1880s and 1890s carried news of the Way to Afrikaners, South African gold diggers, Zulus and Scandinavians. D. M. Maartens had been dissatisfied with the Dutch Reformed Church when he stumbled across a copy of *Elpis Israel* in a little town on the Great Karroo. It confirmed what he had learnt by his own studies, and he appealed for a Christadelphian to visit him. The nearest—150 miles away by ox-wagon—made the trip willingly, but the dry season caused the two to wait weeks before there was sufficient water in the Sundays River for the baptism to take place. The event stirred the Boer community for miles around. Adam Shrosbree learned of the Truth in Tarkastad, a remote rural outpost at that time, and travelled 600 miles to be baptized. He travelled widely over the Eastern Cape and Natal preaching everywhere and, before chaotic conditions were brought about by the Boer War, was tending several small ecclesial groups over a wide area. James Markham was a typical roving pioneer of the period, putting his hand to any kind of job and rarely staying still for very long. He had received literature from a Christadelphian in Pietermaritzburg before going north to the hill country where he made the acquaintance of a Boer farmer. He could not speak Afrikaans, the farmer could speak no English, but over their meals they traded passages of Scripture on subjects such as the nature of man and baptism. One day the farmer asked Markham if he had ever been baptized, and received a negative reply. Then the two men baptized each other. Afrikaner and Briton then worked together in proclaiming the Faith. Some local Zulus heard of these things and invited them to give an account of their new found hope, which they did to an audience of over a hundred. The local ministers of religion put a stop to these proceedings; all, that is, except one. A Wesleyan Zulu preacher, Ndokoza Sibisa, was profoundly disturbed, and set about studying his Bible diligently to see "if these things were so". Ndokoza was baptized and earned the respect of all for his Christlike character.

Markham later joined Cecil Rhodes' band of pioneers who

were carving large farms out of what is now Zimbabwe. He obtained a farm himself (some 6000 acres), left it in the hands of a manager, and set off on a missionary tour of the whole new colony. He visited every farm in the country and actually canvassed practically the entire white population in the course of his rounds. Behind him, in farms and lonely homes on the veld he left copies of the *Declaration* and other books and tracts. Then he returned home and like a good farmer waited for the seed to germinate. After a space he set off again and revisited every home where he had left his books. He found generally greater interest in loaves and fishes than in the bread which endureth; but on arriving at a farm about 55 miles south of his home in a locality which even today cannot boast a road, he found an answer to his prayer. An Afrikaner farmer, influential in his neighbourhood, had become convinced of the Way, and he and two other members of the Dutch Reformed Church were baptized.

From Norway to Burma

In the 1880s Olaf Wettergren left his native Arendal in Norway and went as a missionary for the "Free Christians" to preach to the Zulus. Soon afterwards he and several friends of his of the same nation and church became Christadelphians, and together they vowed to take their new appreciation of the teaching of Christ to their native land. Several "missionary journeys" were made by one or more of this group at enormous personal cost. On one such trip seven thousand copies of the *Declaration* and two thousand *Bible Companions* were given away, besides many other tracts in Norwegian of which we now have no knowledge. Finally, *Kristenheden paa Vildspor,* a translation into Norwegian of *Christendom Astray* was completed. In 1907, 7000 copies of this book were distributed "from Vodra to Lindesnes" (the Norwegian equivalent of "from Dan to Beersheba"), including every major town in Norway, personally and through booksellers. 300 newspapers were asked to review it, and carried advertisements. Thousands of large billboards advertised it, even church notice boards announced it! Leaflets and brochures were distributed to any and to all. In Arendal itself, almost the whole town turned out and packed the largest building to hear the man who had gone away to preach to the Zulus and then decided that his own countrymen needed converting also. At the end of the meeting, a vociferous adversary had to be ejected, and the town authorities refused further use of the hall, but a spirited defence

THE FAITH AT THE END OF THE AGE

of the returned preacher was made by the editor of the local press. The cost of all this effort, based on a country half a world away, cannot even be estimated, and only the Lord Himself knows the result of all this sowing. But with shame it must be said that earnest appeals from these South Africans to their British fellow-pilgrims so much nearer Norway largely went unheeded, as did many other appeals as the 20th century waxed.

Shortly before the death of Robert Roberts, a convert in Burma suggested the establishment of a press in the East for dissemination of Christadelphian literature. "Come over and help us", he wrote. "Will you work only in England and America while we are left alone? Surely hath not God so blessed you for so many years that you might send at least one man to the East?" The hardpressed editor gave the appeal prominent publicity, but it met with no result.

Despite many problems, towards the close of the 19th century it seemed as if a genuinely international fellowship was growing. Christadelphian literature and the annotated list of Bible passages known as the *Declaration* were being distributed by zealous members at their own expense in French, Bulgarian, Cape Dutch (Afrikaans), Zulu, Norwegian and German. There were Christadelphians among the first gold-diggers on the Witwatersrand, with the earliest settlers in Rhodesia, on the frontiers of European settlement in South America, Australia, and elsewhere. There were small but vigorous groups of non-European members in the Caribbean, Brazil, Africa, China, India and the United States. Scott to the South Pole and Amundsen to the North carried with them *Christendom Astray* and other works in their respective languages. At the first South African Fraternal Gathering in Durban in 1897 Britons, Afrikaners, Zulus, Norwegians and Swedes rejoiced together for all that the Lord had done for them.

Promise Unfulfilled

Sadly, in the 20th century the promise for the community latent at the end of the 19th did not appear to materialise, although ecclesias continued to grow strongly in certain metropolitan areas of the British Empire and the United States. The death of Robert Roberts was undoubtedly a major factor, but there must have been others. Controversy and divisions certainly wreaked havoc in some areas. Did zeal for material well-being so characteristic of the century from its beginning replace zeal for extension of the Gospel? Distant ecclesias were often neglected and forgotten, and promising work in various countries was not followed up. Two world wars in this century, however, did test and try the community and even brought some Christadelphians into national prominence for a time, since the body remained true to the long traditions and refused to be militarily conscripted. One Christadelphian at the time of the first world war had almost legendary powers, and there were occasions when one word from him opened His Majesty's prisons and released detained fellow-members.

The two major evangelising ventures in new countries to be undertaken before mid-century were the establishment of Christadelphian communities in Germany and the Soviet Union. They are of particular interest in that in both cases this work to a large extent was carried out against the background of alien and atheistic political ideologies in two totalitarian nations. The Christadelphian ecclesias in Germany owe their origin to the work of Albert Maier, an employee of the Daimler plant near Stuttgart, who was baptized while on a lengthy visit to Portland, Oregon, U.S.A. in the 1890s. Although the earliest German members were baptized before the turn of the century, the period of most vigorous growth was in the troublous days of the Weimar Republic. The records make exciting reading, and the community there has never been as large since that time. A Dr. von Gerdtell of the Berlin ecclesia, excommunicated by the Baptists for rejection of the trinity and other doctrines, became the most dynamic preacher during the pre-Nazi period. The most outstanding event in all the work in Germany was the campaign in Stuttgart in 1930, when he lectured in the Schiller-Realgymnasium to crowds averaging six to seven hundred night after night. On the fourth night Nazi stormtroopers burst into the hall and broke up the meeting, and with each successive night they became more and more menacing. Eventually, police appeared and there was a tense confrontation which ended the campaign. It was a shadow of the fiery trial which was to follow.

Esperanto — Language of Hope

The initial medium of penetration into the Soviet Union in the 1920s was the artificial language Esperanto, then as now more popular in eastern Europe than in the west.[4] By painstaking effort the Christadelphian faith began to take root, mainly in an area of the northern Ukraine. Vladimir Doubrovsky and his wife were among the earliest converts and they proved to be a quite extraordinary couple, undaunted pioneers of the faith in the most difficult of circumstances, the Stalinist transformation of their country. Vladimir was fluent in Russian, Esperanto and English, and his correspondence radiates an insatiable thirst for the things of the Truth. Single-handed he translated the whole of *Christendom Astray*—all 200,000 words of it, along with any other Christadelphian publications that got to him past the censors—while trying to eke out a spartan living from "pioneer" farming and experiencing intense persecution from the authorities. By 1929 there were several small ecclesias totalling around fifty members and it was reported that "the seed of the Truth has fallen into good ground and is producing fruit bountifully".

Vladimir Doubrovsky, translator of *Christendom Astray* into Russian

[4] Today, Bibles and literature in Esperanto are crossing frontiers into Eastern Europe, South America, even China, opening doors and reaching many who otherwise would have no opportunity to hear the Word.

Regrettably, the harvest time was short-lived. In Stalin's terrible purges which began in 1932 between five and eleven million peasants died. The brethren suffered in common with their neighbours, Vladimir Doubrovsky himself being one of the early victims. He died of starvation in September 1933, not yet thirty years old. Other believers were shot, or sent to Siberia. Nevertheless, the ecclesias struggled on until the 1940s. Then, as if the years of privation had not been enough, even worse sufferings then burst upon them—a storm of fire and blood as the Nazi hordes rolled over their land. "Then complete silence", as a correspondent in Britain put it. Very little is known about them after that time. In the late 1970s, during a period when Jamaica, the author's home, had close ties with the Soviet Union, he was able to work with both a co-operative KGB official and an authority on religious groups in communist countries in an effort to locate any surviving Christadelphians. But the word came: "Officially, they do not exist."

A 20th Century Revival

What shall we more say? In recent years the same questing spirit of Bible-inspired, earnest enquiry which has been the dominant theme of these pages has been the spark to revive Christadelphian work and fellowship in some areas and brought them to many new areas in Africa, Asia, the Americas and the Pacific. The Christadelphian body has far greater resources, both relatively and absolutely, than it had at the close of the 19th century. Also and even more urgently—now is our salvation nearer than when either we or they believed. Shall they who rejoiced at the shoot rise to reprove the sloth of us who behold the blossoming?

The two great challenges which face the body of Christ today are not from rationalism, science, orthodox religion or oecumenism—even though all these have brought problems to us as they have to previous generations. They are materialism and the unfinished work of witness which lies upon us. Materialism implies that the present span of mortal existence is the supreme goal of human effort. In this connection, perhaps the Bible School movement may be viewed as one of the most important in our generation—offering a reminder that man does not live by bread alone, and providing an all too rare haven from a world seeking wealth, status, power and fame. And in relation to the second challenge, of worldwide witness, in the formation of the several Bible Mission committees and the work of those who voluntarily assist them, we may hope to see a new determination to discharge our present responsibilities to a world adrift.

It is surely a cause for thankfulness that in the 1980s half the number of those taking on the Saviour's Name in baptism as members of Christadelphian ecclesias in at least forty-five countries worldwide, worship and witness in languages other than English. At an exhibition in Jamaica in 1978, Christadelphian preaching literature was displayed in more than fifty tongues from Afrikaans to Zulu—a reason to rejoice but not to boast. For it is God who gives the increase.

The end of the age, as many students of the prophetic Word mentioned in these chapters recognised, is the convergence of two great events. The Lord Jesus Christ said of his own people of Israel: "They will fall by the edge of the sword, and be led captive among *all nations;* and Jerusalem will be trodden down by the Gentiles, *until* the times of the Gentiles are fulfilled" (Luke 21 : 24). The Apostle Paul wrote: "A hardening has come upon part of Israel, *until* the full number of the Gentiles come in (Rom. 11 : 25). Both the scattering and the worldwide witness to the nations continue *until* in the last day "all Israel shall be saved", and out of Zion shall come the deliverer. We have watched every sign of the fulfilment of the Olivet prophecy. Yet Jesus our Lord also said: "This gospel of the Kingdom will be preached throughout the whole world, as a testimony to *all nations; and then the end will come"* (Matt. 24 :14).

20

EPILOGUE

IN his drama *A Man for all Seasons,* the playwright Robert Bolt presents to us in Sir Thomas More a man who loved life in great variety and seized its sweetest and highest fruits to the full, yet who, when at last driven to retreat from "that final area where he located his self, could no more be budged than a cliff". And in his preface, Bolt diagnoses the desperate sickness of our generation, that more and more people act only from expediency and fewer and fewer from principle and rooted conviction. To adapt a metaphor which runs through the play, the rodent of rationalism has gnawed through the lifeline that moors our selfhood and we are left drifting helplessly over the wild, dark waters. It is significant that, rationalist and humanist though he is, Bolt had to utilise a man of deep religious conviction and piety for his hero of unshakable conviction.

More was a Romanist; the heroes of this study were not. They were, for the most part, as stubbornly convinced that the Roman church is the harlot woman of the Apocalypse as More was that they were unspeakable heretics. Yet, in a profound sense, there was more in common between them, despite their utterly irreconcilable beliefs and manner of life, than between both of them and our own generation.

It has been related in this book how an entire region, because its inhabitants preferred to accept death and exile rather than betray their true selves and their convictions, became so depopulated that a dispensation of polygamy was promulgated by the Roman church. This appears as madness to our generation, dedicated as it is to expediency and conformity. "These people must have been cranks, religious maniacs, fools, masochists in love with martyrdom."

But the evidence is overwhelming that they were nothing of

the sort. True, some of them, perhaps a majority, were drawn from social classes beset by powerful economic frustrations. But, in the main, they were people who had a love and zest for life, ennobled by a rich spiritual fellowship among themselves. Many of them were the flower of their generation, if the deeper qualities of mercy, brotherly kindness, tolerance, human sympathy and sensitivity are considered the yardstick of character. Friends and enemies alike, in an age when religion begat as much brutality and foulness as politics does today, bore insistent testimony that here were people who dared to be different, not for the stubbornness of pride and vain-conceit, but for the meekness and gentleness of Christ. They lit a lamp for their day and generation.

The Salt of the Earth

"You are the salt of the earth." Jesus of Nazareth invested the tiny band that he called apart to testify to him and all he stood for with a staggering responsibility. Into all the world they were to go. Not with the hope of converting the world, but with the aim of creating and forming a redemptive society that would be as the savour of salt in a world of corruption. In parable, metaphor and allegory, the Gospels illuminate the Master's teaching as embodying the one element of permanence and true selfhood in a world of doubt, changeableness and transcience. To build on it was to build on rock; by it one entered the light and joy of the bridal festivities while outside was the darkness; to bear witness to it was to be bearing lamps which shone with divine illumination; it was enduring bread and living water. In the wild darkness of the stormy night human guidance was in vain, and all their rowing brought no aid to a boat sinking with water. They were unable to discern any ethical landmarks; in all their doubts and fears they were in jeopardy. It was the voice of the Lord which stilled their storm.

The world has had—so it is said—an age of gold, an age of faith, an age of reason. Now perhaps we are in the age of uncertainty; which is strange since we know more about things than ever before. Yet we do not know what to give in exchange for our souls. "For what will it profit a man if he gains the whole world and forfeits himself?" That is true enough now, but in the day of reckoning if our self has been compromised and sacrificed to the Moloch of expediency, what will there be left to perpetuate?

"You are the salt of the earth." Many of the characters in

this book, most of them virtually unknown, worked and struggled to season their generation with the savour of sincerity, charity and faith, and they are their own commendation. Many of them wrote, not with the cool pen of the academic theologian, but with the passionate intensity of tested conviction and a love that overflowed from a source which they felt was infinitely more precious than anything that this world affords. There is much we can learn from them.

SELECTED BIBLIOGRAPHY OF SOURCES

Annales Anabaptistici.
Archiv für Reformationsgeschichte. Periodical.
ASHWELL, GEORGE. *De Socino et Socinianismo Dissertatio.* Cambridge, 1680.
AUER, FAGGINER. *Lowell Institute Lectures.* Boston, 1933.

BAILLIE, ROBERT. *Anabaptism, the True Fountaine of Independency, Brownisme, Antinomy, Familisme, and the Most of the Other Errours, which for the Time doe Trouble the Church of England, Unsealed.* London, 1647.
BAINTON, ROLAND. *Hunted Heretic.* Boston, 1953.
BAINTON, ROLAND. *The Reformation of the 16th Century.* London, 1953.
BAINTON, ROLAND. *The Travail of Religious Liberty.* New York, 1958.
BEARD, CHARLES. *The Reformation of the 16th Century.* Hibbert Lectures, 1883.
BECKER, B. *Autour de Michel Servet.* Haarlem, 1953.
BEGG, JAMES. *A Connected View of some of the Scriptural Evidence of the Redeemer's Speedy Personal Return.* Paisley, 1831.
BENDER, HAROLD S. *Conrad Grebel* (c. 1498-1526): *The Founder of the Swiss Brethren.* Goshen (IN), 1950.
BENDER, HAROLD S. ed. *The Mennonite Encyclopaedia.* 4 vols. Scottdale (PA) 1955.
BENDER, HAROLD S. *Theologische Zeitschrift.* 1952, pp. 262-278.
BERGSTEN, TORSTEN. *Balthasar Hübmaier.* Valley Forge, 1978.
BEST, PAUL. *Mysteries Discovered, etc.* London, 1647.
BETTENSON, HENRY. *Documents of the Christian Church.* London, 1943.
Bibliotheca Fratrum Polonorum. Amsterdam, 1660.
BIDDLE, JOHN. *A Twofold Catechism.* London, 1654.
BIDDLE, JOHN. *Confession of Faith Concerning the Holy Trinity.* London, 1653.
BIDDLE, JOHN. *The Testimonies of Irenaeus, etc.* 1649.
BLANKE, FRITZ. *Brüder in Christo.* University of Zürich, 1961.
BLANKE, FRITZ. *La Préhistoire de l'Anabaptisme à Zürich* in *Mélanges Historiques Offerts à M. Jean Meyhoffer.* Lausanne, 1952.
BOHMER, H. *Urkunden zur Geschichte des Bauernkrieges und der Wiedertäufer.* Bonn, 1910.
BONET-MAURY, AMY. *Des Origines du Christianisme Unitaire.* Paris, 1881.
BRAGHT, T. J. van. *The Martyr's Mirror.* Amsterdam, 1660.
BRANDT, G. *Histoire abrégée de la Réformation aux Pays-Bas.* The Hague, 1726.
BRONS, A. *Ursprung, Entwicklung und Schicksale der Täufgesinnten.* Norden, 1883.
"BROOER JANZ" (publ.). *The Racovian Catechism* (in English). Amsterdam, 1652.
BURRAGE, H. S. *History of the Anabaptists in Switzerland.* Philadelphia, 1882.

CALVIN, JEAN. *Brieue Instruction pour armer.* Geneva, 1545.
CALVIN, JOHN. *A Short Instruction to Arm.* London, 1549.
CALVIN, JOHN. *Letter to Viret.* Geneva, 1546.
CHEWNEY, NICHOLAS. *A Cage of Unclean Birds.* London, 1656.
Christadelphian, The. Periodical. C.M.P.A., Birmingham, England.
CHRISTADELPHIAN, THE (publ.). *One Hundred Years of "The Christadelphian".* Birmingham, 1964.
CHURCH ASSEMBLY (ANGLICAN), THE. *Towards the Conversion of England.* London, 1945.

CHURCH OF GOD OF THE ABRAHAMIC FAITH. *Our Confession of Faith.* Miami (FL) 1954.
COUTTS, A. *Hans Denck, Humanist and Heretic.* Edinburgh, 1927.
CRELL, J. *The Unity of God.* London, 1665.
CROSBY, THOMAS. *History of the English Baptists.* London, 1738.

DA PORTA, P. D. R. *Historia Reformationis Ecclesiarum Raeticarum.* Coire, 1774.
D'ARGENTRÉ, C. *Collectio Judiciorum de Novis Erroribus.*
DENCK, JOHANNES. *He who really loves the Truth.* 1525.
Die Religion in Geschichte und Gegenwart (Dict.—article "Wiedertäufer").

EGLI, EMIL. *Die Züricher Wiedertäufer.* Zürich, 1878.
EPPS, JOHN. *The Church of England's Apostasy.* London, 1834.
EPPS, JOHN. *The Devil: A Biblical Exposition.* London, 1842.
EPPS, MRS. *Diary of John Epps.* London, 1875.
EYRE, JOSEPH. *Observation upon the Prophecies relating to the Restoration of the Jews.* London, 1771.

FEATLEY, DANIEL. *The Dippers Dipt.* London, 1645.
FOSDICK, E. *Great Voices of the Reformation.* New York, 1952.
FRIEDMANN, ROBERT. "The Encounter of Anabaptists and Mennonites with Anti-Trinitarianism". *Mennonite Quarterly Review.* XXII, 1948, p. 139 ff.
FROOM, LE ROY. *The Conditionalist Faith of our Fathers.* Washington, 1965.
FROOM, LE ROY. *The Prophetic Faith of our Fathers.* Washington, 1954.
FULLER, THOMAS. *Church History in Britain.* London, 1655.

GERARDI and DE RYS. *Confession of Waterland.* 1580.
Goshen College Record Review. Periodical, Goshen (IN).
GREBEL, CONRAD. *On Scripture.* Zürich, 1525.
GREBEL, CONRAD. *On the Church.* Zürich, 1525.
GUICHARD, LE P. ANASTASE. *Histoire du Socinianisme.* Paris, 1723.

HARTLEY, THOMAS. *Of Christ's Glorious Reign on Earth.* London, 1764.
HATCH, PAUL. *The Church of God in America (Abrahamic Faith): A Historical Sketch.* Restitution Herald, 1956, Oregon (IL).
HAVERSTICK, J. *The Progress of the Protestant.* New York, 1968.
HILLERBRAND, HANS J. *A Bibliography of Anabaptism, 1520-1630.* Elkhart, 1962.
HOMES, NATHANIEL. *The New World.* London, 1641.
HOMES, NATHANIEL. *The Resurrection Revealed.* 1653.
HORSCH, JOHN. *Menno Simons: His Life, Labours and Teaching.* Scottdale (PA), 1916.
HORSCH, JOHN. *The Hutterian Brethren.* Goshen (IN), 1931.
HORSCH, JOHN. *Origin and Faith of the Swiss Brethren.* Private Publication.
HORSCH, JOHN. *The Principle of Non-resistance.* Scottdale (PA), 1940.
HORST, I. B. *The Radical Brethren.* Nieuwkoop, 1972.
HÜBMAIER, B. *Complete Works,* ed. W. O. Lewis. Liberty, Missouri.
HÜBMAIER, B. *An Open Appeal.* 1525.
HÜBMAIER, B. *Concerning Heretics and Those That Burn Them.* 1525.
HÜBMAIER, B. *"Ein Gesprech."* Discourse on baptism. Mikulov, 1526.
HÜBMAIER, B. *Form for Baptising.* 1525.
HÜBMAIER, B. *The Sum of a Perfect Christian Life.* 1525.

HÜBMAIER, B. *The Twelve Articles of Christian Belief Set Forth as a Prayer in the Water Tower at Zürich.* 1527.
HULME, E. M. *Persecution and Liberty.* New York, 1931.
Humble Apology of Some Commonly (Though Unjustly) Called Anabaptists. London, 1660.
Instructor of the Ecclesias in the Kingdom of Poland Which Believe in One God. Racow, 1605, 1652.
KELLER, LUDWIG. *Die Reformation und die alteren Reformparteien.* Leipzig, 1885.
KLAASSEN, WILLIAM. *Anabaptism in Outline.* Kitchener, 1981.
KLASSEN, W. and KLAASSEN, W. *The Writings of Pilgram Marpeck.* Kitchener, 1978.
KNOWLES, JOHN. *Brief Discourse Concerning the Ends and Intents of Christ's Death and Passion.* London, 1668.
KOT, STANISLAW. *Socinianism in Poland.* Boston, 1957.
KRAJEWSKI, EKKEHARD. *Leben und Sterben des Zürcher Täuferfuhrers Felix Mantz.* Kassel, 1957.

LAMBERT, MALCOLM. *Medieval Heresy.* New York, 1976.
LANGENMANTEL, EITELHANS. *An Exposition of the Lord's Prayer.* 1527.
LATOURETTE, K. SCOTT. *A History of Christianity.* New York, 1953.
LECLERC, JOSEPH, S. J. *Toleration and the Reformation.* London, 1960.
Lightstand, The. Christadelphian Periodical, South Africa.
LITTELL, FRANK. *The Anabaptist View of the Church.* Boston, 1956.
LIVERMORE, HARRIET. *Millennial Tidings.* Periodical. Philadelphia.
LOCKE, JOHN. *The Reasonableness of Christianity.* London, 1695.

M'CRIE, THOMAS. *History of the Reformation in Italy.* Edinburgh, 1827.
MCGLOTHLIN, W. J. *Baptist Confessions.* Philadelphia, 1911.
MCLACHLAN, HERBERT, ed. *Sir Isaac Newton's Theological Manuscripts.* London, 1950.
MCLACHLAN, HERBERT JOHN. *Socinianism in 17th Century England.* London, 1951.
MCLACHAN, HERBERT. *The Religious Opinions of Milton, Locke and Newton,* Manchester, 1941.
MARSH, JOSEPH. *Expositor and Advocate.* Periodical. Rochester (NY).
MARTINI, M. *Pierre Valdo.* Genève, 1969.
Mennonite Quarterly Review: Periodical.
MILTON, JOHN. *Complete Prose Works.* New Haven, 1953.
MURALT, L. VON und SCHMID, W. *Quellen zur Geschichte der Täufer in der Schweiz.* Leipzig, 1926.
MUSTON, ALEXIS. *L'Israël des Alpes.* Paris, 1851.

NATIONAL BIBLE INSTITUTION. *The Church of God of the Abrahamic Faith: Its History, Organisation and Belief.* Oregon (IL), 1952.
NEWMAN, A. *A History of Anti-Pedobaptism.* Philadelphia, 1897.
NORRIS, J. B. *The Christian and War.* Birmingham, 1954.
NORRIS, J. B. *The First Century Ecclesia.* Birmingham, 1951.
NYE, STEPHEN. *A Brief History of the Socinians.* London, 1687.

OCHINO, BERNARDINO. *Certaine Godly and Very Profitive Sermons.* London, 1580.
OVERTON, RICHARD. *Man's Mortalitie.* London, 1643.

PAYNE, E. A. *The Anabaptists of the Sixteenth Century.* London, 1949.
PERRIN, J. P. *Histoire de Vaudois.* Geneva, 1618.
PREGER, W. *Beitrage zur Geschichte der Waldensier.* München, 1833.
PRZYPKOWSKI, S. *Vita F. Socini.* 1636.
Racovian Catechism—see "Brooer Janz" (publ.).
REDWOOD, JOHN. *Reason, Ridicule and Religion.* London, 1976.
REES, T. *The Racovian Catechism with Introduction.* Edinburgh, 1818.
Restitution Herald, The. Periodical. N.B.I. Oregon (IL).
RIDEMANN, PETER. *Appeal to the Lords of Liechtenstein.* 1545.
ROBERTS, ROBERT. *City Hall Lectures, Birmingham.* Birmingham, 1897.
ROBERTS, ROBERT. *Christendom Astray.* Birmingham, 1884.
ROBERTS, ROBERT. *Dr. Thomas: His Life and Work.* Birmingham, 1873.
ROTONDÒ, ANTONIO. *Per la Storia dell'eresia, etc.* Bologna, 1962.
RUAR, MARTIN. *Epistolarum Selectarum.* Amsterdam, 1677.
RUTH, JOHN L. *Conrad Grebel, Son of Zürich.* Scottdale, 1975.

SABATIER, AUGUSTE. *Religions of Authority and the Religion of the Spirit.* New York, 1903.
SACHSE, CARL. *Dr. Balthasar Hübmaier Theologe.* Berlin, 1914.
SATTLER, MELCHIOR. *Dissertatio erroris Chiliastarum.* Hanover, 1670.
SATTLER, MICHAEL. *Brüderliche Vereynigung, etc.* Rottenburg-am-Neckar, 1527, pub. Walther Kohler, 1908.
SATTLER, MICHAEL. *Two Kinds of Obedience.* 1527.
SAURAT, D. *Milton, Man and Thinker.* London, 1925.
SCHAFF, PHILIPP. *History of the Christian Church.* New York, 1859.
SCHOMANN, GEORG. *Confession of Faith of the Congregation Assembled in Poland.* Kraków, 1574.
SCUDERI, GIOVANNI. *Studio sulle Dottrina dei Valdesi.* Roma, 1956.
SERVETO, MIGUEL. *Christianismi Restitutio.* Lyons, 1553.
SMITH, ELIAS. *Sermons Concerning Prophecies to be Accomplished, etc.* Exeter (NH), 1808.
SMITH, ELIAS. *The Doctrine of the Prince of Peace and his Servants.* Portsmouth (NH), 1805.
SMITHSON, R. J. *The Anabaptists: Their Contribution to our Protestant Heritage.* London, 1935.
SOET, H. I. (publ.). *'t Kleyn Hoorns-Liet-Boeck.* Amsterdam, 1646.
SOZZINI, LAELIO. *Confession of Faith.* 1555.
SPALDING, JOSHUA. *Sentiments Concerning the Coming and Kingdom of Christ.* 1796.
SPALDING, JOSHUA. *The Divine Theory.* 179?.
STEGMAN, JOACHIM. *Brevis Discussio.* 1633.
STEMLER, ABRAHAM. *The Hope of a Better Time.* 1712.

TAZBIR, J. *A State without Stakes.* Warsaw, 1973.
TEDESCHI, JOHN A. *Italian Reformation Studies.* De Kalb, 1970.
THOMAS, JOHN. *Eureka.* Birmingham, 1866.
THOMAS, JOHN. *The Revealed Mystery.* Virginia, 1836. Reprinted Birmingham, 1869.
TORREY, WILLIAM. *A Brief Discourse Concerning Futurities.* Boston, 1757.
TOULMIN, JOSHUA. *Life of John Biddle.* London, 1789.
TROELTSCH, ERNST. *The Social Teaching of the Christian Churches.* Vol. III. London, 1931.
TRUEBLOOD, D. ELTON. *Alternative to Futility.* New York, 1948.

TURNER, WILLIAM. *Lives of Eminent Unitarians.* London, 1840.
TUROBINCZYCK, ALEXANDER. (publ.). *Confession of Faith of the Congregation Assembled in Poland.* Kraków, 1574.
TYNDALE, WILLIAM. *Exposition upon Certain Words in Holy Scripture.* 1520.
TYNDALE, WILLIAM. *A Pathway into the Holy Scripture.* 1525.
TYNDALE, WILLIAM. *An Answer to Sir Thomas More's Dialogue.* 1531.

UNDERHILL, E. B. *A Martyrology.* 2 vols. London, 1850.

VEDDER, H. C. *Balthasar Hübmaier: The Leader of the Anabaptists.* New York, 1905.
VERHEYDEN, A. L. E. *Anabaptism in Flanders.* Scottdale, 1961.
VOLKEL, J. *De Vera Religione.* 1630.

WALLACE, ROBERT. *Antitrinitarian Biography.* London, 1850.
WEIGEL, VALENTINE. *Of the Life of Christ.* London, 1648.
WEIS, F. L. *The Life, Works and Teaching of Johannes Denck.* Strasbourg, 1924.
WEIS, F. L. *The Life, Works and Teaching of Ludwig Haetzer.* Dorchester, Mass. 1930.
WILBUR, E. M. *A History of Unitarianism, Socinianism and its Antecedents.* Cambridge, Mass., 1945.
WILLIAM, GEORGE HUNTSTON (ed.). *Spiritual and Anabaptist Writers.* S.C.M. Press, London, 1957.
WILLIAMS, GEORGE HUNTSTON. *William Tyndale.* London, 1979.
WILLIAMS, GEORGE HUNTSTON. (ed.). *The Polish Brethren.* Missoula, 1980.
WILLIAMS, GEORGE HUNTSTON. *Camillo Renato.* Firenza (Florence), 1968.
WISZOWATY, ANDREW, (ed.). *Library of the Polish Brethren.* (Bibliotheca Fratrum Polonorum). 10 vols. Amsterdam, 1665.
WOLKAN, RUDOLF, etc. *Geschicht-Buch der Hutterischen Brüder.*
WRIGHT, E. NEEDLES. *Conscientious Objectors in the Civil War.* Philadelphia, 1931

YODER, JOHN. *The Legacy of Michael Sattler.* Scottdale, 1973.
YODER, JOHN (ed.). *The Schleitheim Confession.* Scottdale, 1973.

ZILVERBERG, S. B. J. *Geloof en Geweten in de Zeventiende Eeuw.* Bussum, 1971.
Zionspilger, Der. Periodical. Switzerland.

NOTE: The most accessible sources for references in the first chapter to early Christian writers—Cyprian, Eusebius, Hippolytus, Justin, Papias, Tertullian—are possibly:

COXE, A. C. (ed.). *The Ante-Nicene Fathers to 325* (Translations).
SCHAFF, P. (ed.). *A Select Library of Nicene and Post-Nicene Fathers.*

Several other collections are, however, available in different countries.

INDEX

In the following, names of people and places and other general topics are in normal type; publications are in *italic*; doctrinal subjects in **bold** type. The publications are those actually referred to in the book: for a bibliography of other literature see preceding pages.

Aargau 69
Aberdeen 194
Abraham (Promises to, Faith of), see **Promises of God**
Adventists 159
Africa 201, 205-207, 210, 211
Alba-Iulia 130
Allobrex, Claudius 108
American Civil War 188, 191
American Frontier 176, 181
Amsterdam 82, 122
Anabaptism, the True Fountaine of ... Errours ... Unsealed (Baillie) 104
Anabaptists (see also **Baptism**, Baptists) 23, 24, 46, 67, 77, 81-82, 93, 97, 103-104, 126, 145, 150, 187
Anderson, Albert 189
Angels 84, 86, 94
Antichrist 12, 15, 87, 147, 172
Antwerp 88
Apocalypse, see Revelation
Apostles' Creed 5, 43, 45, 107, 129, 166, 190
Appenzell 35, 47
Are the Dead Conscious? (Doycheff) 204
Arendal 206
Argula of Stauffen 106
Arles 16
Armageddon 163
Ashwell, George 95, 96
Assheton, John 96
Assisi, Francis of 89
Athanasian Creed 112
Atonement (see also **Jesus Christ, Sacrifice**) 92, 98, 129, 136, 160

Augsburg 15, 20, 48, 52, 77
Augustine 47
Australia 1, 183, 199, 201, 207
Austria 18, 49-51, 54-55, 67-70, 94-95, 108-109, 186
Authorised Version of Bible 88, 140
Avignon 16

Baillie, Robert 104, 105
Baptism 6, 13, 20, 24-28, 33-37, 41-42, 45, 48, 52, 60, 80, 82, 83, 86, 102-104, 114, 116-118, 122, 129, 137, 144, 146, 147, 154, 157, 173, 203
Baptists 139, 145, 146, 187, 203, 204
Barbados 203
Basel 20, 35, 47, 48, 67, 79
Begg, James 176-180, 193
Belgium 88, 112
Berlin 208
Bermuda 201
Bern 67
Best, Paul 150
Biandrata, Giorgio 114, 130
Bible, see **Scriptures**
Bible Campaigns 170, 173, 199
Bible Companion 204, 206
Bible Mission, Christadelphian 201, 210, 211
Bible Schools 210
Bible Translation 15, 19, 47, 77, 78, 83, 85, 88
Bicheno, James 88, 186
Biddle, John 4, 128, 131-141, 150, 184, 185, 199

Birmingham 199, 201, 204
Blaurock, George (Cajacob) 28-40, 199
Blenman, John 203
Blood of Christ, The (Roberts) 197
Bockelszoon, Jan 81
Boers 205
Bohemia 15, 50, 54
Bologna 90
Bolt, Robert 212
Book of Martyrs, The (Foxe) 2
Borneo 202
Brandenburg 130
Brazil 207
Breaking of Bread 11, 28, 31, 34, 37, 45, 86, 118, 122, 129, 157, 183
Brenius, Daniel 123, 152
Brethren in Christ 2, 11, 13, 27, 28, 36, 45, 67, 87, 90, 91, 94, 99-104, 111, 180, 188, 189
Brethren in Christ (Eyre) vi
Brevis Discussio (Stegman) 123
Brief Discourse Concerning Futurities or Things to Come, A 158
Brieue Instruction (Calvin) 103, 104
British-Israelism 200
Brötli, Johannes 28, 30-32
Brown, B. B. 182
Brüder in Christo (see also Brethren in Christ) 27, 28
Brüderliche Vereynigung (Sattler) 71
Brussels 88
Bulgaria 204, 207
Burma 207

Cage of Unclean Birds (Chewney) 150
Cajacob, see Blaurock
Calcutta 202
Calvin, John 8, 93, 94, 101-105, 107, 123
Calvinism, Calvinists 44, 78, 123, 138, 146, 163, 165, 168, 169, 183
Calvinist Baptists 168
Cambridge 12, 84, 150, 152
Campbell, Alexander 174, 185
Campbellites 174, 185, 194
Canada 181, 191, 201
Caribbean 201, 203, 207

Casimir, King of Poland 125, 126
Caspano 91
Castelberger, Andreas 6, 19, 20, 28, 100
Catechism for the Instruction of Youth 16
Catechisms 16, 118-123, 136-139, 149, 168
Catholic, see Roman Catholic
Catholic Apostolic Faith 177
Celibacy 15, 23, 57, 63
Cellarius, Martin 79
Champion, William 193
Charles V, Emperor 88
China 207, 209
Christadelphian, The 179, 196
Christadelphians 1-4, 83, 166, 177, 185-211
Christendom Astray (Roberts) 197, 203, 204, 206, 209
Christening (Infant Baptism) 13, 20 22, 24-27, 31, 33, 36, 37, 41-42, 48, 97, 102-104, 136, 144, 203
Christian and War, The (Norris) 10
Christian Physician and Anthropological Magazine, The (Epps) 183
Church Fathers 7, 11, 133
Church of God Conference 187
Cluj 74, 116, 123, 130
Cochin China 202
Coire 47
Cole, Peter 97
Cologne 85
Commandments of Christ 31, 99, 107, 129, 137, 147, 213
Community of Goods 107
Concerning Divorce (Sattler) 60
Concerning Evil Overseers (Sattler) 60
Concerning Heretics (Hübmaier) 56
Confession of Faith of the Congregation Assembled in Poland (Schomann) 117
Connected View, A (Begg) 177
Conscription (see also **War**) 10, 106, 188, 208
Cooper, John 151
Cranmer, Thomas 97

INDEX

Cromwell, Oliver 139, 146
Curio, Celio 94

David, Ferenc 129, 130
Day of Judgement, The (Smith) 170
Death, see Mortality of Man, Immortality
Declaration 206, 207
Denck, Johannes 59, 77-79
De Vera Religione (Volkel-Locke) 143, 153, 190
Devil, Demons 50, 61, 75, 77, 95, 96, 160, 183-184
Devil, The (Epps) 183
Dialogue with Trypho the Jew (Justin) 8
Dippers Dipt, The (Featley) 150
Discourse on Eternal Life (Thomas) 191
Divine Theory, The (Spalding) 166
Doctrine of the Prince of Peace and his Servants, The (Smith) 170
Dominicans 70, 90
Doubrovsky, Vladimir 209-210
Doycheff, Peter 204-205
Drummond, William 177, 180
Durban 207

Early Church and the World, The (Cadoux) 10
Eberli, Heinrich 19, 30, 35, 36, 39
Ecclesia Minor, Poland 95
Ecclesial Discipline 60, 82, 105
Ecclesial Organisation 10, 11, 19, 45, 57, 60, 77, 82, 94, 101, 105, 114, 115, 120, 122, 156, 194
Edinburgh 159, 177, 183
Ein Gesprech (Hübmaier) 41
Elliott, Edward 186
Elizabeth I, Queen 97
Elpis Israel (Thomas) 164, 166, 179, 190, 193, 201, 205
Emmaus, Baptistry 6
England 18, 83-88, 95-98, 103, 118, 128, 131-155, 182-183, 191-192, 196-204
Epps, John 182-184, 189, 193
Erasmus, Desiderius 20, 77, 84, 112, 114

Esperanto 208, 209
Essay Explaining the Revelation (Biddle) 140
Eton 149
Eucharist, see Breaking of Bread
Eureka (Thomas) 14, 16, 180, 186, 190
Eusebius 7
Exeter (NH) 170
Exposition upon Certain Words in Holy Scripture (Tyndale) 84
Expositor and Advocate (Marsh) 182
Eyre, Joseph 160-162

Fabri, Johannes 55
Ferdinand I, Emperor 54, 68, 70, 109
Fellowship 3, 6, 11, 34, 59, 82, 94, 95, 104, 105
Ferrara 91
Fifth Monarchy Men 146
Firmin, Thomas 153
Flekwijk, Herman van 112
Flemings, Flanders (see also Netherlands, Belguim) 88, 97
Florida 201
France 12, 16, 204, 207
"Free Christians" 206
Freiburg 20, 57
Frieberg 20

Gardiner, Stephen, Bishop 88
Geneva 12, 16, 204
Gentilis, Valentino 93, 96, 114
Gerdtell, Dr. L. von 208
Germany 18, 20-23, 38-39, 48, 51-52, 57-67, 69-70, 75-82, 85, 114, 128, 130, 150, 176, 208
Gibbon, Edward 186
Glasgow 103, 193
Gloucester 131-134, 151
Glorious Reign of Christ and the Church on this Earth, The (Brenius) 123
God, Unity and Character 4, 13, 44, 45, 79, 92, 108, 111, 112, 114, 117, 118, 129, 137, 140, 151

THE PROTESTERS

God-manifestation 4, 197
Grebel, Barbara 47
Grebel, Conrad 19-39, 46, 47, 78, 85, 100, 102, 104, 106
Grebel, Jacob 47
Greek Philosophy 6, 8, 135, 186
Grisons 34, 47, 95
Groningen 82
Grüningen 37, 38, 47-49, 57
Guinness, Grattan 188
Guyana 201, 203

Habsburgs 54, 60, 69, 70, 114
Halbmayer, Jacob 62-65
Hartley, Thomas 167
Hatch, Paul 181, 188
Hätzer, Ludwig 25, 28, 30, 59, 78, 79
Haynes, Hopton 151
Hearing of False Prophets, The (Sattler) 60
Heaven (see also **Immortality, Kingdom**) 8, 84, 123, 172
Hedworth, Henry 123, 151
Hell 8, 84, 95, 104, 123, 137, 148, 153, 172, 183-184
Henry VIII, King 84, 88
Hepburn, James 203
Herald of Gospel Liberty, The (Smith) 170
Herald of the Kingdom 188
Hetz, Hans 51, 52
Hinwyl 38
Hippolytus 7
Hirslanden 31
History of Baptism (Crosby) 145
History of the Roman Empire (Gibbon) 186
Hobbes, Thomas 186
Hofmann, Eberhard 62-65
Hofmann, Melchior 79-81
Hohenzollerns 62, 66
Holy Roman Empire 46, 67, 74, 87
Holy Spirit 6, 19, 44, 45, 53, 79, 94, 96, 109, 111, 112, 118, 122, 129, 133, 134, 137, 144, 149, 197
Hong Kong 202
Hope of a Better Time, The (Stemler) 167

Hope of Israel 160, 161-167, 169, 171
Horae Apocalypticae (Elliott) 186
Horb 60, 61
Hottinger, Elizabeth 39
Hottinger, Claus 19
Hottinger, Jacob 32, 35
Hottinger, Margareta 39
Hübmaier, Balthasar 20-56, 78, 85, 102, 184, 199
Hübmaier, Elizabeth 22, 54, 55
Huddersfield 198
Huguenots 152, 187
Humble Apology of Some Commonly (Though Unjustly) Called Anabaptists 146
Hungary 50, 54, 74, 79
Hutterites 107
Hymns 54, 100, 101, 106, 157, 174

Illinois 187
Immortality (see also **Resurrection**) 7, 8, 22, 44, 45, 86, 90, 118, 122, 123, 148, 151, 172, 181, 190-191
India 201-202, 207
Inquisition 89-91, 96, 112, 142, 156
Investigator 182
Ireland 177
Irenaeus 8
Iron Curtain 15, 204, 208-210
Irving, Edward 176, 177, 180
Iseppo of Asola 94
Israel, see **Hope of Israel, Jews**
Italy 14-16, 18, 51, 89-98

Jamaica 203, 210, 211
James I, King 88, 142
Japan 202
Jerusalem 145, 146, 161, 165, 173, 175, 211
Jesuits 115, 125, 128
Jesus Christ, Sacrifice, Saviour 4, 11, 22, 44, 45, 78, 86, 92, 98, 109, 118, 137, 141, 151, 160, 197
Jesus Christ, Second Coming 7, 80-84, 97, 109, 122, 129, 137, 169, 171, 173, 176, 177, 180

INDEX

Jesus Christ, Son of God, Man, Nature 4, 9, 13, 44, 45, 79, 93, 94, 108, 109, 112, 117, 118, 121, 127, 129, 135, 141, 144, 151, 160, 184, 197-198
Jewish Expositor 179
Jews, Regathering 123, 160, 161-164, 171, 177, 179-180, 190
Johnson, Lyndon 202
Jones, Abner 174
Jones, Isaac 201
Judgement 8, 21, 24, 44, 45, 51, 85, 90, 92, 95, 112, 123, 124, 137, 153, 154, 160, 163, 172, 180, 195, 200
Justin 'Martyr' 8

Kautz, Jakob 85
Kessler, Johannes 35
Kingdom of God 2, 7, 44, 45, 80, 81, 91, 97, 123, 129, 140, 144, 146, 154, 155, 160, 161, 165-170, 173, 176, 179-181, 195, 200, 211
King James Version of the Bible 88, 140
Kingston 203
Knowles, John 123
Königsberg 130
Kraków 111, 114, 116, 125
Krell, Johann 122
Krell, Samuel 151

Lavaur 16
Legate, Bartholomew 142
Library of the Polish Brethren 122
Lichfield 144
Liechtenstein 70
Lingg, Martin 32, 38
Lismanin, Francis 114
Lithuania 118, 125
Livermore, Harriet 180
Locke, John 143, 153, 156, 186
Lollards 100
London 96, 97, 103, 132-138, 147-153, 183, 201, 203
Love 9, 78, 82, 95, 98, 133, 137, 214
Lovingkindness of God Displayed, The (Smith) 170

Luther, Martin 9, 23, 24, 75, 83, 102, 104, 107, 123
Lutherans 18, 43, 64, 75-88, 107, 117, 121, 123
Lyons 12
Lynn (MA) 168

Maartens, D. M. 205
Maienfeld 47
Maier, Albert 208
Malan 204
Malaya 202
Man's Mortallitie (Overton) 148
Manz, Anna 39
Manz, Felix 19-39, 46, 48, 49
Mariolatry 20, 63, 64, 91, 137
Markham, James 205
Marpeck, Pilgram 109
Marriage (see also **Celibacy**) 105, 106, 157, 159
Marsh, Joseph 182
Martin, Rudolph 111
Mass 11, 20, 22, 31, 91
Matthys, Jan 81
Mede, Joseph 152
Melbourne 199
Mennonites 111
Messenger 182
Mikulov 41, 50-56
Millennial Harbinger (Campbell) 174
Millennial Tidings (Livermore) 180
Millennium, see **Kingdom of God**
Military Service, see **Conscription, War**
Milton, John 149, 186, 187
Minden 82
Ministry, Clergy 15, 105, 136, 147
Modrevius, Andrew 111
Moore, Richard 138, 139
Moravia 48, 50-56, 67-74, 93, 94, 114, 128
More, Thomas 84, 212
Mortality of Man, Soul 7, 8, 14, 17, 83, 84, 90, 95, 104, 120, 123, 135, 144, 148, 153, 159, 183, 204
Moskorzowski, Hieronim 118
Münster 81, 82
Müntzer, Thomas 23, 52, 106

225

THE PROTESTERS

My Days and My Ways (Roberts) 196
Mysteries Discovered (Best) 150

Naples 90
Napoleonic wars 176
Nazis 73, 208, 210
Negri, Francesco 94
Netherlands 80-83, 96, 97, 111, 112, 122, 128, 142, 145, 151
Neuchâtel 102
Newgate Prison 139
Newton, Isaac 88, 151-153, 169, 176, 186, 187
New York 202
New Zealand 201
Nisbet, James 177
North Pole 207
Norway 205-207
Norwich 97
Nürnberg 77

Observations upon the Prophecies relating to the Restoration of the Jews (Eyre) 160
Ochino, Bernardino 96, 98
Of the Torments of Hell 148
One Hundred Years of The Christadelphian 196
Open Appeal, An (Hübmaier) 36
Oregon (IL) 188
Origen 8, 47
Overton, Richard 148
Oxford 83, 84, 95, 131, 152

Pacifism, see **War, Conscription**
Padua 90
Paisley 177, 193
Papias 7
Paradise Restored (Hartley) 167
Paradoxical Questions Concerning the Morals and Actions of Athanasius and his Followers (Newton) 152
Paris 204
Parravicinis 91
Parris, George van 97
Pastor of Hermas, The 6

Pathway into the Holy Scripture, A (Tyndale) 84
Paul, Gregory 114
Paul, Letters of 19, 84, 124, 211
Peasants' War 23, 52, 107
Peeters, John 97
Persecution 2, 9, 16, 24, 36, 39, 41-98, 126-128, 142, 163
Phanerosis (Thomas) 197
Philadelphia 180
Philippines 202
Phillips, Obbe 111
Phocas, Emperor 87
Picart, Bernard 156-159
Pinczów 114, 115
Plato 135, 186
Plovdiv 204
Poland, Polish Brethren 13, 16, 69-70, 79, 94-96, 111-130, 133, 136, 139, 140, 150-152, 166, 176, 191, 197, 199
Popes (see also Roman Catholics) 15, 87, 109
Portland (OR) 208
Portsmouth (NH) 170
Pottawatomie Indians 202
Pra del Tor 15
Prayer 13, 28, 44, 117, 133, 141, 194-195
Prison Confession (Hübmaier) 43
Promises to Abraham etc. (see also **Kingdom of God**) 80, 97, 118, 121, 155, 160, 164-167, 169-170, 173, 190, 200
Prophecy 109, 117, 123, 160-164, 170, 171, 173, 179, 182, 186, 211
Protestant, see Reformation
Prussia 128, 130
Przypkowski, Samuel 123
Pur, Bartlime 19

Raków 114-121, 125, 151, 152, 191
Raków (Racovian) Catechism 118-123, 149
Reasonableness of Christianity, The (Locke) 153
Reformation, Protestant 13, 16, 18-20, 22, 25, 52, 59, 84, 85, 89, 90, 93, 99, 100, 107, 125, 126, 156, 186

INDEX

Regensburg 20, 37
Renaissance 89
Renato, Camillo, see Ricci, Paolo
Resurrection, Eternal Life (see also **Immortality**) 7, 8, 14, 44, 45, 85, 86, 91, 97, 109, 123, 124, 129, 137, 141, 145, 148, 151, 154, 160, 166, 169-170, 177, 183
Revealed Mystery, The (Thomas) 190, 191
Revelation, Apocalypse 88, 109, 133, 140, 161, 163, 180, 186, 212
Rhegius, Urban 77
Rhineland 81
Ricci, Paolo 89-92
Richmond (VA) 191
Robert Roberts (Collyer) 196
Roberts, Jane 201
Roberts, Robert 191, 192, 194, 199, 200, 201, 207
Robinson, D. I. 182
Rochester (NY) 182, 187
Roman Catholic 12, 14, 15, 18-26, 35, 42, 54, 57, 63, 70, 75, 81, 83, 85, 87, 89-93, 99, 115, 126, 150, 156, 184, 212
Romania 74, 116, 123, 130
Roman Law 7, 46
Rottenburg 61, 65-66, 75
Röubli, Wilhelm 28, 32, 59, 60, 61
Roznów 128
Russia 74, 128, 130, 208-210
Rutschmann, Rudolf 33

Sacred Massacre 92
St. Bartholomew Massacre 72
St. Gallen 20, 25, 35, 36, 38, 47, 77
Saints, Invocation of 20, 64, 90, 91
Salem (MA) 165
San Francisco (CA) 200
Sattler, Michael 38, 57-66
Schaffhausen 32, 35, 48, 60
Schleitheim 48, 60
Schomann, Georg 116
Schumacher, Fridli 31
Schwenckfeld, Caspar 75
Schwyz 36
Scilly Isles 140
Scotland 103, 159, 160, 176, 177, 183, 193, 194

Scriptures, Basis of Faith and Truth 1, 6, 13, 19, 21, 34, 37, 47, 53, 64, 77, 78, 91, 94, 96, 99, 100, 114, 117, 120, 124, 131, 133, 136, 137, 140-142, 152, 168-169, 182, 185, 204
"Seekers" 142, 182
Separation (see **Society and the Believer**)
Serfs 115
Seripando, Girolamo 90
Serpent in Eden 95
Serveto, Miguel 93
Shrosbree, Adam 205
Siberia 210
Sibiza, Ndokoza 205
Sicily 89
Sienienski, Jakob 114, 115
Silesia 128
Simons, Menno 82, 83, 111
Simple Explanation (Hübmaier) 53
Sin, Original Sin, Remission of Sins (see also **Jesus Christ, Sacrifice**) 15, 52, 86, 109, 118, 129, 137, 151, 154, 183
Singapore 202
Slavic lands 96
Smaltzy, Valentyn 118
Smith, Elias 168-175
Society and the Believer 60, 61, 66, 104, 106, 114, 115, 129, 146
Socinians 93-96, 116-122
Sonntag, Christoph 167
Soul, see **Mortality of Man**
South Africa 205-207
South America 201, 203, 207
South Pole 207
Soviet Union (see Russia)
Sozzini, Darius 93, 96
Sozzini, Fausto 95-96, 116, 120-122
Sozzini, Laelio 93-96, 114
Spain 18, 93, 112
Spalding, Joshua 164-166, 169
Spitalmaier, Ambrosius 108
Stalin, Josef 210
Statements of Faith 5, 13, 14, 22, 44, 45, 71, 97, 108, 109, 116-120, 128, 129, 137-139, 151, 153-155, 159-160
Stegman, Joachim 120, 123, 124, 176

Stemler, Abraham 167
Strangers' Church 96
Strasbourg 59, 77, 79, 81
Stuttgart 208
Sum of a Perfect Christian Life, The (Hübmaier) 37
Sweden 18, 125, 126, 207
Switzerland, Swiss Brethren 12-69, 78, 84, 93-95, 100-102, 107-110, 114, 167, 188, 199, 204
Syracuse 89
Szlichtyng, Jonas 122

Tahiti 204
Tarkastad 205
Tarshish 171
Täufer-Jaeger 67
Tertullian 7, 9
Texas 201, 202
Theophany (Walker) 197
Thirty Dialogues (Ochino) 98
Thomann, Ruedi 31, 32
Thomas, John 1-2, 14, 16, 88, 145, 164, 166, 174, 179, 182, 185-195
Thuanus, Jacques 14
Tims, R. T. 177
Tirano 91
Torre Pellice 14
Torrey, William 158
Towards the Conversion of England 7
Transylvania 128-130, 150
Tricessius, John 111
Trinity 4, 9, 63, 78, 79, 92, 93, 96, 97, 108, 111-114, 121, 127, 134, 135, 139, 142, 144, 149, 152, 169, 184
Tübingen 61, 62, 65
Tunstall, Cuthbert 88
Turin 14
Turks 54, 128, 171, 186
Turwert, Henry 97
Twelve Arguments (Biddle) 134
Twenty-two Queries Regarding the Word 'Homoousios' (Newton) 152
Twofold Catechism (Biddle) 136-138, 190

Two Kinds of Obedience (Sattler) 60
Two Notable Corruptions of Scripture (Newton) 152
Tyndale, William 83-88
Tyrol 49, 51, 67-70, 94, 95, 108, 109
Tyshkovych, Jan 125

Ukraine 209
Unitarians 4, 9, 121, 130, 141, 159
Universalists 169, 174
Uollimann, Wolfgang 32, 35, 36
U.S.A. 1, 156-175, 180-185, 187-189, 191, 193-194, 200-202, 207, 208
Ussher, James, Archbishop 134

Valdensian Church 16
Val-Louise 16
Vaud 15
Vaudois, Valdensians 12-17, 83, 100, 114
Venice 16, 90, 94
Verbizier, Victorine de 204
Vicenza, Vicenza Society 15, 92, 93
Vienna 30, 50, 55, 56, 69, 70, 73, 186
Vilvoorde 88
Virgin Birth 44, 64, 93, 108, 109, 129, 154
Virginia 191, 193
Vogel, Catherine 125
Voice of Truth and Glad Tidings of the Kingdom, The 182
Volkel, Johannes 118, 143, 153
Vulgate 14, 15, 18

Waldenses, see Vaudois, Waldo
Waldhaus 15
Waldo, "Peter" 12-17
Waldshut 20, 22, 32, 38, 39
War, Non-Participation, Pacifism (see also **Conscription, Society and the Believer**) 10, 24, 60, 61, 97, 98, 106, 136, 137, 146, 188, 191, 208
Warsaw 125
Washington (DC) 193, 202
Washington, George 164

INDEX

Watt, Joachim von 20, 25, 36, 38
Weimar Republic 208
Wellenberg Prison 33, 34, 46
Weniger, Martin 69
West Indies (see Caribbean)
Wettergren, Olaf 206
Wiederkehr, Anna 39
Wightman, Edward 142, 144
Wiszowaty, Andrew 120, 122, 128, 184, 191
Witness for Christ (Walker) 197
Woburn (MA) 168
Wolsey, Thomas 88
Women in the Ecclesia 105, 106
Worms 77, 85
Wotton-under-Edge 131

Yamboli 204

Zimbabwe, Rhodesia 206-207
Zollikon 31-35, 110
Zulus 205-207, 211
Zürich 9-51, 57, 59, 67, 69, 78, 84, 100, 101, 107, 110
Zwingli, Huldrich 9, 19-21, 24, 36-52, 78, 102, 109